Sartre's *Nausea*

Text, Context, Intertext

Edited by

Alistair Rolls
and
Elizabeth Rechniewski

Rodopi

AMSTERDAM - NEW YORK, NY 2005

Cover design: Pier Post

Cover illustration: reproduced with kind permission of The Old Island Stamp
Company ιοο5ᑫᎥՏᏮᎥ᠆ᏲᏮᏉ

The paper on which this book is printed meets the requirements of
'ISO 9706: 1994, Information and documentation - Paper for documents -
Requirements for permanence'.

Le papier sur lequel le présent ouvrage est imprimé remplit les prescriptions
de 'ISO 9706: 1994, Information et documentation - Papier pour documents
- Prescriptions pour la permanence'.

ISBN: 90-420-1928-X
©Editions Rodopi B.V., Amsterdam - New York, NY 2005
Printed in The Netherlands

Contents

Editors' Foreword

The chapters in this volume have been developed from papers presented at 'Nausea 2004: Why Study Jean-Paul Sartre's *Nausea* Today', a conference held at the University of Newcastle, New South Wales, in July 2004 at the initiative of Dr Alistair Rolls, whose experience of teaching *Nausea* both in French (to students in French Studies programmes) and in translation (to students of English literature) convinced him of the necessity to consider the novel afresh, freed from the baggage of traditional interpretations and the perspectives of hindsight. Students from different disciplines have correspondingly different expectations of the text, and its teachers, too, develop an understanding of it that is drawn from their own pedagogical as well as research-focussed commitments. We felt that certain aspects of the text – notably its value as a piece of creative writing and the artistic and literary context out of which it evolved – have been eclipsed by its iconic status as an Urtext of French Existentialism. It was our particular design, therefore, to recognise *Nausea*'s status as a trans-disciplinary chameleon and to reveal the dynamic role that it can continue to play in dialogue with a wide range of texts, when placed in new literary and disciplinary contexts. The chapters in this volume, contributed by writers from a range of academic and literary areas, seek to offer fresh perspectives on the text and to show how much it has still to offer.

Because our authors are generally working with the English-language version of the text, references will be made throughout to the translation by Robert Baldick (Penguin 2000) and will be given by using a page number in brackets after each quotation.

The Editors would like to thank the School of Language and Media at the University of Newcastle, and particularly Professor Hugh Craig and Karyn Asher, for their support, and the University of Sydney for financial assistance. We also express our appreciation to Melanie Safon for her careful editing of the text.

E.R.
A.R.

Alistair Rolls, Elizabeth Rechniewski

Uprooting the Chestnut Tree: *Nausea* Today

Twenty-five years after his death, critics and academics, film-makers and journalists continue to argue over Sartre's legacy. But certain interpretations have congealed around his iconic text Nausea, *tending to confine it within the framework provided by the later philosophical text,* Being and Nothingness. *In this opening chapter we seek to problematise interpretations of the novel that benefit from hindsight, to open up the text to a range of new approaches, in order to avoid too narrow a categorisation of the text.*

In the interest of broadening the appeal of Nausea *we have collected together in this volume authors whose approaches to the text spring from four principal areas: French Studies, Philosophy, English and Comparative Literature. All four discipline areas have their own contribution to make in terms of the written text (the textual strategies at work within the novel), its context (be it literary, cultural or philosophical) and the intertextual web within which it is situated, and this chapter offers an overview of the contributions of this volume to these three topics.*

* * *

2005, the centenary of Jean-Paul Sartre's birth, is an opportune time to re-engage with his most famous creation, a book that has marked readers around the world since its publication in France in 1938. This is a time to celebrate the ongoing success of this most famous of French thinkers, and to re-consider what *Nausea* has come to 'mean' and what the future holds for it as a reading, teaching and researching experience. Twenty-five years since his death, everything is still to be said about the most renowned of his orphans. For Sartre's masterpiece of French fiction still has the potential to proliferate academic discourse across university departments and across continents. The essays that follow do not treat *Nausea* as a set of readings that need to be conveyed or passed on to posterity; they explore the living text, exposing its potential to generate new discourse well into the new millennium.

In April 2000 the French television network Arte aired, as part of their series *Le Sens de l'histoire*, a programme dedicated to Jean-Paul Sartre. The programme — a discussion of Sartre the philosopher and phenomenon — was prefaced by a short film directed by Guy Seligmann, *Sartre: Vingt ans d'absence*. This film brought together leading French philosophers and Sartrean academics in order not so much to discuss twenty years of the void left by Sartre's death in April 1980, but his continued importance in the twenty-first century. Michel Contat, a researcher with the CNRS, opens the film by challenging the need to "bury Sartre again" that seemed to him to be prevalent in the French media at the time the film was made. In questioning the thesis of Bernard-Henri Lévy's prodigious volume, *Le Siècle de Sartre* (Paris: Grasset, 2000), in which, Contat resumes, a desire is expressed to redeem Sartre from purgatory, he suggests that it is absurd to talk of purgatory in our discussion of a philosopher whose posthumous works have been so widely collated and published, and whose whole *oeuvre* is still so avidly read. This would, indeed, appear to be the very opposite of a writer's purgatory. We use the word 'writer' advisedly; for what is left of Jean-Paul Sartre — and Seligmann's documentary is at pains to highlight this point (with close-up shots of the various editions of Sartre's works) — is a daunting collection of books.

The question that the film raises for the reader of *Nausea* is the eternal one: is this a work of philosophy or a novel? *Sartre: Vingt ans d'absence* puts forward an ambivalent image of *Nausea*. It showcases the novel, giving it pride of place (it is the first text discussed after Contat's preamble) and quoting it both directly and indirectly (and it is important to state that we consider Sartre's own discussion of the text to be indirect commentary despite his privileged relationship to the novel, as writer); it also emphasises *Nausea* as philosophy, depicting its status as novel as almost incidental, as a vector — albeit the ideal one — for Sartre's early philosophy. In footage of the two mandarins of Existentialism, sitting before a group of the next generation of French philosophers (Beauvoir is shown sitting behind Sartre, as if both intently listening to him and watching over him), Sartre describes nausea as a feeling that comes with existing in the world; it is, he explains, a pathological intuition of the way things are. He had never felt nausea, or experienced Roquentin's visceral reaction in quite this way. Had his thoughts been clearer, more fully formed at that time, he would have written a philosophical text. In order to convey his thoughts on existence in the world — *pour le rendre au lecteur* — he needed to adopt the apparatus of the novel, *une forme plus romanesque*. This, too, is double-edged: *Nausea* could not have been (i.e. in the form that exists today, as the novel that is the focus of our discussion), had it not been for the need to communicate with the reader; and yet the role of this reader, and Sartre is quite clear on this, is subordinated to that of the writer. *Nausea* is portrayed as a sketch of a phenomenology that will come of age in its 1943 avatar, *Being and Nothingness*. The chestnut tree roots hold the key. Sartre was seeking to expose Roquentin's guilt (of existing) in the form of a detective novel (interestingly, Sartre's status as reader is not discussed in the film, and he was a great reader of this particular genre); he veiled his thoughts in a web of novelistic techniques in order better to unveil them, exposing the guilty party with the crushing evidence that is contingency. The novel is a necessary form in 1938 if he is to impart his feelings (Beauvoir's role in the fictionalising of *Nausea* is — logically — not broached in this film). The tree roots are the key, then, and the film quotes this famous passage at length, with close-up shots panning around a *jardin public* (in Paris, interestingly). At no point is it suggested that either the writer, as novelist or thinker, or the reader, as fan of literature and philosophy, actually gained anything more from the novelistic (or diary that becomes novel) form that Sartre adopts than an accessible expression of an inchoate phenomenological gut feeling. Philosopher Jean-Toussaint Desanti sees in *Nausea* a striking rendering of phenomenology "*en situation, sur le tas*", in which the role of Roquentin is to provide the eyes through which the reader will discover the world not as we are told that it is but as it actually exists. The fictional form, it would appear, has the perverse effect of conveying reality.[1]

In this volume, it is our contention that the novel has an existence that lies apart from its author. It is, indeed, interesting that, in the twenty-first century, a novel should continue to exist in relation to

---

[1] We might think here of strategies inside the novel itself that exploit this fictional reality / external reality tension. The 'Editors' note', for example, stands ostensibly as a proof of the text's status as 'genuine' diary; by following a well established literary tradition of such devices, however, *Nausea* sends up – and, in fact, emphasises – its status as fiction (Nicholas Hewitt, for example, discusses this eighteenth-century tradition in his article "Looking for Annie"). Indeed, one might argue that the 'Publishers' note, links *Nausea* intertextually to such particular examples of the French canon as Laclos' *Les Liaisons dangereuses*.

which it is still necessary to discuss Barthes' famous appropriation of Nietzsche. It is not that we wish to join those grave-digging commentators against whom Michel Contat argues for the continued life of Jean-Paul Sartre. In some form, however, it seems to us necessary to allude to the death of the author in order to breathe some life back into *Nausea* as novel.

For a student reading *Nausea*, and possibly Sartre, for the first time, the sheer weight of knowledge and writings for which this text has become something of a flagship can be daunting. For the teacher, too, the challenge is considerable, and it is doubtless to some degree for this reason that *Nausea* has tended to become a tool or vehicle for studying clearly defined and demarcated fields of knowledge, such as French culture or philosophy, by which it subsequently becomes subsumed. This tendency can be seen variously as logical, defensible or lamentable. As a fixed part of the French syllabus in secondary and higher education, it is a hugely important text: within the discourse of French studies, *Nausea* is prefixed with such epithets as 'a seminal novel of the twentieth century', and is a valuable point of entry into *la pensée sartrienne*. It is a novel, in short, that has been appropriated by French studies around the anglophone world as a way of teaching Existentialist thought. In France it continues to endure within a philosophical framework. In *Sartre: Vingt ans d'absence* high-school teacher Charles Pépin bears witness to the difficulty of making *Nausea* accessible to French adolescents. They are more able to engage with the image of a philosopher sitting in a café, smoking a pipe, drinking coffee and popping amphetamines than with the prose voice of Antoine Roquentin. But, admits Pépin, *Nausea* is still — with or without amphetamines — a powerful tool for explaining what it means to exist. But what of *Nausea* the novel? Our aim here is to avoid too narrow a categorisation of the text and to open it up to new approaches, new functions and new purposes.

In the context of the modern Anglo-Saxon university system, with its constant appeals to interdisciplinarity, permeability and economic reality, it is clear that *Nausea* can exist perfectly well outside the disciplines of French Studies and Philosophy. It is in the interest of broadening the appeal of *Nausea* that we have collected together in this volume authors whose approaches to the text spring from four principal areas: French Studies, Philosophy, English Studies and Comparative Literature. All four discipline areas have their own contribution to make in terms of the written text (the textual strategies at work within the novel), its context (be it literary, cultural or philosophical) and the intertextual web within which it is situated. In this volume, then, *Nausea* will be considered by academics from diverse backgrounds both for what they can do for it and what it can do for them.

Nausea *as Text*

As has already been suggested, Sartre, unlike his character Anny, has not spent the last twenty-five years 'outliving himself'; he has continued to act on the world stage as a philosopher, political commentator and novelist. The works that continue to be published (both under his own name and by philosophers and literary scholars) attest to his importance as a figure greater than the sum of his collected works. Perversely, the awe in which Sartre is held has been one of the key factors behind the tendency to delimit the textual possibilities that a reading of *Nausea* should bring forth.

The famous words "J'étais Roquentin" ("I was Roquentin"), coupled with the fact that Sartre has become too big for us to consider him as dead in any but the most physical sense, have resulted over the years since the novel's publication in the conviction that there is something that *Nausea* 'is about'. In particular, the declaration that Sartre "was Roquentin" acts to foreclose interpretative analyses of *Nausea*. The major problem in seeking to make Sartre and Roquentin coincide is that, as scholarship shows, the Sartre who wrote *Nausea* has become synonymous with the Sartre of 1943 who published *Being and Nothingness*. Roquentin has, thus, acquired philosophical baggage — and *Nausea* a whole philosophical framework — that Sartre's own words belie. To conflate the pre-war Sartre and the wartime Sartre appears to contradict his admission that at the time of writing *Nausea* he chose the novelistic form because *his own* understanding of existence was not clear enough to him to allow him to ideate his thoughts in the form of a purely philosophical work. If he were Roquentin, then we might suggest that this undermines scholars' attempts to read *Nausea* via *Being and Nothingness* (i.e. by understanding *Nausea* through *Being and Nothingness* we are perhaps guilty of putting the cart before the horse: we should use *Nausea* to explicate *Being and Nothingness*).[2] If we assume that Roquentin represents Sartre, we must, therefore, consider that he was just one historically specific instance of Sartre's incarnations. Bernard-Henri Lévy writes at length on this point. In *Le Siècle de Sartre*, Lévy demonstrates the extent to which Sartre changes between the writing of *Nausea* and the position he adopts vis-à-vis humanism after his experiences as a P.O.W. during the Second World War. Indeed, according to Lévy, if Sartre were Roquentin, he was also — just a matter of a few years later — the Autodidact. And yet, if we read his post-Liberation lecture, *Existentialism is a Humanism*, which he gave at the club Maintenant in Paris in 1945, we find a Sartre who is still at pains to distance himself from the cult-of-humanity humanism, according to which men are to be praised for the wondrous achievements of mankind. By placing his own humanism within the context of a subjectivist philosophy (there is no other universe than that which is human, he writes), Sartre not only distances himself from the Autodidact; he also critiques certain misinterpretations of *Nausea*. As early as 1945, then, Sartre himself claims *Nausea* to be a misunderstood text, a victim, as it were, of its own success — very much like Existentialism itself, a word which he declares to be all but meaningless in the mouths of most people.

There is also a philosophical problem at the root of Sartre's claim. To what extent can ontological parallels be drawn between Jean-Paul Sartre and Antoine Roquentin? In what way can he have *been* Roquentin? If we consider *Nausea* to be a philosophical novel inasmuch as its narrative tension derives from the text's constant negotiation of the philosophy / fiction dichotomy, then we should do well to question its way of existing as novel. As a being *for-itself* Sartre existed before he could be said to have an essence. There was no essential Sartreness possible until the day of his death, at which time he finally coincided with the sum total of his past actions. Be that as it may, in order for Sartre(ness) to be said to have some kind of meaning, it is necessary for inferences to be drawn by Others (it is we who must decide what he means). To equate Roquentin and Sartre is

---

[2] This is, of course, not a suggestion that we wish to push too hard, counter-hegemonically, as it were. To apply *Being and Nothingness* in order to explicate aspects of *Nausea* can, of course, be not only relevant but immensely fruitful, even within the framework of a specifically literary study of the work (see Alistair Rolls' chapter in this book).

to suggest that the novel can be said to 'mean something' upon its completion. And yet, this seems to us to be missing a vital stage in the process of 'meaning'. The novel is initially drafted according to a plan; to this extent, its essence precedes its existence. As the writer puts pen to paper, however, the text begins to develop — to a certain extent — of its 'own free will'. That is to say that there is a degree to which the formulation, in words, of an idea takes that idea into a written form that is removed from the author's initial design. Much has been said in reference to *Nausea* of the tension between the resultant novel and the philosophical treatise that was at the centre of its inception (and which Sartre himself admitted was too inchoate in 1938 to be expressed other than by fiction). Jean-Toussaint Desanti paints a picture of a thinker writing too fast for his thoughts, of a cogito, as it were, spilling out beyond the control of its body, perhaps to be written down in order to be recaptured, composing his text *au courant de la plume*, or 'as the pen took him'. So, despite the best laid plans, it seems that a text begins to come alive, as an existent, even as the author tries to forge it according to a pre-defined *telos*.

And upon the novel's completion? Whilst it is true that the novel can be likened to the piece of jazz in *Nausea* inasmuch as we readers cannot touch it, if we burn our copy, it cannot be said that *Nausea* no longer exists. As a series of words, it is untouchable. It is not for this reason, however, that its meaning is set in stone. The words can only produce meaning in the minds of *Nausea*'s readers. And so, it is upon its passing into the public domain (the moment of its separation from authorial power) that it exists fully. For it is at this moment that it becomes a *being for-Others*, exposing itself to them as an object of their interpretation.

The existential(ist) novel, like any *being for-itself*, can only exist in situation. Unlike Descartes' dualism, according to which one thinks therefore one is, existentialist man 'thinks therefore he is what he is not and is not what he is'. *Nausea* is a projection onto the world, frozen beyond the control of authorial consciousness, and accessible only to the Other. An existential(ist) novel is, therefore, one whose meaning(s) must be constantly (re-) negotiated not at the interface of the author / text but at that of the text and its readers. The reader is the Other who holds the key. This empowers the reader — who acquires the authority and freedom to dare to infer meaning — whilst retaining the novel's freshness: the reader can only ever understand the text's 'shallow level of being', to borrow a term from Neil Levy's *Sartre*; the novel cannot *be* in a 'profound' way any more than can a human being. To seek to impose a retrospective essence on a living text is, to continue our use of Sartrean vocabulary, to read in bad faith. As readers of *Nausea* we must seek to apprehend the text in the ways that it is, in full knowledge of the fact that we can only ever unveil layers of possibility. To impose hegemonic meaning upon a novel (to tell people what 'it is all about') is to glue it in place.

It is the aim of this volume to give readers access to a number of potential readings. For the novel does have meanings. Just as we who are writing this introduction are not French lecturers in any essential sense, there is clearly a way in which we are French lecturers. And so it is for *Nausea*: it is not because it is not only and essentially a treatise on contingency that it is not a treatise on contingency. For *Nausea* is still a treatise on contingency inasmuch as this is one of the ways in which it *is in situation*, in which it *is in relation* to the Other (reader); in short, this is one way in which it *exists*. This realisation that the meanings of the text are there to be made does not devalue the novel — or Sartre via the novel — rather it liberates the text, from the rigid framework of existing critical dogma, and provides new structures of meaning from within which it can be free.

In the light of these opening comments, the first chapter of this collection is a remarkably liberating reading. Lawrence Schehr draws on all his expertise (in the fields of the nineteenth- and twentieth-century French novel, Queer Theory and — even — French cuisine) to reread the figure of the Autodidact. Just as the self-taught man becomes one with the books that he internalises, he leaves himself exposed to a keen eye. Schehr opens him up, exposing Sartre's description of him for what it is. For the Autodidact is there to be read, and it is almost as if Sartre is taking pleasure in surrounding him with words that he knows the reader will misconstrue. Schehr does not draw our attention to the words of the Corsican librarian, who attacks the Autodidact for his violation of the schoolboy, in order to offer up the possibility that Roquentin may himself be a homosexual; rather, he exposes the scene in the library as the climax of a long sequence of exchanges between Roquentin and the Autodidact, in which the (body-) language is not only suggestive of homoeroticism but actually simulates sexual intercourse. The reader can only feel some of the Autodidact's shame: we have read the pages but have not understood the words. Schehr points to Sartre's use of juxtaposition, through which a glimpse of truth is hushed up, buried beneath apparently clumsy bursts of, often obscene, monologue. The text's textuality is shown to be its sexuality. *Nausea* has a coy, provocative side; it will kiss and tell as long as you do not avert your gaze.

A good example of this is the scene where the two men meet for lunch. It does not take a massive leap of imagination to read the Autodidact's 'love of men' as an avowal of homosexuality. Where Schehr's reading is so powerful is in its revelation that this admission of humanism is a rewriting — by a man who is made of text — of events that have already taken place in *Nausea*. Readers are once again made to realise that they were indeed present at the moment of intimacy between men which the Autodidact recounts. This diary that Roquentin designs to be a setting out of events in a permanent present (the truth aired *en direct*) becomes a forum where the Autodidact and Roquentin revel in invented tales of their past (the former as a P.O.W. and the latter as Anny's lover). This monument to bad faith all begins to look like an avoidance of sexuality; or, rather, sexuality becomes redirected, veiled and transposed. Schehr's conclusion is almost a remake, the last instalment of 'Sex in the Library'. As such, this chapter sets the scene perfectly for this collection of essays: Schehr's translation of what is on the menu at lunch is picked up by Debra Hely (who arrives at similarly homoerotic conclusions by intertextual means), whilst the caress in the library will be revisited in Rolls' hands-on reading. As Schehr notes, the Autodidact's language "does not seduce through the contents but through the form"; and it is this language of forms that Schehr enables us to read.

The remaining chapters in this section all address the question of Roquentin's nausea, each approaching the question from a different perspective. George Woods' chapter is all about perspectives; her chapter posits nausea within the framework of the visual arts, revealing the root of the nausea to lie in the tension created by Roquentin's opposition of visual perception and mental conception. In this way she questions 'meaning' as the application of abstract understanding to a world-canvas where objects are simply present. Tom Martin's chapter acts as a rejoinder, seeking to investigate the way in which the world may be considered to be always already meaningful. And finally, Peter Poiana elevates the nausea to the level of protagonist; by approaching the text from both a Freudian and

Lacanian angle, he is able to offer a different analysis of the body language that is central to Schehr's reading whilst rehabilitating the discourse of psychoanalysis as a means of opening the Sartrean novel.

Woods demonstrates how meaning in Roquentin's world depends on the correct light settings. *Nausea* gradually exposes as illusory the feeling of well-being that comes from moody, ambient lighting; Roquentin will reject the dimmer-switch, favouring instead the close-ups on individual objects picked out by the contrast of bright light on a dark background. Diffused light, Woods reveals, offers a visual overview that the brain must supplement; mental constructs seek to impose an understanding of what has been perceived by overlaying a map of abstract 'knowledge'. Meaning is thus shown to be created by an individual reading the real world through a preconceived set of values. The diffused lighting that allows this conception of the world becomes, for Roquentin, a sinister fog. The atmosphere of Bouville, when the nausea overwhelms him, replicates the darkly realistic description of noir literature, in which life is shown in all its brutality and nuances (in the noir novel, as in *Nausea*, life is not 'black and white'; events are always ambiguously couched in shades of grey). By contrasting the uses of light in the novel, which are in turns Cubist and Impressionist, Woods arrives at a definition of the nausea as Roquentin's "[rumination] over the gulf between perception and interpretation."

Tom Martin follows on from Woods by introducing a third element into the meaning equation. For it is not enough for us to say that an object's meaning is a mental appraisal made by the subject of that object's existence in the world; that we are able to consider the object in abstract terms is made possible by an understanding of meaning which is independent of us. Meaning is, Martin argues, intersubjective; and, as such, it precedes our individual existence. The nausea is therefore Roquentin's realisation that meaningful relations are not born of necessity or internal logic. Where Martin seeks to innovate is not in a search to justify a reading of nausea as a state that accompanies a revelation of the nature of existence; rather, he aims to explain the disappointment that Roquentin feels, which seems to stem from a set of implicit *a priori* expectations of how the world ought to be. He discusses, in philosophical terms, the way in which meaning is generated by the interaction of subject and object (i.e., the being in-itself cannot 'mean' in the absence of a subject, but neither can the subject bear sole responsibility for producing meaning in the object). The meaning that we need in order to act in the world (our projects help us to create meaning but we are also shaped by them[3]) is made possible by our interaction with others. Martin considers Roquentin's problem to lie in his Manichean attitude towards meaning, according to which it shall be essential or it shall not be. The fog that Woods reads in terms of diffused light, and which accompanies the nausea, becomes, in Martin's analysis, the grey area through which Roquentin cannot find his way. And it is in this grey area that the possibility for some kind of meaning lies.

In the final paper of this section Peter Poiana follows what appears to be a familiar trajectory: like Martin, he begins his reading with the pebble scene and, like so many philosophical interpretations of *Nausea*, concludes with the famous incident of the chestnut tree. In 'The Subject as Symptom in *Nausea*', however, Poiana offers an analysis of Roquentin's drives that differs radically from phenomenological interpretation. He begins, in a similar tone to this introduction, by justifying a move away from the discourse of Sartrean Existentialism. The unconscious, he argues, is fundamental to the novel, however much the Sartre of that period may have denied its reality in terms of the being for-itself. As such, *Nausea* teems with material for the psychoanalyst, and Poiana's reading focuses on its potential as a site of (continual instances of) resistance to impulses recognised by the subject as dangerous. The nausea functions accordingly as symptom.

In light of his reading, the drives that Poiana exposes can be seen as subterranean currents running through this volume. For example, his discussion of the importance of substitution — the act whereby, in Freud's view, the subject replaces one object with another in an act of sacrifice before a dangerous impulse — is picked up by the discussion of fetishism in Rolls' chapter. Indeed, both Poiana and Rolls reveal the narrative to be driven by a lack of catharsis, where writing replaces — unsatisfactorily — more carnal urges. This concept is also clear in Schehr's chapter where acts of sex are shown to be fleeting, disguised and always disappointing. Where Rolls and Schehr focus on the language of the hands and face, Poiana concentrates his reading around the throat, revealing the famous encounter over lunch to be one

---

[3] In the same way we make free choices because we are free, but it is only through the choices we make that we can be free…

of a number of scenes driven by the tension of a pleasure/displeasure binary (in this case, based on ingestion). In his discussion of Roquentin's loss of language, Poiana moves from a Freudian analysis of hysteria towards a Lacanian reading of loss of the expression of desire. He thus shows how the diary works against its own stated purpose: the idea of speaking out, of opening up (to a reader), instead of producing a catharsis, only points to a vague solution that may or may not happen in the future. Indeed, not only does the symptom not abate over the course of Roquentin's production of text, it actually takes over; as he offers up his throat to the symptom, the nausea speaks in his stead. And the very fear that he expresses when confronted with scenes of *jouissance* (Poiana cites Roquentin's ambivalent attitude towards the Autodidact's submission to his symptom in the library) is ultimately abandoned before the tree root that both disgusts him and holds his gaze. Nausea is shown to be a quicksand that pulls one further in the more one struggles; and the very act of giving this suffocation the name 'existence' seems to bear witness to the victory of the symptom over the subject.

Nausea *in Context*

The work of Jean-Paul Sartre, and *Nausea* in particular, is amongst the most extensively studied in the world and yet there has been remarkably little published about the context within which his work was produced. Indeed, rarely has what Bourdieu describes as the myth of the 'créateur incréé' been better illustrated than in the case of Sartre. On its publication *Nausea* was greeted by many critics as a work of novelty and originality; they described it as a starting point, oriented towards a future which it would help to construct.[4] The danger is to follow their lead, to refuse to see what links *Nausea* to its situation. This section seeks to fill a gap in scholarship which still remains in relating the novel to its literary and intellectual context and predecessors. Bourdieu's category of the literary field provides the over-arching theoretical framework within which these chapters seek an understanding of the characteristics of *Nausea*: not only those which the novel may share with other literary forms and intellectual positions, but its originality, its innovations both generic and thematic

---

[4] D. Hollier, '*La Nausée*, en attendant', in *La Naissance du phénomène Sartre, raisons d'un succès 1938-45*, ed. by I. Galster (Paris: Seuil, 2001), pp. 86-100.

that reflect Sartre's struggle against existing conventions to express his own position.

The most extensive attempt to place Sartre within the literary and intellectual field of his time, and one which adopts a Bourdieusian perspective, is Anna Boschetti's *Sartre et les Temps modernes* (1985) which argues that his dominance resulted from his unique positioning at the summit of both the literary and intellectual fields. As the title suggests, however, Boschetti focuses on the decade following the Second World War rather than on the context of *Nausea*. The recent collection of articles edited by Ingrid Galster, *La Naissance du phénomène Sartre, raisons d'un succès 1938-1945* (2001) takes up the debate with Boschetti, who contributes an article to the volume. *La Naissance du phénomène Sartre* brings together articles by many leading Sartre scholars and allows us to assess the latest contributions of Sartrean scholarship in this area. The articles help to position Sartre in the intellectual and literary field of his time but tend to concentrate, as the title suggests, on the reception of his works rather than on their production. Moreover, by bracketing together the pre- and immediate post-war period, the articles risk losing sight of the specificity of *Nausea*. The danger is then to view the novel through the subsequent work of philosophy, *Being and Nothingness,* and to lose sight therefore of both the specifically literary qualities of *Nausea* and of its possible divergence from the philosophical positions of the later work.

The authors in this section 'Context' attempt, on the contrary, to dispense with the perspectives of hindsight and seek to understand the emergence of *Nausea* in the context of the literary and intellectual fields of its time — which is not, moreover, the period of its publication but the twenties and early thirties, when the work was conceived. The challenge is to recognise in the difficulties Sartre encountered as he wrestled throughout the thirties with the text — the difficulty of writing attested in his letters to Beauvoir and the length of its gestation — his struggle to carve out his own space within these fields. The chapters in this section seek to identify the influences accepted or rejected, the forms adopted or transformed, the references whether implicit or explicit to other works.

Denis Hollier defines the challenge of understanding *Nausea* as that of identifying: "la transgression de la loi du genre sous tous ses aspects (un non-conformisme à la fois générique et génétique) [qui] est sans doute le véritable noyau générateur de *La Nausée* [the transgression of the law of genre in all its aspects (non-conformism, both generic and genetic) which is no doubt the true generative kernel of *Nausea*]" (Hollier, p. 95). What were the generic forms, the literary styles available to Sartre as he began his career as a writer? What hierarchy of genres might have dictated his choices, what themes were seen as valid, which predecessors might be called on to legitimise his enterprise? How did he mark his difference from the accepted norms? Only a close textual reading of *Nausea* in the context of the literary and intellectual fields of the early twentieth century can begin to answer such questions.

The challenge in relating *Nausea* to its context lies in the limitless extent of that context: whether literary or philosophical, political, social or personal. All aspects of Sartre's personal and intellectual itinerary are relevant to the study of *Nausea* in its context: the scope of his reading (attested to by *Words*), his studies within and outside the academy, the influence of the dominant literary movements of his youth, especially Surrealism, his work as a teacher, his philosophical studies in Berlin and the occasional lectures that he gave on contemporary American fiction at Le Havre library, to which Annie Cohen-Solal draws our attention.[5] The topic certainly deserves a book to itself, yet here we are able only to hint at some of the less explored aspects of the context of his early work.

The question of the title affords perhaps a way into the discussion to which these chapters contribute. As is well known, *Nausea* was not Sartre's choice at all: the text submitted to Gallimard was entitled *Melancholia*. If inspired by the Dürer engraving, the romantic overtones associated with this term are also strong: 'mélancolie', 'spleen', 'ennui' (the latter term appears in notes for the early drafts[6]) — who could pretend that the distaste for ordinary life, the sense of monstrous otherness, the self-absorption, are not tropes of the nineteenth-century romantic and post-romantic literature in which Sartre was steeped?

The boredom and frustration of long days spent in front of a blank sheet of paper; the contempt for the bourgeoisie, their respectability, their rituals, their smugness and philistinism; the condemnation of art that flatters and gives them a good conscience, that hides their faults; the revelation of the music that saves the world, the creator and the

---

[5] A. Cohen-Solal, *Sartre: 1905-1980* (Paris: Gallimard, 1999), p. 186.
[6] J.-P. Sartre, *Œuvres romanesques* (Paris: Gallimard, 1981), p. 1684.

singer; the final project of writing a novel which will be as bright and hard as steel and will make people ashamed of their existence and bring salvation: "le salut auquel aspire Roquentin, *in fine*, est celui de l'artiste qui oppose à la pesante et fade contingence de l'existence le fil tranchant de l'œuvre d'art [the salvation to which Roquentin aspires is, in the end, that of the artist who opposes to faded, heavy existence the sharp cutting edge of the work of art]."[7] These features of *Nausea* — however transformed by the particularities of setting and character — can be found in many a nineteenth-century novel.

But rather than romantic, to be more precise, *Nausea* is redolent of late Romanticism, the disenchanted Romanticism of the late nineteenth century which finds expression in the symbolist project of Mallarmé, the poet who will be for Sartre the exemplary figure of the writer in search of the absolute.[8] Critics have not, in our view, paid enough attention to the persistence of the symbolist conception of art and the artist, which continued in the decades following the First World War: it is not merely a nineteenth-century mode relegated to the museum of literary movements but is represented by one of the best known writers of the period, André Suarès. Elizabeth Rechniewski seeks to trace the parallels between the preoccupations of this second-generation symbolist writer and Sartre's literary and philosophical works of the thirties. Through close textual analysis and broad conceptual comparisons she demonstrates that the two writers share a vision of the world which developed in the second half of the nineteenth century amongst the artists and writers of the restricted field of literary production, and which has its roots in the growing alienation of the artist from the general public. As the 'restricted' and 'mass' fields of artistic production become increasingly distinct and antagonistic, founded as they are on contradictory principles and aims, a vicious cycle of mutual incomprehension and hostility opposes avant-garde artist and mass public. The former's 'search for distinction' finds few more stark expressions than in the work of André Suarès whose tortured aspiration to achieve transcendence through art has as its counterpart his horror of the contingent: the material forces which seek to abase and destroy the artist.

---

[7] M. Contat, 'Sartre et la gloire', in *La Naissance du phénomène Sartre, raisons d'un succès 1938-45*, ed. by I. Galster, (Paris: Seuil, 2001), pp. 29-41 (p. 32).
[8] J.-P. Sartre, *Mallarmé: La Lucidité et sa face d'ombre* (Paris: Gallimard, 1986).

It can be argued that the preoccupation with contingency — in its literary, philosophical and personal forms — is an essential component of the situation in which *Nausea* was conceived. Beauvoir refers in *Mémoires d'une jeune fille rangée* to the 'theory of contingency' that Sartre was elaborating in 1929 and which contained "déjà en germe ses idées sur l'être, l'existence, la nécessité, la liberté [already in germination his ideas on being, existence, necessity, freedom]".[9] When Sartre began work in 1931 on what was to become *Nausea* he described it as his 'factum on Contingency'. For Contat and Rybalka his early writings are essentially an exploration of the theme.[10] They consider his reflection on contingency as "le noyau d'originalité le plus décidé, le fondement le plus radicalement personnel et c'est à cette intuition originaire qu'il cherche des confirmations dans ses lectures littéraires et philosophiques [the most pronounced kernel of originality, the most radically personal foundation and it is to confirm this original intuition that he searches in his literary and philosophical readings]" (p. 1660). The chapters in this section, 'Context', are characterised by recognition and exploration of the unresolvable antagonism of contingency and the absolute that can be said to lie at the heart of *Nausea*. Rechniewski contests, however, the originality of Sartre's formulation of contingency, arguing that it had found highly developed metaphorical, literary and conceptual expression in earlier writers. The other chapters in this section similarly relativise the claim of originality.

The impossibility of transcendence except through art; the polarisation of the writer and society which positions the former as monstrous outsider; the objectification of the self, these are some of the forms of alienation which stem from the fundamental antagonism of contingency and the absolute and which characterise the universe of *Nausea*. The chapters in this section illustrate these forms of alienation, alienation from the self, from others and from the world: for Rechniewski, it is the alienation of the artist from society which underlies the *vision du monde* of both Sartre and Suarès. Amanda Crawley-Jackson explores the alienation from the self that awaits Roquentin at his journey's end, in the city. Chris Falzon argues that

[9] S. Beauvoir, *Mémoires d'une jeune fille rangée* (Paris: Gallimard, 1958), p. 342.
[10] M. Contat and M. Rybalka, '*La Nausée*: Notice, Documents, Notes et Variantes', in J.-P. Sartre, *Œuvres romanesques* (Paris: Gallimard, 1981), pp. 1655-1678 (p. 1661).

Roquentin's impossibly strict demand for meaning has its roots in his alienation from others and their socially constructed meanings.

Falzon argues that *Nausea* allows Sartre to undertake a radical philosophical critique of existing beliefs, to explore the limits of previous theories of the foundation of meaning including those of Descartes and Husserl. Roquentin's process of discovery unfolds through an exploration of the travails and the limits of consciousness and the gradual revelation of the fragility of the categories and concepts on which unreflecting consciousness is based. As against Descartes, Roquentin's exploration of the cogito results not in certainty but in doubt: introspection is not a 'safe place' a fortress of sure knowledge, but a place of irreality, of surreal images and nightmarish landscapes. Husserl's 'philosophical reduction': the "suspension of all empirical existential considerations and all a priori assumptions about entities external (transcendent) to experience" in order to transform consciousness into a transcendental consciousness, or transcendental subjectivity, a transcendentally purified stream of experiences from which a genuinely phenomenological constitution of the world can begin[11] is also shown to be an inadequate basis for founding meaning, for in *Nausea* the things-in-themselves haunt and colonise consciousness, they refuse to be purified and tamed, to reveal their transcendental meanings.

Falzon argues that *Nausea* — through its implicit rejection of these attempts at founding meaning — clears the way for Sartre's own philosophical account of being, undertaken in *Being and Nothingness*. This treatise presents itself as overcoming the negative stage of critique of foundational theories of meaning through postulating a radically free subject that exists insofar as it negates itself and all forms of determinism. But Falzon argues that the heroic subject of *Being and Nothingness* does not offer a solution to the grounding of meaning but a new set of problems: the Sartrean subject "reigns supreme but it is also wholly unsupported, strangely unlocated, problematically abstract". Falzon suggests that *Nausea* provides the key to understanding the problematic nature of Sartre's philosophical position: Roquentin's growing alienation from all forms of social contact and common project, his physical isolation so tellingly described as the novel unfolds, illustrate in literary form the

---

[11] E. Pivcevic, *Husserl and Phenomenology* (London: Hutchinson, 1970), p. 65.

philosophical consequences of detachment from the meanings created in social contexts. *Nausea* illustrates the 'phenomenological problem': "it is inevitable that the belief that truth resides in the interiority of Man should create a problem of others" (Pivcevic, p. 149). Roquentin has set up an impossibly high criterion — the demand for an absolute foundation — and discards as inadequate 'too human' attempts at constructing meaning. In this 'all-or-nothing' universe, the lack of an absolute foundation of meaning plunges life and the world into meaninglessness.

Crawley-Jackson's chapter draws attention to the context of travel and adventure: the myth of the adventurer, the lure of action, these were common themes of the inter-war years — and indeed of Suarès who was fascinated by the man of action and even more by figures such as d'Annunzio who were both men of action and artists. That Sartre wished to foreground the wrestle with the temptation of adventure is made clear by the phrase contained in the publicity band which he himself suggested for *Nausea*: "Il n'y a pas d'aventures". We remember too that the alternative title that Sartre had proposed, when Gallimard ruled out *Melancholia*, was *Les Aventures extraordinaires d'Antoine Roquentin*. If there is to be found there a reference to Robinson Crusoe, as Contat and Rybalka suggest (p. 1720), it is just as possible that Sartre had the examples of more recent adventurers in mind, the case of Malraux perhaps, who had already contributed so much to the myth of the adventurer through his life and his novels, and yet who had also already done so much to deconstruct it. As early as 1926 in *La Tentation de L'Occident* Malraux had suggested the futility of the Western fascination with the East, the risk of disintegration of the Western spirit, the malaise of the post-war generations who did not know where to direct their energy, the disenchantment with the myths and legends of fabulous explorations. If his early novels — *Les Conquérants* (1928), *La Voie royale* (1930), *La Condition humaine* (1933) — plunge their protagonists into the extremes of 'extraordinary adventures', they nonetheless suggest the ultimate futility of human action.

Early in *Nausea* Roquentin recounts the sudden disenchantment which overwhelms him as he sits in the office of a French civil servant, discussing an archaeological mission: on the table stands a Khmer statuette. This scene almost certainly echoes the one in *La Voie royale* where Claude describes his project to Albert Rameges, director of the Institut français: on his desk are photographs of Khmer and Cham statues.[12] While Claude presses on with his adventure, but discovers in the death of Perken the nullity of human effort, Roquentin returns to France, to the stultifying existence of Bouville, and 'la nausée des fins de voyage'. Crawley-Jackson situates Roquentin's experience within that of the protagonists of Sartre's earlier fiction and compares it to the dystopias that the latter find at their journey's end. If the early protagonists reach a heterotopia of irreconcilable opposites, Roquentin's journey's end is in the stagnant liminality of Bouville. (We should note that Bouville recalls not only 'Boue-ville' but 'Bout-ville'). As the forms of the city disintegrate around him, he is engulfed in the very condition he had sought to escape: ambiguity, incompletenesss, a kind of perpetual in-betweenness, caught forever in a process of becoming, trapped in the web of process and flux, symbolising the ambiguity of Man who is what he is not and is not what he is.

Nausea *as Intertext*

Intertextuality — as a new critical practice for reading text — was born in the late 1960s, the term being coined by Julia Kristeva.[13] The main thrust of intertextuality is an opening up of the term 'text' itself: instead of seeing individual novels, poems, etc. as closed, autonomous systems, Kristeva considers all individual examples of text to belong to one 'text', the whole system linking all its constituent parts to one another. This system of interrelations, she defines as intertextuality. The principal difference between intertextuality and other negotiations of textual networks (such as influence, for example) lies in the emphasis that it places on the active engagement of the reader. Whereas examples of author influence can often be easy to spot (the influential text being clearly signposted in the new text), it is not always clear what purpose they serve or what the reader should 'do with them'. Intertextuality empowers the reader to construct the network outside the parameters of the written text, between one book and another. This practice recalls (post-)structuralist theories of the

---

[12] A. Malraux, *La Voie Royale, Romans* (Paris: Gallimard, 1976), pp. 201-5.
[13] J. Kristeva, *Séméiotikè: Recherches pour une sémanalyse* (Paris: Editions du Seuil, 1969).

writerly reader (as defined by Barthes in S/Z[14]), where the reader does not so much understand (*read*) the meaning of a work as actually generate (*write*) it. There are various advantages, as far as textual analysis is concerned, that an intertextual approach to text offers over one guided by the principles of author influence: firstly, the reader adopts a broader critical perspective, importing a whole new set of codes — which are no longer external to the text, but existent within the broader Kristevan text — to read the novel, poem, etc. under examination; secondly, the reading practice is no longer inhibited by troublesome chronological details (whereas *Nausea* cannot be influenced by a work written after 1938, the intertextuality linking it to any other text, irrespective of its place in history, can be used to inform a reading of both).

There are clear links between intertextuality and postmodernism; both have radical implications for the concept of identity. Postmodernism has effectively dissolved the structures through which an individual's identity was constructed (Queer theory is a more recent off-shoot of such fluidity, the way in which we view our own sexuality now being far less dependent on binary structures of male/female, hetero-/homosexual, etc.). In terms of textual identity, Kristevan intertextuality brought about a radical change in our attitudes to the objects that we read. Whereas Modernism had already made full use of self-referential writing techniques — readers being constantly made aware of the status of the text that they are reading as fiction — intertextuality moved beyond any need for the text to be self-consciously literary. That the text is one piece of literature within one giant text called literature would henceforth be a given: the onus would no longer be on the writer to encode this status into the text (via such techniques as the *mise en abyme*, for example); instead the references to the broader (inter)text would always already exist to the extent that the reader could recognise them.

And yet, in practice it is not always the aim of the reader to engage with a text at the level of its intertextual status. And, indeed, as Michel Riffaterre has pointed out in his work on reader-response theory, the reader can only bring to his or her critical engagement with a given text the sum total of his or her previous reading: clearly no intertextuality can exist between Freud and *Nausea* for the reader if the reader has not read Freud. As such, the texts that tend to yield the

---

[14] R. Barthes, *S/Z* (Paris: Seuil, 1970).

most interesting intertextual analyses are those that expose themselves appropriately to the reader (i.e. a text often has to be self-consciously modernist in order for the reader to be empowered to read it in a postmodern way). The chapters in both the 'Text' and 'Intertext' sections of this present volume will reveal *Nausea* to be such a text.

Whilst work has been done on the postmodern aspects of Sartre and his writing, the tendency has been for *Nausea* not to figure prominently. In his approach to the subject, for example, Nik Farrell Fox emphasises the standard philosophical landmarks: *Being and Nothingness, Critique of Dialectical Reason* and *Search for a Method.* This is only to be expected given the troubled status of *Nausea* as 'somewhere between novel and philosophy'. Indeed, there are only three references to the novel in *The New Sartre*. For example, Fox explains how Sartre's theorisation of the self changes progressively (towards postmodernism) throughout his career. He writes as follows of the relationship between identity and the Rollebon project:

> Sartre's early work (*The Transcendence of the Ego, Nausea, Being and Nothingness*) theorizes the subject in isolation from language and presupposes that any linguistic determination of the self will not affect it in any substantive way. This can be seen in *Nausea*, for instance, when Roquentin becomes aware that his self is not identifiable with the referent 'historian', giving rise eventually to the experience of nausea itself.[15]

There is nothing wrong with what Fox is suggesting. What has happened is that *Nausea* has (again) been appropriated as a philosophical text. Fox is able to use *Nausea* this way because there is an understanding shared between him and his readers as to what the text is all about. This is an appropriation of *Nausea* to a postmodern end, which, perversely, denies the novel its own postmodern identity. For Roquentin's self can be seen to be born directly of the Rollebon project. His very name, *Roqu*entin, can be found in the pseudo-historical evidence from the Rollebon case, which not only draws physical similarities between Rollebon and his historian but also contains the following homonyms: Mlle de *Roque*laure and *Roque*fort cheese[16]. Sartre is deliberately setting *Nausea* up as a text about texts,

---

[15] N. Fox, *The New Sartre: Explorations in Postmodernism* (New York; London: Continuum, 2003), p. 22.

[16] A. Rolls, "'This Lovely, Sweet Refrain": Reading the Fiction back into *Nausea'*, *Literature and Aesthetics*, 13: 2 (2003), 57-72.

made out of texts. This textuality has so often been denied by philosophers for the simple reason that they have tended to see the novel as informing the philosophy, thus becoming blinded to alternative interpretative possibilities. The only other substantive reference to the novel in Fox's text is once again doubly interesting in this respect: firstly, it is a valuable remark (which we should like to see followed up in due course); and secondly, it draws on the famous chestnut tree scene, which has become a metonym for the (frozen meaning of the) novel:

> This [the tendency for an 'order of things' to be imposed by the socially and historically conditioned frameworks of human society] is well illustrated in *Nausea* where Roquentin tries to apprehend the objective, unmediated reality of the roots of a chestnut tree but ends up feeling nausea prompted by the recognition of the stark separation between the brute, viscous reality of the thing and the words and concepts we use to capture it. In this respect it is possible to view Sartre's epistemology in *Nausea* as a (postmodern) reaction against the (modern) scientific idea of *representation* in which it is thought that we can authentically represent or 'picture' the true, essential nature of things. (Fox, p.171, fn 13)

Nausea has not always been appropriated to philosophical ends. It has been adopted by authors of fiction, usually in a way that might more properly be termed influence than intertextuality. One of the most famous, and oft-quoted, examples is the use made of both *Nausea* and Jean-Paul Sartre as textual import. In his novel *L'Écume des jours* (1947) Boris Vian showcases grossly caricatural aspects of Existentialism, not so much as philosophy but as post-War phenomenon. Sartre the icon of the Parisian Left Bank becomes Jean-Sol Partre, and his famous conference of 1945 is parodied with ample punning on *la nausée*, including displays of stuffed vomit being presented to those in attendance. This clearly exposes *L'Écume des jours* to intertextual analysis via *Nausea*, and also opens a possibility of importing the novelistic strategies at the heart of Vian's work (back) into Sartre's text.[17]

According to Kristeva's vision of the text, *Nausea* joined the intertextual network from the very moment that Roquentin was first read. Sartre himself became a truly intercultural artefact a year before the publication of Vian's *L'Écume des jours*. 1946 saw publication of

---

[17] For an example of an intertextual analysis of these two texts, see A. Rolls, *The Flight of the Angels: Intertextuality in Four Novels by Boris Vian* (Amsterdam; Atlanta: Rodopi, 1999).

Robert Scipion's *Prête-moi ta plume*, a novel-cum-pastiche that presents — through anagrams — the whole cast of the Left Bank at the time of the Liberation. Foremost among these are "les Genpolçarthres" who sit around cafés smoking pipes and "sucking on nausea".[18]

A less well known example of intertextuality linking a later novel to *Nausea* can be found in Georges Simenon's novel *Maigret et la vieille dame*, in which Maigret reminisces about the predictions that were printed in the almanacs of his youth:

> Each day of the month was followed by a prediction. One would read, for example:
> 17 August. Melancholia
> 18 August. Undertake nothing. Do not travel.
> 19 August. Morning will be happy, but beware the evening.[19]

The similarity between these lines (right down to the expression of Melancholia, the term that famously stood as title for Sartre's novel before 'Nausea' was finally chosen) and various diary lines from *Nausea* is striking. The authors in this section use examples such as these to read *Nausea*, opening the way into the enormous potential for meaning that intertextuality makes available.

Keryn Stewart's chapter, '"I Have Finished Travelling": Travel, Displacement and Intertextuality in Jean-Paul Sartre's *Nausea*', displays the way in which a novel can point simultaneously inside and outside the bounds of its own pages. By drawing on the exercises in intertextuality performed by Michel Riffaterre, Stewart provides provocative examples of *Nausea*'s ability — by virtue of its deliberate construction — to elicit reader response; and by so doing, she explores the creative potential that lies at the interface of reader and text whilst, at the same time, indicating the power of the novel's construction (the author-text interface) to kindle such production of meaning. It is important to underline this dual perspective, for all too often intertextual analyses fall prey to accusations of seemingly random comparisons being drawn between two unrelated texts. It is the duty of the critic to establish the 'relatedness' of her texts, to establish her

---

[18] "Fumeurs de pipe [...] et suceurs de nausées, voilà les Genpolçarthres", R. Scipion, *Prête-moi ta plume* (Paris: Gallimard, 1946), p. 211.
[19] G. Simenon, *Maigret et la vieille dame* (Paris: Presses de la Cité, 1951), p. 144 (authors' translation).

intertext. Stewart's choice of David Wilson's novel *Love and Nausea* will ruffle few feathers; it is a novel that explicitly declares its debt of influence to Sartre's text from the front-cover to the last page. Stewart is thus able to use this link as a seal of approval, drawing on its authority to reverse the flow: the influence that *Nausea* has on Wilson's novel is put to creative use through the revelation that *Love and Nausea* can retrospectively inform our understanding of Sartre's text.

Having established the intertextual potential of *Nausea* — and the fruitfulness of intertextual criticism itself — Stewart is able to steer her work into uncharted, and unexpected, waters. Her examination of Wim Wenders' film *Paris, Texas* is an exemplar of double-edged intertextual criticism: whilst the parallel drawn between the road movie and Roquentin's diary leads the reader of *Nausea* out of the novel in search of new illumination, there is a constant pull back to the novel. For Stewart is able to demonstrate how her intertext, far from inventing meaning *ex nihilo*, highlights words that are already there.

Given the revelations of the essays in this volume, one might wonder whether *Nausea* is a novel in good or bad faith. This is an extremely difficult question to answer, especially since bad faith itself is such a complicated term. It is this very question, however, that Debra Hely asks implicitly in 'Fact or Fiction? Reading through the Nothingness behind *Nausea*'. Implicitly — because the concept of nothingness is her starting point, just as it lies at the heart of every role that our consciousness plays in our every dealing. And our ability to be in bad faith — that is, our ability to lie to ourselves — depends upon this void that separates us from ourselves. This void is, of course, nothing, which makes the very concept of lying to oneself more complicated than it may at first appear. In his study of bad faith as expounded in *Being and Nothingness*, Marc Wetzel explains that the standard definition of this concept as a case of 'lying to oneself' depends on an understanding of what it means to 'lie', which is less clear than first appears:

> Indeed, the essence of lying implies that the liar is completely aware of the truth that he is disguising. One does not lie about what one does not know; one does not lie when one propagates an error to which one has oneself fallen victim, and neither is one lying when one is mistaken. [...] The liar's intention is to deceive,

and he does not seek to hide this intention or to mask the translucidity of consciousness.[20]

And yet it is not Hely's purpose here to examine the nature of truth. Neither is it to ascertain to what extent the author/narrator is duped by his own game. Rather she takes it as a given that this nothingness that intervenes between us and the world in which we are situated (that which simultaneously joins us to it and distances us from it) is the same as that which distances the reader from the text that she is reading.

Not only can we not be sure whether or not the facts being divulged are true; we cannot know either to whom the truths or lies are being told. This parodied diary form introduces a duality into the consciousness of the narrator: in terms of bad faith, Roquentin is set up as the teller (writer) of the lie and the receiver (reader) of the lie. As Wetzel writes: "[I]n bad faith it is from myself that I mask the truth. Therefore the deceiver/deceived duality does not exist here" (p. 50). As the Autodidact will rightly point out, one writes with an audience in mind. And, as a writer writing to be read, Roquentin inverts the strategies of the Autodidact whose aim is to read in order to find that his thoughts have already been written. In appearing to lie to himself (to be in bad faith), Roquentin is lying to his reader, transferring responsibility for the truth of the text onto us. And in so doing, he is offering to the reader the truth of our existence in the world: as the world only offers a truth that is relative, and which hinges upon our interpretation of it, so too the facts on which *Nausea* is constructed have no basis in some empirical concept of truth. This is, as we have already suggested, the paradox of the philosophical novel: it is only as hard as steel inasmuch as it responds entirely to the plans written by its author. If *Nausea* only means what Sartre wants it to mean, then it can appeal to some idea of purity. But the intertextual reading puts the reader to the forefront; it is she who makes the novel 'mean something'. Yet clearly it is not enough just to say that 'everything is relative'. Hely takes this as her starting point, and seeks to reveal how Sartre-Roquentin consciously exploits, or points up, this relationship by offering a selection of details that correspond to or

---

[20] M. Wetzel, *Sartre: La mauvaise foi (L'Etre et le Néant)* (Paris: Hatier, 1985), p. 49 (authors' translation).

diverge from what may be considered historical accuracy in various degrees. She takes the examples of the recordings to which Roquentin listens, comparing lyrics and biographical details to historical records. And by revealing the surprising incoherence of Roquentin's account, she applies the concept of the unreliable narrator to other aspects of his relations in the text. In Hely's chapter, intertextuality is thus shown to reflect the nothingness that is around the novel, that *is* the novel in the sense that it is the meeting point where reader and author negotiate meaning.

It is this same concept — of the convergence in the pages of the book of the author and reader — that subtends 'Seduction, Pleasure and a Laying on of hands: A Hands-on Reading of Sartre's *Nausea*'. Indeed, the aim of Rolls' chapter is to draw attention to the novel's self-referentiality, demonstrating the affective power that is released through the process of reading. Those passages that declare themselves to be conscious of their own literariness have a double role vis-à-vis the reader that can be compared to the role played by nothingness, as analysed by Debra Hely: they point up the way in which the text links the reader to Roquentin's tale, situating her within it, whilst at the same time acting as a barrier, forever holding her at bay with the same film of words that draws her in. The fact that the novel resides in this secretion of words that exist ultimately both inside and outside the text — that are and are not the text — serves to posit the reader in a relationship with *Nausea* that may be said to be intertextual.

This is not an intertextual reading in quite the way that Stewart's paper is; an illumination of *Nausea* is not sought via a text written by another author. The material that is imported into *Nausea* is largely that provided by Sartre himself. This sounds a little like traditional *Nausea* criticism: the novel can be understood in the philosophical terms outlined in *Being and Nothingness*. And yet, Rolls' aim is to show that the philosophy that lies outside *Nausea* (i.e. concepts that are not fully expounded explicitly in the novel – concepts other than contingency and superfluity, etc.) is brought into it by the reader. Reader response itself is seen to be something wilfully set up by the author. The novel, through its pervasive use of self-referential techniques, constantly spills beyond its own pages; its meaning appears to become frozen and known by the reader. And whilst only the reader who reads the text freely, who engages head-on with the seductive text, can know its secrets, the text reserves the right to reel back in its being-for-the-reader, both violating the bond of trust and making the reader feel the frisson not only of reading but of being read. This is not simply a case of philosophy in a novelistic wrapping; the novel, in our approach to it and its appeal to us, reveals itself in the colours of the ontological struggle that is our lot as beings in the world. This is a case of intertextuality as existential reading praxis.

TEXT

Lawrence R. Schehr

Sartre's Autodidacticism

This chapter analyses how homosexuality is articulated through and around the character of the Self-Taught Man, the Autodidact. With the Autodidact, Sartre creates one of his first important homosexual figures for whom there is no real psychological or situational explanation. The Autodidact is also a mental masturbator, an intellectual auto-eroticist, who attempts to fill what he perceives as his lacks. Through an analysis of a series of scenes in which the Autodidact figures prominently, I shall show how Sartre conceives of homosexuality, bad faith, and engagement even at this early point in his writing.

* * *

> *Cette quantité de désœuvrés vulgaires, de bourgeois retirés, d'hommes veufs, de solliciteurs sans places, d'écoliers qui viennent copier leur version, de vieillards maniaques, – comme l'était ce pauvre Carnaval qui venait tous les jours avec un habit rouge, bleu clair, ou vert-pomme, et un chapeau orné de fleurs, – mérite sans doute considération, mais n'existe-t-il pas d'autres bibliothèques, et même des bibliothèques spéciales à leur ouvrir ?*
> Nerval, Angélique, 1ère lettre

In the film, *Sartre par lui-même*, directed by Alexandre Astruc and Michel Contat, Jean-Paul Sartre, along with Simone de Beauvoir, reminisces about his life, his work, and his engagement in the politics and culture of the twentieth century. In telling that there was a real-life model for the Self-Taught Man, l'Autodidacte, Sartre tells that part of the model was himself:

> La contingence, la première fois que j'en parlais, c'était dans un carnet que j'avais ramassé dans un métro. C'était un carnet vierge, il y avait dessus « Suppositoires Midy », c'était évidemment un carnet distribué aux médecins. Il était fait comme un registre avec A – B – C – D, etc. et – c'est peut-être ça qui m'a donné l'idée de faire de l'Autodidacte, un des personnages de *La Nausée*, un homme qui s'instruit alphabétiquement – je mettais mes pensées par ordre alphabétique, pour une simple raison, c'est qu'il y avait l'ordre alphabétique dans ce registre.

[The first time I spoke of contingency was in a notebook I had found in the
Metro. It was a virgin notebook, "Midy suppositories" was written on the cover;
it was obviously a notebook handed out to doctors. It was in the form of a ledger,
with A, B, C, D, etc., and it was perhaps that that gave me the idea of making the
Autodidact, one of the characters in *Nausea*, a man who teaches himself
alphabetically. I put my thoughts in alphabetical order for the simple reason that
there was an alphabetical order in this ledger.][1]

The editors of the Pléiade volume recount the anecdote with even
greater precision:

On sait que l'une des caractéristiques de l'Autodidacte est de consigner avec
soin dans un carnet ses pensées et surtout les pensées des autres. Rappelons à ce
propos que Sartre, vers 1922-1923, faisait la même chose dans un carnet à
couverture « Suppositoires Midy » qu'il avait trouvé dans le metro.

[We know that one of the characteristics of the Autodidact is to write his
thoughts and especially those of others down with care in a notebook. Relative to
this, let us remember that Sartre, toward 1922-1923, did the same thing in a
notebook with the cover "Midy Suppositories", which he had found in the
metro.][2]

But something is amiss: Midy suppositories did not appear on the
market until 1938, the year of the publication of *La Nausée*. So if
Sartre wrote about contingency in 1922-23 it certainly was not in that
anal retentive notebook. And he could not have written about
contingency for the first time in such a notebook, for that could have
been no earlier than 1938. While this is a minor point of literary
history, it does provide a nice means of entry to talking about buggery
in the novel, a work that does, in the end, depend on straight-shooting
and classification in anal retentive, alphabetical order.[3]
    In an earlier study, 'Sartre as Midwife',[4] I focused on the visual

---

[1] *Sartre* (1977), Film directed by Alexandre Astruc and Michel Contat, Screenplay
(Paris: Gallimard). With the exceptions of translations of *La Nausée*, all translations
in this article are my own.
[2] J.-P. Sartre, *Œuvres romanesques* (Paris: Gallimard, 1981), p. 1726.
[3] As Kershaw points out, Sartre addresses the question of autodidacticism in an
earlier, unfinished work, 'La Semence et le Scaphandre' (A. Kershaw,
'Autodidacticism and Criminality in Jean-Paul Sartre's *La Nausée* and Edith Thomas'
L'Homme criminel', *Modern Language Review*, 96:3 (2001), 679-92 [p. 679n3]). On
autodidacticism, also see R. Chapman 'Autodidacticism and the Desire for Culture',
Nottingham French Studies, 31:2 (1992), 84-101.
[4] L. Schehr, *Alcibiades et the Door: Gay Discourses in French Literature* (Stanford:
Stanford Univerity Press, 1995), pp. 68-112.

component to male homosexuality in Sartre's writing, a kind of scopophilia necessary for him to guarantee the existence of the category through a perception of 'the' act and essential to his analyses of the matter. Here I am not proposing a change of paradigm, but rather a change of perspective: an analysis of the affects of homosexuality as it is articulated through and around the character of the Self-Taught Man, the Autodidact. The Autodidact is but one of a series of gay characters in Sartre's writing and as all readers of Sartre know, Sartre was endlessly fascinated with the articulations of male and female homosexuality, though in different ways. Characters in works from *Les Chemins de la liberté* to *Huis clos* turn out to be queer. And that matter makes its way into his philosophy as well: the third example of bad faith in *L'Etre et le néant* focuses on a gay man who confesses his gayness to a straight friend. Sartre considers both to be in bad faith: the gay man should not have to confess to anyone and the straight man is in no position to forgive him, accept him, or pardon him. Notable as well is Sartre's literary analysis of Jean Genet's prose, a study that depends to a great extent on the bad faith that comes out of Genet's twin problematic of crime and homosexuality.

Thus it comes as no surprise to anyone that the pivotal counter-figure to Roquentin's existential crisis is the Autodidact, truly the only other well-limned figure in the novel, aside from Roquentin himself. Rather than being a fully-fledged character, Anny is an affect of Roquentin's (and Sartre's) vague (or not so vague) misogyny and his "phallonormative model of masculinity".[5] In any case, she is seen mostly retrospectively as a site of melancholia and loss, so much so that the scene with her is a rewriting and reinscription of the pain of the past.[6]

---

[5] L. Kritzman, 'To Be or Not to Be: Sexual Ambivalence in Sartre's *La Nausée*', *L'Esprit Créateur*, 43: 3 (2003), 79-86 (p. 81).

[6] On Roquentin's heteronormativity, see S. Vanbaelen, 'Anny, Syrinx de Roquentin : Musique et érotique dans *La Nausée* de Jean-Paul Sartre.' *Romanic Review*, 90: 3 (1999), 397-408 (p. 402). In his article, 'Nausea and Desire in Sartre's *La Nausée*', Andrew Leak writes of "the jeopardizing of the masculine attitude, the loss of gender-identity and, ultimately, castration" (A. Leak, 'Nausea and Desire in Sartre's *La Nausée*', *French Studies*, 43:1 (1989), 61-72 [p. 65]). In his excellent volume, Robert Harvey discusses Sartrean "ontological androgyny or, perhaps, even sexual 'betweenness'" as well as what he calls "the erosion of masculinity" (R. Harvey, *Search for a Father* (Ann Arbor: University of Michigan Press, 1991) pp. 110-18). See also S. Doubrovsky, 'Phallotexte et gynotexte dans *La Nausée* : "Feuillet sans

With the Autodidact, Sartre creates one of his first important homosexual figures for whom there is no real psychological or situational explanation. Homosexuality — or same-sex desire — is thus initially pitched as another component of being thrown into the world, although it can lead to opprobrium in the form of what the late twentieth century somewhat all too easily labels homophobia, be it external or internalised. As those words can often be misleading, I would define external homophobia as moral opprobrium from another directed toward a homosexual individual (or someone perceived to be such, whether it is the case or not). Internalised homophobia would describe a situation in which a homosexual individual has consciously or unconsciously taken in the negative image that society often paints of the homosexual and of homosexuality; that internalised mechanism would be seen psychologically in some forms of self-loathing. Sartre would shortly classify such behaviour as one form of bad faith involving the *pour-autrui*: what the homosexual is for others, s/he expresses as his/her own identity, as if that were the *pour-soi*. Even more than Daniel, in *Les Chemins de la liberté*, the classic example of the self-loathing homosexual in Sartre's work is Inès in *Huis clos*.

The Autodidact, it will turn out, is in many ways a Baudelairean *bourreau de soi-même*; he is also a mental masturbator, an intellectual autoeroticist who attempts to fill what he perceives as voids, gaps, blanks, or lacks in himself. These are attempts to plug his gap, one shared by Roquentin: the nausea within him, the gap of emptiness, the alienation from self, the absurdity of existence, or the void. These are so many metaphors for the absence of meaning, certainly not always sexual; they nevertheless function according to a mechanism of the metaphysics of desire. While Roquentin may try to fill his emptiness by engaging his own nausea or by nostalgically returning to Anny, albeit farcically, the less advanced Autodidact tries to fill his gap or gape with mental masturbation, fraternity, and ultimately, pederasty or ephebophilia.

The very first image presented of the Autodidact is a well-crafted, pointed, and dehumanizing characterization: "Je voyais un visage inconnu, à peine un visage. Et puis il y avait sa main, comme un gros ver blanc dans ma main [I saw an unknown face which was barely a face. And then there was his hand, like a fat maggot in my hand]" (9;

14).[7] Unrecognizable as a person or even as a part of a person, the Autodidact has always already been transformed into a fleshy, phallic monster in Roquentin's hand. A handshake — a greeting — turns into a masturbatory and homosexual moment in which Roquentin is forced to caress the Autodidact's limp phallus, displaced into his hand. This displacement will become important in the Autodidact's final appearance in the novel, where he reaches out with his hand and caresses the adolescent. So at that latter point, he is not just making an improper advance with his hand, which itself would be problematic but forcing his displaced phallus onto the adolescent boy, an act that at least metaphorically, is an act of indecent exposure or molestation.[8]

The image of extension and retraction is repeated in the library as the Autodidact turns from reading his current volume in "L" to contemplating a high-school student next to him:

> Il regardait en souriant son voisin de droite, un collégien crasseux qui vient souvent à la Bibliothèque. L'autre s'est laissé contempler un moment, puis lui a brusquement tiré la langue en faisant une horrible grimace. L'Autodidacte a rougi, il a plongé précipitamment le nez dans son livre et s'est absorbé dans sa lecture.
> [He was looking with a smile at his neighbour on the right, a filthy-looking schoolboy who often comes to the library. The schoolboy allowed himself to be looked at for a while, then suddenly put his tongue out at him and pulled a horrible face. The Autodidact blushed, hurriedly plunged his nose back into his book, and became engrossed by his reading.] (48; 60)

A penetrating look on the part of the Autodidact is followed by a sign of male bravura, as the student sticks out his tongue. If we remember the flaccidity and the interchangeability of the Autodidact's body parts, we may impute that metamorphosis to all characters – such is the case with Roquentin's examination of his own face in the mirror or his own hand as a "bête à la renverse [an animal upside down]" (118; 143-44), as well as his transformation into the root of the chestnut tree. With its tensed muscles, the teenager's tongue is briefly an erect phallus that repels the longing glance, the amorous attack of the

---

[7] All references to the novel give the French page reference first followed by the English translation. The French text is the Pléiade edition, taken from J.-P. Sartre, *Œuvres romanesques* (Paris: Gallimard, 1981), pp. 1-210.

[8] Sartre seems vague about the age of the two young men and whether they have entered puberty or not. Kershaw for one sees the molestation scene as a scene of "homosexual paedophilia." I tend, as will be seen from the rest of the article, to consider that the boys have at least begun to enter manhood.

Autodidact. It is a sign of male territoriality or a figure of alpha-male dominance: the extended erect tongue repels the Autodidact, pushing him toward himself and within himself, and that forces his own amorous attention back on himself. The Autodidact blushes; his head turns red, thereby permitting a momentary conflation with the red-headed Roquentin and allowing for a momentary queering of Roquentin. The Autodidact retreats: he puts 'his' nose into 'his' book. But that book is what is gradually becoming part of him. He plunges his nose into himself, in an act of autoeroticism that turns, depending on what angle one takes, into an act of self-buggery.

Somewhat later, the Autodidact hints that "il m'arrive une histoire abominable [something abominable happened to me]" (91; 111) and that the guard at the library is somehow involved, but that he will not tell Roquentin the story in front of the guard. Witnessing implicates a reinscription of the scurrilous event, and moving away from the sexualized locus of the library might allow the Autodidact to forget the reality, to bury his actions, or to translate them — as he will indeed do — into a lofty, noble discourse of desexualised fellowship. Instead, he invites Roquentin to lunch the following Wednesday. The invitation is made with the following description of a character somewhat akin to Proust's Charlus: "Il rougit et ses hanches ondoyèrent gracieusement [He blushed and his hips swayed gracefully]" (91; 112). Blush for blush: now when inviting Roquentin on a date, earlier when having been caught looking lovingly (or leering perversely) at the high school student, who Roquentin has already indicated is not a suitable object of desire because he is "filthy". Thus does the Autodidact shift, albeit briefly, his lustful attention to Roquentin the arbiter of taste, of knowledge, and seemingly, of boys as well. Though the Autodidact cannot read Roquentin's mind, he can certainly feel the necessity to displace desire and perhaps even to do away with it.

Yet why? Is it that he has penetrated Roquentin's space? For this is the first meeting after the scene in Roquentin's room, a scene to which I now turn. As readers know, Roquentin has been remembering past events as he is transported to other times and other places. As he is lying there in the room with the lights off, he is roused by a knock at the door. The Autodidact enters and sits down:

Il s'assied sur une chaise ; ses fesses tendues touchent le dossier et son buste roide s'incline en avant. Je saute en bas de mon lit, je donne de la lumière :

"Mais comment donc, monsieur? Nous étions fort bien."
[He sits down on a chair; his buttocks spread out and touch the back of it while his stiff torso leans forward. I jump off my bed and turn on the light.
"Do we need that, Monsieur? We were all right as we were."] (42; 53-54)

The room is light enough for Roquentin to notice the Autodidact's behind, but why does he focus at first on that part of the body? Sartre has deliberately sexualized the scene: stiffening the Autodidact's bust and moving it forward presents the front part of the guest's body as if it were a hard phallus. Similarly pushing his butt cheeks back into a chair seems to be a thrust of his behind. As in the situation in the library in which he symbolically commits an act of self-buggery, the Autodidact takes both roles in a situation of simulated anal intercourse. The simulated enactment of that scene is threatening to the overly heterosexual Roquentin who not minutes before has been thinking about his past and in part, his past with Anny: this is a queer interruption into heterosexual nostalgia. Finding himself in a dark room with a man who is attracted to other men is just too problematic for Roquentin who needs to turn on the light to extricate himself from a seemingly compromising situation. It little matters that no one would see, whatever the ambiguity. But Roquentin is pressed, afraid, worried about himself, not about the Autodidact. Arguably, Roquentin fears his own possible homosexuality, in what Lawrence Kritzman calls Roquentin's "inability to come to terms with the dangers of homoerotic desire and the challenges of bisexuality" (Kritzman, p. 79). Roquentin fears going "gay all of a sudden."

One might very well raise two objections here: the first is that Roquentin does not 'know' that the Autodidact is homosexual and the second is that I am over-reading a simple action. Yet Sartre knows that the Autodidact is homosexual and he does nothing to disambiguate the scene for Roquentin: he could have left the lights on for his narrator/protagonist; he could have not had Roquentin recently muse on his heterosexual past; he could have had Roquentin remember his rendez-vous with the Autodidact; he could have had the Autodidact sit differently. Sartre's choices are wilful, and his construction of the scene queers the entry into the private space of Roquentin's bedroom. It is a space that is now potentially and dangerously the locus of a migration or mutation of that solipsistic, masturbatory, heterosexual nostalgia into a coupled queerness.[9]

At the same time, Sartre lets the Autodidact bathe briefly in his illusion. The Autodidact has already thought or at least unconsciously felt that being in the dark with Roquentin is a good thing. The Autodidact has formed a bond in the shadows; they have, in his mind, formed a 'we', and that 'we' is in a good place. While I am not suggesting that the Autodidact has imagined any sexual congress, he has, at least in terms of emotional proxemics, gotten closer to Roquentin. And even when the light is on, as soon as the pictures are shared, the Autodidact will repeat his forward gesture.[10] Just as he has entered Roquentin's private space and just as he has thrust his torso forward, he now thrusts his jaw forward: "il pointe vers moi sa grande mâchoire d'âne [he juts his great ass's jaw-bone towards me]" (43; 55).[11] As Sartre or Roquentin oralizes the Autodidact — the author is sketching the picture of a stereotypical bottom — Roquentin heads into the world of sexual fantasy, as he displaces the present, not into the past but into the exotic, configuring the Autodidact thinking about Samoyeds and Tierra del Fuegans. But Roquentin does not merely stop at displacing things geographically, he fantasizes a sexuality that many would say violates taboos far more than mere homosexuality does: the exotic figures "s'accouplent au hasard, mère et fils, père et fille, frère et sœur, se mutilent, se châtrent, se distendent les lèvres avec des plateaux, se font sculpter sur les reins des animaux monstrueux [copulating at random, mother with son, father with daughter, brother with sister, mutilating themselves, castrating themselves, distending their lips with plates and having monstrous animals carved on their backs]" (43-44; 55). Monstrous indeed. It seems that it is easier for Roquentin to entertain thoughts about heterosexual incest and castration than to engage the question of his own possible homosexual penchants or at least his sexuality being put momentarily into question. As safe figures of comforting heterosexuality, castration and incest replace the unspeakable

---

[9] I add in passing that in that time and place it would have been extremely unlikely for a non-intimate acquaintance to enter someone's bedroom. Rather they would have met in a café, with Roquentin having brought his photographs and postcards to a neutral, public location

[10] On the body movements of the Autodidact, see Chapman, who remarks that "His bodily movements and gestures often suggest femininity" (p. 98).

[11] Judges 15. 15-16 is an intertext here, with the reference to a jawbone of an ass, but the reference is ironic, as the Autodidact is anything but Samson-like.

homosexuality that Roquentin has just flashed on and rejected.

There will be one more thrust in this short scene, after Roquentin reveals the truth of the Autodidact and regrets having done so because it must be "un délire secret [a secret madness]" (44; 56). He has shown the Autodidact's truth to himself, outing him intellectually, showing the truth in his mind; it is as if he were revealing the truth of his sexuality to him. And the Autodidact's response, yet again, is to thrust part of his body forward: "ses grosses lèvres s'avancent d'un air pleurard [thick lips jut out as if he were going to cry]" (44; 56). The movement has narrowed itself over the course of these pages from bust to jaw and then to lips. The forwardness of the thrust described by Sartre is unmistakable as the arc of the movement moves the Autodidact toward an act of fellatio with Roquentin. The more the latter penetrates him, and this by revealing his deepest, darkest secrets, the more the Autodidact moves toward performing oral sex on Roquentin.

Finally, though, it is the Autodidact's entire self that moves in for the act as he asks Roquentin if the latter has had "aventures [many adventures]" (45; 57). Whilst the word *aventures* can quite simply mean 'adventures', it also has the specific meaning of sexual escapades, one-night stands, anonymous tricks, or encounters. If Roquentin chooses to understand the question in the general sense, the specific sexual sense is not lost on the reader who surmises that this is where the textual unconscious is headed and where the real and emotional proxemics have also been heading. The Autodidact is now so close that Roquentin can smell his bad breath, so close that the Autodidact's mouth is too near him. The event is over. Bad simulated sex has come to an end.

Eighty pages later it is time for lunch. Two global things should be noted in passing before an examination of the scene with the two hapless figures. First, the obvious must be stated: the scene in the restaurant continues the orality of the photograph scene but adds to it with several perverse twists including the Autodidact's intense determination, albeit out of a misguided sense of etiquette, to decide exactly what Roquentin has in his mouth. And second, the scene in the restaurant happens the same day as the scene with the chestnut tree root. It is a double realization, a double illumination, and a double nausea. The scene of the chestnut tree root is usually perceived as the culminating point of the novel's philosophical trajectory, that is true;

yet it is preceded by the restaurant scene, and ultimately followed by
the final scene in the library, the only scene in which Roquentin truly
takes action. The nausea of the chestnut tree scene continues the
nausea of the restaurant scene; the actions of the final scene in the
library stand in opposition to all the previous moments of stasis and
paralysis.

The long scene in the restaurant is an excuse for Sartre to allow
Roquentin to reflect in general about human existence and to produce
an implicit and explicit critique of a kind of weak socialism/humanism
of the sort to which the Autodidact adheres. This socialism seems to
be based in a kind of shared fellowship, an idyllic, primitive
Christianity that has no real sense of politics or class. The scene is
explicitly constructed for Roquentin to be able to expatiate on his
ideas, as Roquentin indicates that he was looking forward to seeing
the Autodidact and that he needed to talk. Figurations of the
Autodidact's sexuality continue to bubble to the surface and this
occurs despite the fact that Sartre seems not yet to be clear about
whether the Autodidact is attracted to Roquentin or, as will be the case
the following week, if he is attracted to adolescents. Sartre's confusion
may be wilful or not, but he seems not to distinguish nuances here
between various modes of same-sex desire.

Sartre places the scene under the sign of the abject, the petty, and
the provincial. And it starts with Roquentin killing a fly for no
apparent reason, and this despite the humanist protest of the
Autodidact. The white innards come out of the fly's abdomen, guts
that strangely resemble the Autodidact's worm-like white hand. This
is a strange way to start a food scene, to say the least. And the food
itself is remarkable. No manly, phallic sausage for Roquentin, the
Autodidact insists, only invertebrate snails or oysters. No manly, red
meat of a *bœuf en daube* for him, but rather the less manly *poulet
chasseur*, while the Autodidact permits himself to order the beef. And
there is not even robust red wine, but rather the less manly *rosé
d'Anjou*.

The most interesting moment in the scene is the missing
conversation that happens right after the food is ordered. The purpose
of the lunch was ostensibly for the Autodidact to tell Roquentin about
the trouble the Corsican guard in the library is making for him. At this
point, the naive or the first-time reader will probably not know what is
going on, but we all recognize that what the guard has said, hinted, or

somehow implied that the Autodidact is a "sale pédé." What would have led the guard to this conclusion? Lingering stares or actions by the Autodidact? Untoward comments? A gut reaction? Effeminacy? Gaydar? It is difficult to say, but in any case, the Autodidact cannot bring up the situation and merely settles for saying that the story consists of rumours.

This is the day for the truth: this will be the day of the chestnut tree. So Sartre cannot have the Autodidact speak the love that dare not speak its name, for that would put Roquentin in an extremely difficult position. If the Autodidact explains the rumours while either confirming or denying them, Roquentin will have to take verbal action, either accepting the confession, rebuking it, tolerating homosexuality or false heterosexuality, or even not deciding. All of these are problematic because each would put him in a situation of moral superiority to the Autodidact, either now or later as he reflects on existence, on nausea, and on the chestnut tree root. And now, as has just been seen, the important thing is not to exist: killing the fly is doing it a favour, indicates Roquentin at the beginning of the scene. For the purposes of the narrative, the existential solution is not yet to be found and Roquentin must remain in a nihilist funk, far from the humanist existentialism that he and Sartre will eventually embrace.

As has been noted, the Autodidact's humanism is more than directly based on Christian fellowship and Popular Front socialism; Roquentin specifically says, "Je salue au passage l'humanisme catholique à qui l'Autodidacte a emprunté, sans le savoir, cette formule [I salute in passing the Catholic humanism from which the Autodidact has unknowingly borrowed this formula]" (142-43; 173); a nice little Hail Mary — *Je vous salue Marie* — from the atheist. Most importantly, this position gives the Autodidact a vocabulary he can safely use to talk with impunity about others. So it is necessary to love people. And it allows for what we know is an act of self-deception: "'Comment pouvez-vous, dit l'Autodidacte, *arrêter* un homme, dire il *est* ceci ou cela ? Qui peut épuiser un homme ? Qui peut connaître les ressources d'un homme ? ["How can you," says the Autodidact, "limit a man like that, how can you say that he *is* this or that? Who can drain a man dry? Who can know a man's resources?"]" (142; 173). In an inversion of an inversion, the Autodidact seems to be miming the position or situation of the author himself: one cannot name a man, saying he is this or that, because the naming can never exhaust him, explain everything.[12] But it is not really Sartre's own position, because that position is determined by change — an individual is always changing — and by existence; there is no essence that can be known until after the change has stopped, i.e., after the individual has died.

Refusing to see that Roquentin's position depends on contingency and existence, the Autodidact is determined that there be an essence, and specifically, this is a secret essence that is multilayered, multifarious, and unplumbable.[13] He is determined that part of this essence remain a secret, one known to him and undoubtedly to his god. This means two things. First, this humanistically determined core essence — an *en-soi* — is fundamental to human nature for the Autodidact (whilst, for Roquentin, whatever is contingent — i.e., everything — is only tangential and accidental). For the Autodidact, there is an unchanging and unchanged nature in each of us, and it is undoubtedly that that reaches out to others in humanity and in friendship. Second, it relates to the matter at hand. Rather than facing some version of self that is as absurd as any other – sexual orientation in this case — some of which may be related to nature, but all of which is as accidentally fixed as any other feature, the Autodidact can compartmentalize it, burying it, not naming it, and metaphorizing it in his humanism. At no point then does the Autodidact come to face with his own otherness to himself and for himself.

While seemingly continuing his lines of thought, Roquentin articulates the slippage and makes a statement that can easily be construed, and that indeed must be construed as being about same-sex desire:

> Je contemple l'Autodidacte avec un peu de remords : il s'est complu toute la semaine à imaginer ce déjeuner, où il pourrait faire part à un autre homme de son amour des hommes. Il a si rarement l'occasion de parler. Et voilà : je lui ai gâché son plaisir.
> [I look at the Autodidact with a little remorse: he has been looking forward all week to this luncheon, at which he would be able to tell another man about his

---

[12] I follow Sartre's use of the word 'man' here because the discourse is fundamentally androcentric. In the abstract, one would make the argument about the individual, be it a man or a woman, even if Sartre's treatment of women in his texts does not always seem totally egalitarian.

[13] Christina Howells writes of the "'useless passion' of attempting self-influence" on the part of the Autodidact and Daniel of *Les Chemins de la liberté* in *Sartre: The Necessity of Freedom* (Cambridge: Cambridge University Press, 1988), p. 54. It is, I would add, an attempt that will fail because of secrets and believed essences.

love of man. He so rarely has the opportunity of talking. And now I have spoilt his pleasure.] (143-44; 174)

If the Autodidact is not fully out to himself or if he has translated a sexual discourse into an emotional discourse of fraternity, Roquentin does not share the same naïveté or blindness. He now knows what the Autodidact refuses to know, what cannot be said, and what will be acted on in a week's time.

The scene ends as it has started: with an act of violence. In this case, it is only imagined, as Roquentin thinks of shoving his cheese knife into the Autodidact's eye, an act that would be followed by an attack on him from the onlookers. If he is stopped, it is not by the sociopathic nature of the proposed act, but rather by the superfluity of all parts of that event. And yet it is a neat frame for the lunch, repeating the violence with which it began, making the inside come out, even if it is with an act of imagination. Up to this point, the entire book has been about making the inside come out, letting it ooze its way out, so that it is visible on the surface: the nausea is about that as well. Rather than being the banquet of the truth, the lunch is a meeting in which the truth remains hidden: Roquentin's true thoughts and his potential violence, the Autodidact's homosexuality mistranslated into acceptable fraternity or homosociality, and the fact that there is never any love of man that can come out. And finally, the fantasized stabbing of the Autodidact in the eye is a proleptic announcement of the act of violence that is to come: the bloodying of the Autodidact's nose after the latter has caressed the hand of an adolescent in the library.

But I go too fast, in imitation of Roquentin's retrospective announcement of the end of the scene, the first words he writes at the beginning of the scene, a writing to which I shall briefly turn after having looked at the initial explanation set undoubtedly to defuse the reader's possible shock. After all, this is not the queer twenty-first century but rather, provincial, Catholic France in the thirties:

A vrai dire, je n'ai guère été surpris quand la chose est arrivée : depuis longtemps, je sentais que sa tête douce et craintive appelait sur elle le scandale. Il était si peu coupable : c'est à peine de la sensualité, son humble amour contemplatif pour les jeunes garçons – une forme d'humanisme, plutôt.
[To tell the truth, I was scarcely surprised when the thing happened: for a long time I had felt that his gentle, timid face was positively asking scandal to strike it. He was guilty in so small a degree: his humble, comtemplative love for little boys

is scarcely sensuality – rather a form of humanism.] (189; 228)

In writing the summary of the scene up front, Sartre/Roquentin makes an apology for what is doubtless not as innocent an act as Roquentin makes it out to be: the act is certainly a violation of personal space and non-consensual activity on the person of a minor. And even if nothing results and even if *minima non curat lex* — the Autodidact is not going to be arrested — Roquentin does recognize that this is not a guiltless action: he finds the Autodidact "guilty in so small a degree." Still that guilt is there. Indeed this minimum defense in which he calls it "barely sensuality" and "contemplative love" prejudices the reader perhaps in favor of the Autodidact, but it is certainly not the truth of the situation.

Telling the tale retrospectively, Roquentin retains the image of the blood he had imagined exactly one week earlier. He then feels compelled to write, and goes to the café to do so: whereas he had stopped writing and whereas in the library he had merely been reading the *Journal de Bouville* for the first time since having abandoned his project on the Marquis de Rollebon, Roquentin needs now to narrate. Writing on pages that are part of, yet separate from, his diary, he recognizes that writing has to involve something living and not an *en-soi*. Writing is writing about a crisis. And finally, before the scene opens, this mention of the act of writing connects the preamble to the two monstrations with which Roquentin begins his part of the scene: he returns two books to the assistant librarian and he sits down at the table: "Le *Journal de Bouville* traînait sur la table. J'allongeai la main, je le pris [The *Journal de Bouville* was lying on the table. I stretched out my hand, I picked it up]" (190; 229). Whereas his reaching out does nothing but get him the newspaper, a similar action by the Autodidact provokes – is – the crisis.

Framed by Roquentin's retrospective reading of the entire scene, the Autodidact's own entrance, at the end of the afternoon, is also framed in tragic tones in Roquentin's mind as he thinks, "'Je le vois pour la dernière fois.' Demain soir... ["I am seeing him for the last time." Tomorrow evening...]" (191; 230), which is nothing less than an almost word-for-word quotation of Phèdre's entrance line: "Soleil je te vois pour la dernière fois," this from the tragic protagonist of a play about illicit love and arguably also about a kind of hidden homosexuality in the person of the chaste Hippolytus. In referring the attentive reader back to Racine, Sartre/Roquentin underlines the inevitability of what is going to happen. What I mean here is not that it is going to happen, for we already know this. I mean rather that from the very beginning of the novel, the Autodidact is hurtling down a path where this is the inevitable conclusion, a theme that is played out by repeated comments by Roquentin:

> Pourtant, dès ce moment, j'eus l'impression qu'un événement désagréable allait se produire…
> [Yet, at that moment, I had the impression that something unpleasant was going to happen…] (193; 232)

> Ce qui augmentait ma curiosité et ma gêne, c'est que les autres attendaient aussi…
> [What increased my curiosity and my uneasiness was that the others were waiting too…] (193; 232)

> Je sentis clairement que le drame allait éclater : ils *voulaient* tous qu'il éclatât…
> [I could distinctly feel that the drama was going to begin; they all *wanted* it to begin…] (194; 234)

> L'Autodidacte n'avait pas l'air surpris. Il devait y avoir des années qu'il s'attendait à ce dénouement. Cent fois il avait dû imaginer ce qui se passerait…
> [The Autodidact didn't look surprised. He must have been expecting this to happen for years. A hundred times he must have imagined what would happen…] (196; 236)

Whether it is a projection on the part of Roquentin that this is fated or whether it is a correct reading of the Autodidact's mind, this view of the Autodidact's behavior culpabilizes homosexuality while trying to save it from condemnation. Homosexuality is depicted not just as sexual behavior between two individuals of the same sex; it is also, if not to say fundamentally and existentially, and this despite the Sartrean idea of freedom, guilty behavior. Perhaps it is only a *péché mignon*, but it is not as guilt-free as the heterosexual relationships and events that Sartre has Roquentin describe with overwhelming banality and a dryness of tone elsewhere in the novel. And in that, it is also a measure of Sartre's implicit misogyny, through which he sees women as a reflection of, or a tool for, a man's pleasure. But in any case, though ubiquitous, homosexuality is anything but banal; it is always an event.[14]

---

[14] For lack of space here and as it is not particularly central to my argument, I note in passing that the three authors in this section of the book – Gide, Diderot, and

As Roquentin narrows his focus by pointing the reader toward the event, telescoping his vision to see what is out there, his vision is contrasted, literally and figuratively, with that of the Autodidact whose own gaze is constantly out of focus. Two teenagers enter. Roquentin repeatedly calls them young boys ("jeunes garçons"), although *jeunes gens* would have been more accurate and less scandalous as he indicates that they are *collégiens*. At first after the two teenagers come in, the Autodidact "fixait sur eux un regard fatigué [was staring at them with tired eyes]" (193; 232). If it is a penetrating glance, it is also a tired one that betrays a weariness, perhaps about his own game and martyrdom; or perhaps it is a weariness of hiding who he is. The look quickly changes as he locks eyes with one of the young men:

> Il était penché sur son jeune voisin, les yeux dans les yeux, il lui souriait; je voyais remuer ses lèvres et, de temps en temps, ses longs cils palpitaient. Je ne lui connaissais pas cet air de jeunesse, il était presque charmant. Mais par instants, il s'interrompait et jetait derrière lui un regard inquiet. Le jeune garçon semblait boire ses paroles.
> [He was bending over his young neighbour, eye to eye, and smiling at him; I could see his lips moving and, now and then, his long eyelashes trembling. I had never seen him look so young before, he was almost charming. But, from time to time, he broke off and looked anxiously over his shoulder. The boy seemed to be drinking in his words.] (193; 233)

This scene of seduction involves words unheard by one and drunk in by another. It frames two visions: the locked eyes of the seduction and a literally retrospective glance at the outside world that is perhaps witnessing the action, policing it, as it were, and about to condemn it. In glancing behind himself, the Autodidact splits his vision and his focus, just as the perception of the words he speaks is split: seen by the narrator and heard by the adolescents. At the very least this means that Roquentin is safe from the seduction and not the object of lust for an aging and unattractive homosexual man about to prey on a teenager. Yet, one wonders, what could the Autodidact be saying? For he has not yet, during the course of almost two hundred pages, evinced any oratorical talent; indeed, he has shown minimal communicative skills heretofore. Is he repeating some sententious

---

Baudelaire (192; 231)– all wrote explicitly on homosexuality (as well as on heterosexuality). Authors are not just consigned to the *Enfer de la bibliothèque* for no reason.

remarks that he has read or written down? Is he flirting by means of *marivaudage*? Is he whispering sweet nothings? All we can know is that it is an act of seduction and transfixing. He does not seduce through the contents but through the form.

The seduction is complicated by the counter-current introduced by Sartre. The hand of the one supposedly rapt by the Autodidact's words slides along surreptitiously to pinch the arm of his friend, yet, *mine de rien*, he continues to appear interested in the words of Autodidact. The blond friend, who is older and already has "une ombre de moustache [a hint of a moustache]" and is broad-shouldered, "râblé [strapping)]" (193; 232), is, however, truly caught up in the words of the Autodidact: he is "trop absorbé à jouir silencieusement des paroles de l'Autodidacte [too absorbed in silent enjoyment of the Autodidact's words]" (194; 233). Sartre seems to express what was previously unthinkable: the blond adolescent may indeed, wittingly or unwittingly, be gay and quite simply the Autodidact may have chosen the wrong teenager. Even if the *jouissance* of the older adolescent does not last, at the end of the scene, lingering doubts remain and readers can never be fully satisfied about the dynamics of the seduction.

Roquentin reads the situation and interpellates a *jouissance* come out of nowhere into the mind of the older teenager. And while Roquentin is safe from the seduction by the Autodidact, while he is safely ensconced in his own heterosexuality, he will now describe the scene both by queering it and by straightening it out. He is a passive observer who decides not to interrupt the scene by repeating the gesture just made, but on a larger scale: "Une seconde, j'eus l'idée de me lever, d'aller frapper sur l'épaule de l'Autodidacte [For a second I thought of getting up, going and tapping the Autodidact on the shoulder]" (194; 233). But he cannot; he is transfixed; voyeuristically, he wants the scene to happen as he remains the heterosexual viewer of an act of male homosexuality. In not acting and in staying as transfixed as the two boys, Roquentin is miming their position and acting in what Sartre will eventually term 'bad faith': he abandons himself just as the hand will soon be abandoned.

Body parts are reduced to three: hands, lips, and eyes. The same hand that earlier pinched the friend's arm, thereby confirming the homosocial yet heterosexual masculinity of the boys, now lies upturned on the table, vulva-like, and is feminized both in its vulnerabılıty and in the way Roquentin constructs his description of it: "A présent elle reposait sur le dos, détendue, douce et sensuelle, elle avait l'indolente nudité d'une baigneuse qui se chauffe au soleil [Now it was lying on its back, relaxed, soft, and sensual, it had the indolent nudity of a woman sunning herself on the beach]" (195; 234).[15] Perhaps unwittingly, the young man lets his hand lie in a position that creates a hollow. Roquentin specifically chooses words that relate to feminine sensuality and sexuality, through which he radically straightens out the situation. With the image of a nude sunbather, Roquentin insists on the immediate penetrability and vulnerability of the hand, a penetration that starts in the next sentence and that becomes caught up in a dialectic of sex second to none in the book:

> Un objet brun et velu s'en approcha, hésitant. C'était un gros doigt jauni par le tabac ; il avait, près de cette main, toute la disgrâce d'un sexe mâle. Il s'arrêta un instant, rigide, pointant vers la paume fragile, puis, tout d'un coup, timidement, il se mit à la caresser.
> [A brown hairy object approached it hesitantly. It was a thick finger yellowed by tobacco; beside that hand, it had all the grossness of a male organ. It stopped for a moment, rigid, pointing at the fragile palm, then, all of a sudden, it timidly started stroking it.] (195; 234)

This is the fulfilment of the initial handshake in which the Autodidact's hand becomes a phallic worm. His finger, arguably even more phallic, assumes its role as a disgraceful penis penetrating the nude female sunbather, caressing it, marking, masturbating the boy's hand turned into a female vulva. The phallic reference comes as no surprise, but what is astonishing is the qualification of "disgrace", which seems to suggest that there is something inherently unpleasant or revolting about the penis. Though we know that homosexuality has to be seen to exist in the Sartrean universe, Roquentin does not want to see it and specifically, he does not want to see another penis. In addition to his misogyny, we must add an etymological misanthropy, a misophally rather than out-and-out homophobia.

The text hovers between the straight and the queer reading; the boy's hand is alternately a vagina and a male anus, the finger penetrating it and entering the hollow in which sexuality indecisively hovers. The boy is both man and woman, boy and man, boy and woman, girl and man. Sartre's narrative wavers in a repeated and

---

[15] Serge Doubrovsky speaks of the "feminised hand" (p. 46).

undecidable polymorphous sexual perversity in which the only unchallenged sexual position is that one practised by Roquentin, the act of burying his penis in a woman's vagina, so that the male organ disappears as well. The perversity of the moment is that it erases sex while miming it. For in that very instant Sartre does to the boy what he will repeat in the first case of bad faith in *L'Être et le néant*: he renders the hand inert.[16] But the "inert flesh" in this scene is not produced by the bad faith that Sartre ascribes to the woman whose hand is being caressed by the man. Rather, this is an adolescent boy who is, as Roquentin notes, afraid and overcome: "on aurait dit qu'il se sentait dépassé par les événements [he looked as if he felt that things had gone beyond his control]" (195; 235). So his hand lies there on the table, victimized and frozen at the same time: "Pourtant il ne retirait pas sa main, il la laissait sur la table, immobile, à peine un peu crispée [Yet he didn't draw his hand away, he left it on the table, motionless, scarcely clenched]" (195; 235). And that inertia is followed by a silent scream: "Son camarade ouvrait la bouche, d'un air stupide et horrifié [His friend's mouth was open in a stupid, horrified expression]" (195; 235), as if he too were *interdit* by the act, as if he too were being penetrated by this phallic finger.

Even more telling in the perversion of the scene is the disappearance of the Autodidact's other hand, a disappearance that mimes the disappearance on the previous page of the teenager's hand to pinch his friend's arm. This time, it is for a far less jocular though certainly just as common event, for there is no room for doubt: "Mais il avait clos ses paupières, il souriait. Son autre main avait disparu sous la table [But he had closed his eyes, he was smiling. His other hand had disappeared under the table]" (195; 235). As if in a trance, the Autodidact can be assumed to be masturbating or at least touching himself, just as he is caressing the hand/vulva/anus of the other. No longer is this an innocent gesture, if ever it was, but it is rather what is called an *attentat à la pudeur*. More importantly, this final sequence of actions – the presumed masturbation plus the silent scream by the friend – brings the whole event out of the sphere of voyeurism, a peep show for Roquentin and the other observers, and into the public sphere in which the Corsican guard intervenes.

The fatalistic nature of the event and the transformation of sex and

---

[16] On *La Nausée* as a precursor to *L'Être et le néant*, see K. Gore, 'Lucienne, Sex and Nausea', *Forum for Modern Language Studies*, 26: 1 (1990), 37-48 (p. 40).

sexuality into an invisible and undecidable polymorphous perversity
will have two final effects of interest: inversion and infection. From
being a hidden act performed only for Roquentin's eyes, the queer
caress becomes visible to all, ostensibly after it is over, through the
eyes and language of the Corsican guard. But perhaps they have all
seen it already, not only the guard and Roquentin, but also the woman
next to the latter who says that she has seen the caress. Were they all
then complicitous in this *attentat à la pudeur*? Did they not let it
happen? At what point does the glancing touch of a hand become an
inappropriate caress? As Roquentin describes the scene, the reader
knows from the very first that the act is improper. How many times is
it necessary for the caress to occur before it is self-evident that "ce va-
et-vient obstiné [that stubborn little back-and-forth movement]" (195;
235) is an act of masturbation of a queerly sexed hand?

This Roquentin does not say. In not moving to end the scandalous
action, Roquentin is certainly in bad faith. In letting the Corsican turn
the act into a discourse of homophobia, in permitting homosexuality
(as figured in an individual) to become the *pour-autrui* figure that
homophobia makes of homosexuality, Roquentin fails to stop the
explosion of the private and the exposure of the privates.
Homosexuality inverts therefore into the phantasmatic other created
by those agencies and agents that want to discipline and punish it.
Made public, homosexuality is always reprehensible.

Made public, homosexuality is seemingly also infectious.
Everyone sees it, is complicit with it, and is fascinated by it as all
watch the performance of a probing phallus penetrate the boy's hand
made anus. And yet, it goes further. The Autodidact's penis in his
pants, his finger become a phallus, and now, thanks to the guard's fist,
his nose once again becomes a penis as well: "le nez de l'Autodidacte
commençait à pisser le sang [the Autodidact's nose was beginning to
piss blood]" (197; 238). There are two points here. First, with this
second reference to his nose, it is tempting to think that Sartre is
recalling the Autodidact's learning process: ironically turned inward,
receiving the *logos* of the other, the Autodidact, that monument to
phallogocentrism, is inverted in his learning just as he is inverted in
his sexuality. Second, we certainly know that this is a figurative
expression, but the figurative depends on the literal. The physical
incarnation of homophobia, gay-bashing *avant la lettre*, is the means
by which the gay phallus reproduces. The Autodidact has sprouted a

third phallus; his homosexuality is generalized all over his body, visible in the library that has turned into a panopticon. But in saying that, I am saying nothing new: the discourses of what I am loosely calling homophobia have always generalized the gay sex act to being the only defining moment of a gay person's life: gay people do not eat, drink, work, or sleep; they actively penetrate other men, or worse, they get anally penetrated. And, too, that homosexuality is generalized, at least to Roquentin, is spread infectiously through the discourse of homophobia.

As Roquentin is set to revisit the guard's action on him, in finally rising to action, Roquentin is pegged as a homosexual: "'Lâchez-moi, espèce de brute. Est-ce que vous êtes une tante, vous aussi?' ["Let go of me, you brute. Are you a fairy too?"]" (198; 238). Homosexuality is infectious, turning nice heterosexuals into nasty queers. If the Jews were saved by marking their doors with blood, homosexuality stains the door, marking its denizens for damnation in a *huis clos* from which there will never be any escape: "Le soleil couchant éclaira un moment son dos courbé, puis il disparut. Sur le seuil de la porte, il y avait une tache de sang, en étoile [The setting sun lit up his bent back for a moment, then he disappeared. On the threshold there was a bloodstain in the shape of a star]" (199; 239). And with the gates to hell closed, so does Sartre end his exploration of autoeroticism and homosexuality in *La Nausée*.

George Woods

'Sounds, Smells, Degrees of Light': Art and Illumination in *Nausea*

The qualities that Nausea *borrows from the visual arts supplement its existentialist argument. Throughout the novel, light imagery is manipulated to differentiate between different experiences. There is a striking inconsistency between Sartre's treatment of Roquentin's evenly illuminated experiences and those which rely on high contrast of light and dark. Paradoxically, it is those moments which are dimly lit that are presented as the most trustworthy renditions of phenomenal 'reality': Roquentin's world seems least plausible when it is thoroughly described. By manoeuvring light and shadows, Sartre recreates the fictive construction of reality through perception. Using visual artistic tropes and conventions, Sartre's and Roquentin's struggle with the incompatibility of the ideal and the real are externalised and made visible.*

* * *

> *Voir, c'est déjà une opération créatrice, qui exige un effort...*
> *(Seeing is, in itself, a creative act, and one requiring effort...)*
> Henri Matisse

In the opening passages of *Nausea,* Roquentin sets out his method for understanding the nature of the reality that confounds him. He decides that in order to comprehend his ontological dilemma and intermittent bouts of gripping nausea, he must "neglect no nuances or little details" (9) and faithfully recreate the world around him in his diary. What he does not understand at this point, although he comes to realise it later, is that the plausibility of the perceived world and the suspension of disbelief on the part of the sentient beings who inhabit it, *relies* upon the neglect of detail and the fictive (re)creation of reality through perception. The illusion of plausibility, and the complementary illusion that life has meaning, is constantly interrupted for Roquentin by the incursion of acute sensory experiences, especially bright light, upon dimmed or softened moments. Areas that

are brightly lit, or that create high contrast, comfort him, while grey
and misty scenes with diffuse light make him sick. This directive role
of light in *Nausea* is comparable to its role in the visual arts and can
be read through the role that light and perception play in three visual
art movements, Surrealism, Impressionism, and Cubism.

In the two-dimensional visual arts, as in *Nausea*, diffused light is
associated with softened or idealised reality and creates the illusion
that our environment can appear, in its entirety, in one instant, exactly
as it is. On the other hand, chiaroscuro, a high contrast painting
technique associated with artists like Caravaggio, creates dramatic
emphasis by drawing the viewer's gaze toward patches and planes of
light. Chiaroscuro creates the impression that illuminated figures rise
from or recede back into the shadows that surround them. Similarly, in
Nausea, attention is drawn to illuminated objects because they appear
in a patch of light, bordered by darkness. The alternative use of these
two tricks of the light, patchy and diffuse, are analogical
representations of the difference between perceived phenomena and
images summoned in the mind. Mental images are conceived and
understood instantly, as if light were evenly diffused throughout the
landscape. Conversely, in the perceptive process, the gaze functions as
the limited light source which allows only one or another aspect or
profile of an object to be perceived — or illuminated — at one time.
In *Nausea*, there is a consistent tension created by the multiple
properties of light. At one moment it casts truth upon an object; bright,
harsh or concentrated light exposes the object's tangible existence and
erases the softening effect of diffuse or muted light. It reveals the
terrible fact of our mortality. This can be seen in the following
observation made by Roquentin: "A patch of sunlight on the paper
tablecloth. In the patch of sunlight, a fly is dragging itself along,
dazed" (149-50). He narrates his actions as the light crosses his body
and illuminates his corporeal existence: "I get up. I move about in this
pale light; I see it change on my hands and on the sleeves of my
jacket" (30). Eventually, he comes to the conclusion that "sight is an
abstract invention" (187) and that although light has revelatory
properties, it cannot be trusted because it is always understood
through the medium of sight and the interpretation of consciousness.

In the 'Undated Sheet' that prefaces the novel, where Sartre
recreates the textuality of the diary form, there is a blank space to
indicate a word missing from this sentence: "I ought to try and say

how I saw it before and how I __ it now" (9). This omission mimics the role of consciousness in constructing perceived reality, since the structure of the sentence prompts the reader to automatically supply the missing word, *see.* Throughout the novel, Sartre continues to play with this pattern of lacunae that are filled by consciousness, not so much syntactically, but in descriptive detail. By creating unlit spaces in his descriptions of Roquentin's surroundings, Sartre mimics the lack of complete detail that accompanies perception. In ordinary perception, it is necessary for our minds to 'reconstruct' what we see because things do not present themselves to us in their entirety. Sartre examines this phenomenon in his *Psychology of Imagination.* When we see a cube, we do not see its six faces, its right angles or square sides but our minds nevertheless conceive 'cube' and fill in the disparities between what we perceive and what we understand.[1] Such is the case, in *Nausea,* when Roquentin deceives himself into believing that an adventure is about to happen to him. Sartre prepares the scene by repeatedly specifying the light effects that create Roquentin's stage, and especially the ambiguity that partial illumination can create: "The light grew softer. At this uncertain hour, something indicated the approach of evening" (80). The scene is interrupted suddenly by the sudden shining of a gas lamp: "But it was only a last ray of the setting sun. The sky was still bright, but the earth was bathed in shadow" (81). This ambient lighting creates the perfect conditions for Roquentin's self-deception. Without the glaring light of day, in the shadows of the evening, he must creatively augment his visual perception with his mind. His creative perception of the street scene aids his creation of the psychological fiction of adventure:

> Something is going to happen: in the shadows of the rue Basse-de-Vieille there is something waiting for me [...] I see myself advancing with a sense of fate. At the corner of the street there is a sort of white stone. From a distance it seemed black, and at each step I take it turns a little whiter. That dark body getting gradually lighter makes an extraordinary impression on me [...] It is so close now, that white beacon emerging from the shadows, that I am almost afraid [...] Here is the rue Basse-de-Vieille and the huge mass of Sainte-Cécile crouching in the shadows, its stained-glass windows glowing. (82)

The darkness of the street restricts Roquentin to receiving an "impression" of the scene, and the blazing sunset reflected in its

---

[1] J.-P. Sartre, *The Psychology of Imagination* (London: Methuen, 1972), p. 6.

windows draws the church out of the general gloom. This high contrast allows Roquentin's imagination to embellish what he sees and provides the space for his intellect to interpret perception – leading to the personification of the church.

On the other hand, Sartre claims that when we hold a *mental* image of the cube, it is accompanied by complete knowledge of the cube's properties and we are able to 'see' its essence instantaneously. In *The Psychology of Imagination* Sartre states that "[the imaginative consciousness], which might be called transversal, has no object. It posits nothing, refers to nothing, is not knowledge: it is a *diffuse light* which consciousness releases for itself..." (p.14, my emphasis). Roquentin's nausea is accompanied in the novel by an externalised depiction of this kind of light effect. He tends to prefer the night, because the artificial lighting of the town contrasts abruptly with the darkness. At night, he seeks out the cafés because, as he says, "they are full of people, and well lighted" (33). As he walks along the café stretch of the boulevard Noir, he notes the contrast created by the streetlights. The cafés, which "languish all day long […] light up in the evening and cast luminous rectangles on the roadway. I take another three baths of yellow light" (41). However, his comfort in the café space is eroded by the invasion of a dispersive fog that refracts the light and spreads it dully throughout the room. In this foggy light, Roquentin "floated along, dazed by the luminous mists which were entering [him] from all directions at once" (33). Sartre repeatedly introduces this fog to create diffuse light, and indicate Roquentin's confusion. After making himself anxious about M. Fasquelle, Roquentin recounts his actions:

> I hurried towards the rue Tournebride: I longed for its lights. It was a disappointment: true there was plenty of light, it was streaming down the shop windows. But it wasn't a gay light: It was all white because of the fog and it fell on your shoulders like a shower. (110)

He expects to find "light and warmth" (108) in the library, but the fog that externalised his confusion about Fasquelle also invades that space. In this instance, Sartre uses superfluous detail to invoke the verbal equivalent of diffuse light that bestows complete and instant consciousness of objects and their surroundings. Sartre describes Roquentin's surroundings in meticulous detail, and this aligns the experience more closely with mental imagery than perception, paradoxically creating a sense of unreality. As he recounts it, the fog creates:

> A sort of insubstantiality of things. The books were still there of course, arranged in alphabetical order on the shelves with their black or brown backs and their labels PU fl. 7.996 (Public Use - French Literature) or PU ns (Public Use - Natural Sciences). But... how can I put it? Usually strong and stocky, together with the stove, the green lamps, the big windows, the ladders, they dam up the future. (112-13)

Roquentin cannot actually *see* the subject labels on the books, but in his mind's eye, he knows that they are there. Normally, "these objects at least serve to fix the limits of probability" but under the influence of the diffusive fog, "they no longer fixed anything at all" (113). The fog mutes and disperses the daylight and creates, for Roquentin, an implausible unreality. The presence of unperceived detail indicates that the narrative is in the realm of imaginative consciousness, illuminated to the point of unreality, rather than that of perception, where omission of detail creates the necessary plausibility to suspend disbelief.

Consciousness reconstructs our environment by piecing together sensory information into a plausible picture, but the solipsistic — and nauseous — extension of this argument that Roquentin makes is that the act of perception itself *creates* reality. Of his historical work on Rollebon, Roquentin says, "I have the impression of doing a work of pure imagination" (26). He pieces together information about Rollebon, including some details, discarding others, and recognises it as a creative act. Eventually however, he applies this process to external reality, as in the episode with the fictive death of M. Fasquelle (108). During this episode, too, the lighting arrangements are noted in detail. The waiter turns out the light, and "The café was plunged into semi-darkness. A feeble light streaked with grey and brown was falling now from the tall windows" (107). This is not the comforting, yellow, chiaroscuro of Sainte-Cécile's windows or the street lamps; this is the *grey* light of visual and mental fog. Even during this episode, Roquentin recognises the possibility that the death of Fasquelle is a creation of his consciousness. When the waiter asks him if what he heard sounded like a death-rattle, he replies "I don't know [...] Perhaps it was just because I was thinking about things like that" (110). Sartre has established the role of consciousness in reconstructing reality and even filling gaps in perceptive detail, but the somewhat hysterical suggestiveness of the rumour of Fasquelle's death refutes the possibility that consciousness is entirely responsible for creating reality.

Imagination and perception cooperate to create plausible reality. Where this cooperation is absent in *Nausea*, Roquentin's perception of reality becomes Surrealistic. On the tram, Roquentin loses his ability to reconcile his consciousness of 'seat' with the red plush and leather object before him. He claims that saying the word 'seat' is "rather like an exorcism" (180) and it is familiarity that is being exorcised. He describes the seat moving: "This huge belly turns upwards, bleeding, puffed up - bloated with all its dead paws, this belly floating in this box, in this grey sky, is not a seat" (180). This unnerving dissociation from reality is explicitly correlated with the imaginary death of Fasquelle by Roquentin's observation of the "grey sky". Roquentin watches the scenery flash past the window and shifts his gaze around the tram carriage. As he does so, he observes that "a bright grey light invades the box" (179). The light in the tram carriage is diffused and everything he sees is uniformly illuminated. Roquentin has lost the ability to reconstruct plausible reality with his consciousness because the scene before him has no shadowy or obscured detail, and does not require it. The expedient synthesis between perception and consciousness is indicated here by its absence and by the bizarre pictures that Roquentin creates without it.

In contrast to his terror at the unfamiliar sight of the tram seat, Roquentin is, at times, bored by the predictability of reality. He says that "it is out of laziness, I suppose, that the world looks the same day after day" (114). The word 'looks' in this sentence however, indicates the true nature of Roquentin's anxiety. It implies that the problem lies in our perceptive and reflective laziness rather than the world's failure to change. Semir Zeki writes of this 'laziness', which is the brain's ability to create constancy even though the physical appearance of what we observe is continually changing. Zeki claims that:

> The ability of the brain to assign a constant color to a surface or a constant form to an object is generally referred to as color or object constancy. But perceptual constancy is a much wider phenomenon. It also applies for example to faces that

are recognizable when viewed from different angles and regardless of the expression worn.[2]

Hence we tend to claim absolutely, and somewhat abstractly, that the sky is blue, even though the sky appears to us severally in a spectrum of different colours, or, as Roquentin says "the sea *is* green; that white speck up there *is* a seagull" (182). Roquentin is coming to grips with his brain's penchant for constancy. Sartre demonstrates this process by defamiliarising the reader with what are normally familiar objects — such as a tram seat — thereby showing that the feeling of familiarity and plausibility is a creation of the brain rather than a feature of external reality.

Light imagery is repeatedly used in *Nausea* to differentiate between concrete perception and abstract consciousness. The episode where Roquentin visits the museum and studies the portraits of Bouville's town dignitaries demonstrates the contrast between the two, revealing how light can help the nauseous traveller come to terms with the difference. While Roquentin meditates on the portrait of Parrottin, he recreates his image of the man, his imposing presence and his impressionable wife:

> One day, I imagine, as her husband was sleeping beside her, with a ray of moonlight caressing his nose, or else as he was laboriously digesting [...] stretched out in an armchair, with his eyes half closed and a puddle of sunlight on his chin, she had ventured to look him in the face... (131)

Roquentin imagines that this luminous moment erases the abstract 'greatness' and historicity of the man. His wife sees his illuminated flesh, and the spell of aggrandisement and existence-justification is broken: "From that day on [Roquentin surmises], Madame Parrottin had probably taken command" (131).

These imaginative musings are complemented by the role that the motif of light plays in revealing the fictive nature of portraiture, and the part that consciousness plays in realising that fiction. Roquentin observes that "a pale light falling from the windows was making patterns on the pictures" (122). This time the light betrays the portraits' lifelessness and their consignment to the past. It is clear that the light is not illuminating real flesh, but the representation of flesh.

---

[2] S. Zeki, 'Art and the Brain', *Daedalus: Proceedings of the American Academy of Arts and Sciences*, 127: 2 (1998), 71-104 (p. 73).

Light has the ability to distinguish reality from representation. As Roquentin notes, "here and there a patch of light covered part of a face" (123). In contrast to the revelatory properties of direct light in other situations in the novel, light *covers* these faces, because it is not at faces that Roquentin is looking; it is canvas and paint. The imaginative process of observing a painting and *seeing* its subject is exposed by the incursion of direct light onto the canvas. This illusory process is further elucidated by Sartre in *The Psychology of Imagination* where he discusses a portrait of Charles VIII:

> As long as we observe the canvas and the frame for themselves, the aesthetic object 'Charles VIII' will not appear [...] It will appear at the moment when consciousness, undergoing a radical change in which the world is negated, itself becomes imaginative. (p. 219)

Roquentin continually draws attention to his sensory experiences but in doing so, alienates those experiences from the consciousness that interprets them. At times he takes comfort in his tangible surroundings, but when he ruminates over the gulf between perception and interpretation, he induces nausea:

> I can feel this black wooden handle. It is my hand which is holding it [...] What is the use of always touching something? Objects are not made to be touched. It is much better to slip between them, avoiding them as much as possible. (176)

It is evident that Roquentin's sickness arises from his taste for abstraction. In this moment, for example, the verb *feel* creates a non sequitur out of the optical descriptor *black*. Later, describing the tree root in the park, Roquentin realises that it is not possible really even to see *black*. The climactic scene at the chestnut tree can be understood in a variety of ways. Given Roquentin's close perception of detail throughout the novel, it is possible to understand the scene in phenomenological terms. He narrates his confusion at the gaps between perception and understanding, and understanding and naming:

> Black? I felt the word subside, empty itself of its meaning with an extraordinary speed. Black? The root *was not* black... it was... something else: black, like the circle, did not exist. (186)

His conclusion that contact with objects makes him sick is inaccurate. What provokes his nausea is the discovery that he is continually dealing with abstractions in order to make sense of the world. In the opening passages of the novel he sets out to divest sensory experience of the filtering influence of our subjective perception, but he consistently fails to do so and, hence, experiences nausea. Of the tree root he says:

> That black, there, against my foot, didn't look like black, but rather the confused effort to imagine black by somebody who had never seen black and who wouldn't have known how to stop. (187)

There is an immediacy to this image ("there, against my foot") but this immediacy is nullified by the effect of imagining. There is a sense of removal because "the image as image is describable only by an act of the second degree in which attention is turned away from the object, that is, by *reflection*" (*Psychology of Imagination*, p.1). In truth, Roquentin has realised that black must always be imagined, that the act of perceiving the world is always an imaginary act, just as the immortalisations of the town dignitaries in paint and Roquentin's biography of Rollebon are imaginary.

A new dimension is added to the motif of light in *Nausea* by the emergence of Anny out of the shadows of Roquentin's imaginative memory and into the luminous present of the narrative. In his nostalgia, Roquentin reveals that, in the continuous present of love, the "[s]ounds, smells, degrees of light" (95) that fill the material world are made more immediate and cannot be consigned to the past. Roquentin remembers Anny directing him to "look at the sky, look at the colour of the sunshine on the carpet" and telling him that he should "go back, go and sit in the shadow" (93). These directives indicate that Anny has a significant role in creating meaning from patches of light. When they finally meet, Anny tells Roquentin that her previous theory of 'perfect moments' has been replaced by an obsession with 'physical certainty'. She has forsworn abstraction and embraced the contingent world. However, as the scene progresses and Roquentin's disappointment increases, Anny becomes visually indistinguishable in the gloom: "I can scarcely make out her face. Her black dress merges into the shadows that have invaded the room" (217). The light is failing, and Anny is receding into shadow. This gloom is harshly interrupted when Roquentin steps out of Anny's apartment to find that "the corridor is ablaze with light" (219). All of this suggests that Roquentin's emotional state, specifically his heart-sick longing for Anny, is an alternate source of light and shade in his life alongside his philosophical discoveries.

That visual sensory experiences assume such importance in the philosophical unfolding of *Nausea* underscores its conceptual and stylistic debt to the visual arts. In visual-art terms, the distinction Sartre draws between the perceived and the imagined object is comparable to the tension between the Impressionist and Cubist schools of painting. Impressionism sought to reproduce the landscape exactly as it appeared in one instant, emphasising the effects of light and the changeability of the external world. Impressionism is evoked in *Nausea* when discrete shafts or patches of light illuminate particular objects and, by extension, particular moments. For example, when Roquentin's pipe "is daubed with a golden varnish which at first catches the eye" (27). The eye-catching quality of light is important here as a literary technique for drawing attention to a specific object just as it is on a canvas, when the viewer's eye is drawn toward areas of illumination; this debt to the visual arts is further emphasised by the painterly idiom "daubed". Conversely, according to Kahnweiler, the Cubists were interested in portraying "the *essence*, not the *appearance* of things".[3] They rejected the deceptive influence of light and tried to eliminate perspective by depicting all sides, angles and aspects of their subjects on a two-dimensional plane. In *Nausea*, this multi-perspective approach is indicated where the light is glary or diffuse and every detail is lit by "a pale sky, mottled with white" (27). The Cubist technique — associated with fogs and mists and excessive detail — provokes a kind of vertigo or sensory overload in Roquentin and frequently instigates his nausea. These two schools and their approach to light and perception exemplify Sartre's distinction between perceived phenomena and mentally conceived images. Taking his cue from the Cubists, Semir Zeki claims: "lighting prevents things from appearing as they are. Sight is a successive sense; we have to combine many of its perceptions before we can know a single object well" (Zeki, p.85), Roquentin's confusion can be seen as a manifestation of the tension between these two ways of seeing — essence and existence. He cannot help but notice the patches of light that

---

[3] Quoted in P. D'Espezel and F. Fosca, *A Concise Illustrated History of European Painting* (New York: Harry N. Ambrams, 1961), p. 312.

illuminate certain objects, people and spaces and cast others into obscurity and yet, in his consciousness, the world exists without perspective, uniformly luminous and rendering the external world "cardboard scenery" (113).

The prevalence of light imagery in *Nausea* offers an alternative reading that works against the standard existentialist argument toward a position that could be called phenomenological. Lighting and other sensory experiences direct Roquentin's attention and influence his emotional state as he labours to come to terms with the nature of perception and its relationship to consciousness. Far from being the source of his agony, acute sensory experiences engage Roquentin's imaginative perception and release him from the dull omnipresence of his consciousness: "I should like to pull myself together: a sharp, abrupt sensation would release me" (31). Acute experience is limited experience, which demands that Roquentin engage with the world beyond his mind to fill the voids that perception must leave. While there is variation of light and dark, Roquentin can engage with the world outside him, but when overhead clouds or creeping mists refract the light into a uniform glare the world no longer requires his imaginative engagement, and it becomes, as Roquentin says, "A perfect day to turn in upon oneself." With introspection, comes nausea and the inescapable suspicion that "these cold rays which the sun projects like a pitiless judgement on all creatures enter into me through my eyes; I am illuminated within by an impoverished light" (28).

Thomas Martin

The Role of Others in Roquentin's Nausea

There are several moments in Sartre's narrative when Antoine Roquentin's nausea (an overpowering sense that things just exist, without meaning or connection) is contingent upon others: others as an escape from nausea; others as a cause of nausea; others as the evidence for the absurdity that underpins nausea; others as the objects of nausea. In this chapter I examine the central role played by others in Nausea, *and claim that it is Roquentin's peculiar isolation from others that lies at the heart of his condition, rather than others themselves.*

* * *

Jean-Paul Sartre's *Nausea* is presented as the diary of Antoine Roquentin, whose main aim is to document, describe, and analyze a condition that has befallen him in recent weeks; a condition he names 'the Nausea'. Things — objects, people, even himself — at times make him sick, nauseous. The first instance of nausea that Roquentin describes is an incident on the beach in which he picks up a pebble with a view to skipping it across the surface of the sea.

> At that moment I stopped, dropped the pebble and walked away. [...] There was something which I saw and which disgusted me [...] It was a flat pebble, completely dry on one side, wet and muddy on the other. I held it by the edges, with my fingers wide apart to avoid getting them dirty. (9-10)

This incident could be described as just a matter between Roquentin and the world. Roquentin expects or wants something from the world and gets more (or perhaps it is less) than he bargained for. However such a description neglects to include an important third term: others. In this case, others as a community with shared intentions and a background of intersubjective meaning. Roquentin is, after all, watching children playing a game — a game with particular goals and constraints — and it is the pebble's 'refusal' to limit itself to being a part of this game, through having qualities that extend beyond its function (dry on one side, muddy on the other, and no doubt more), that inspires Roquentin's disquiet. Others play a central role in providing the backdrop of meaning that Roquentin experiences, at times, as a refuge from nausea, at other times, as precisely that, which through its incompleteness, propels him into nausea. Others also figure in the diary as ignorant or mendacious counterpoints to the newly 'enlightened' Roquentin or, less frequently, as fellow-travelers in absurdity. Here I explore the roles that others play in *Nausea* and the importance of Roquentin's solitary life to his condition. I will begin with a general description of Roquentin's nausea before moving on to examine the nature of meaning and how others are involved in it.

Nausea

In our everyday interactions with objects, our relations to those objects are quite 'safe'. We know, by and large what these things are, more or less what to do with them should they be instruments or obstacles, what to ignore about them should they be irrelevant to us. We have no problem placing them, placing them in relation to ourselves and in relation to each other. We are fairly comfortable in our world. In Roquentin's nausea, however, relations with objects are anything but safe or comfortable. Nausea is the experience accompanying the realization that things, including Roquentin, *exist*:

> I exist - the world exists - and I know the world exists. [...] It's since that day when I wanted to play ducks and drakes. I was going to throw that pebble, I looked at it and that was when it all began: I felt that it *existed*. (176)

That things exist might not seem like much of a revelation. After all, in the 'normal' situation I described above there is no doubt that there *are* things: instruments, obstacles, and so on. But 'existence' in the context of nausea goes much further than the acknowledgment that there are things, and in fact is quite the opposite of the 'isness' of things in everyday interactions. The existence that nausea reveals precludes Roquentin from knowing objects, from placing them in relation to each other and himself. Existence, for Roquentin, is characterized by three closely related properties: superfluity, absurdity, and contingency.

The discovery of superfluity is the recognition that things do not bear stable relationships with each other:

> We were a heap of existents inconvenienced, embarrassed by ourselves, we hadn't the slightest reason for being there, any of us, each existent, embarrassed, vaguely ill at ease, felt superfluous in relation to the others. *Superfluous*: that was the only connexion I could establish between those trees, those gates, those pebbles. It was in vain that I tried to *count* the chestnut trees, to *situate* them in relation to the Velleda, to compare their height with the height of the plane trees: each of them escaped from the relationship in which I had tried to enclose it, isolated itself, overflowed. (184)

We order, physically and practically, the elements of our perceptual field. In nausea Roquentin discovers that, in fact, objects escape the meanings imposed on them. Also, and in connection to superfluity, nausea involves recognition of absurdity, utter meaninglessness:

> A gesture, an event in the little coloured world of men is never absurd except relatively speaking: in relation to the accompanying circumstances. [...] But I, a little while ago, experienced the absolute: the absolute or the absurd. That root - there was nothing in relation to which it was not absurd. (185)

Things take on meaning by virtue of their relation to us and to each other. In the absence of those relations (superfluity) things do not have meaning. Finally, there is contingency:

> I mean by that, by definition, existence is not necessity. To exist is simply *to be there*; what exists appears, lets itself be *encountered*, but you can never *deduce* it. (188)

Were objects part of a system of meaningful relations, they would have a place. Within that system they would be, by necessity, some particular things. But Roquentin discovers that this is not so. Things just are (contingent), bearing no necessary relation to each other (superfluous), and are, hence, devoid of meaning (absurd).

So much for the metaphysics and epistemology that underlie nausea. But nausea is not just a matter of belief; it is an experience that accompanies belief. Roquentin's nausea is an intense bodily experience of confused dizziness and immersion in existence. The lack of fixed reference points, the unstable, constantly shifting nature of things in his world, gives him something like sea-sickness. He experiences his body as a fluid, sticky existent, on a par with the other existents in his world. He complains of feeling "full of lymph or warm milk" (14) and being engulfed in a "frothy water" which bubbles up in his mouth, which is both him and something he must deal with (143).

The absurdity of the world is something involving him: "Existence is penetrating me all over" (181). But more than that, he is himself an existent. This feeling of confusion and engulfment is the nausea.

So we have seen the beliefs about the world and the accompanying experience that is involved in nausea. But there is another element that is important to stress; Roquentin is *disgusted* that things should be this way. I suppose we might say that the sea-sick feeling of nausea just is disgusting, but there is surely more to Roquentin's disgust than that. Recalling the incident with the pebble, he says: "there was something which I *saw* and which disgusted me" (10 — my emphasis). What he sees, which disgusts him, is that things are not as he had hoped they would be. He had always, perhaps implicitly, imagined more, or at least something different, with respect to meaning. I suggest that his pre-nausea expectation is a kind of 'spectatorial realism'. He expects the world to just be a certain way – fixed, pure, hard, sharp, constant — and for him to be merely a spectator of it, not touched by it. Anny acknowledges this expectation of Roquentin's when she tells him: "You complain because things don't arrange themselves around you like a bunch of flowers, without taking the trouble to do anything" (215). Roquentin imagines that he should be at a safe distance from his surroundings, which just have the meaning that they have. Regarding his own life, past, present, and future, Roquentin says: "I wanted the moments of my life to follow one another in an orderly fashion like those of a life remembered" (63). However, Roquentin discovers that he has a role in constituting his world, providing the meaning of the objects around him. This throws him toward seeing his understanding of the world and the world itself as bearing little or no relation to each other: "Slow, lazy, sulky, the facts adapt themselves at a pinch to the order I wish to give them, but it remains outside of them" (26). Added to this, he is no longer at a distance from the world: "Objects ought not to touch […] but they touch me" (22). He is immersed in the world, it calls to him, but the call is far from clear. The world demands his attention but it is no longer unambiguously for his benefit.

Meaning

The key elements of Roquentin's discovery seem broadly correct. We do have a role in constituting our world; Roquentin is right.

However, we are not the sole authors of this world. There is a world out there, and our meaning-making practices are answerable to it. The world does make calls to us. Again, Roquentin is right. Where he goes wrong, in my estimation, is in the conclusions that he draws from these observations, conclusions that are driven by his disappointment that the situation is not simpler than it in fact is. Without a clear role for *either* a controlling, constituting subject *or* a world that imparts to us, as passive receptors, its pre-given meaning, Roquentin concludes that there is no meaning worthy of the name. Let us examine each of these sources of meaning — subject and world.

That the subject casts meaning onto the world is captured well in Sartre's example in *Being and Nothingness* of a rocky crag.

> A particular crag, which manifests a profound resistance if I wish to displace it, will be on the contrary a valuable aid if I want to climb upon it in order to look over the countryside. In itself – if one can even imagine what the crag can be in itself – it is neutral; that is, it waits to be illuminated by an end in order to manifest itself as adverse or helpful. Again it can manifest itself in one or the other way only within an instrumental-complex which is already established. [1]

"In itself [...] it is neutral": the world only takes on meaning in relation to us. At a minimum, meaning requires someone for whom something is meaningful; that much is indisputable. But Sartre's point is stronger than this. The subject, through her engagement with the world, *confers* meaningful qualities upon it, qualities it just could not have in her absence. In this way, the subject has a role in constituting her meaningful world.

However, the world must also make its contribution, and human experience bears this out. Expanding on Sartre's example of the crag, Merleau-Ponty writes:

> When I say this rock is unclimbable, it is certain that this attribute, like that of being big or little, straight and oblique, and indeed like all attributes in general, can be conferred upon it only by the project of climbing it, and by human presence. It is, therefore, freedom [that is, the subject] which brings into being the obstacles to freedom, so that the latter can be set over against it as its bounds. However, it is clear that, one and the same project being given, one rock will appear as an obstacle, and another, being more negotiable, as a means. My freedom, then, does not so contrive it that this way there is an obstacle, and that

---

[1] J.-P. Sartre, *Being and Nothingness*, trans. by H. Barnes (London: Routledge, 1958), p. 482.

way a way through, it arranges for there to be obstacles and ways through in general; it does not draw the particular outline of this world, but merely lays down its general structures.[2]

Merleau-Ponty agrees with Sartre that the general structures of the practical field (that is, the world's meaning) are conferred by the subject. But the generation of meaning is not 'one-way traffic'. Objects in the world have subject-independent properties that will make them more or less amenable to particular meaning conferrals.[3] What is more, the nature of the world affects the subject's intentions and practices, such that it in turn affects the meaning conferrals she makes.

> [It is] true that there are no obstacles in themselves, but the self which qualifies them as such is not some acosmic subject; it runs ahead of itself in relation to things in order to confer upon them the form of things. There is an autochthonous significance of the world which is constituted in the dealings which our incarnate existence has with it, and which provides the ground of every deliberate *Sinngebung*. (Merleau-Ponty, p. 441)

This *Sinngebung* ('sense/meaning giving') has two sources; a subject essentially in the world and a world revealed by a subject engaged in it. As such, the *Sinngebung* is both 'centrifugal', as the subject casts meaning upon the world, and 'centripetal', as the world imposes itself on the subject (Merleau-Ponty, p. 439). As Charles Taylor puts it, meaning "refers to the ways in which our world is non-indifferent for us. Features of his world have meaning for an agent because he has purposes, goals, aspirations, and because they touch him in various ways".[4] We have projects, actions to perform as embodied agents, and

---

[2] M. Merleau-Ponty, *Phenomenology of Perception*, trans. by C. Smith (London: Routledge, 1962), p. 439.

[3] It may be claimed that Merleau-Ponty is somewhat unfair to Sartre, in suggesting that he (Sartre) does not accord the world enough of a role in the provision of meaning. While it is true that Sartre does focus heavily on the role of the subject in *Being and Nothingness*, I have argued elsewhere (with respect to idealism and realism – though the point still contributes to the topic under discussion here) that Sartre, even there, certainly does accord the world a significant role (T. Martin, *Oppression and the Human Condition: An Introduction to Sartrean Existentialism* (Lanham, Md.: Rowman and Littlefield), pp. 2-6; 12-14).

[4] C. Taylor, 'Embodied Agency', in *Merleau-Ponty: Critical Essays*, ed. by H. Pietersma (Lanham, Md.: University Press of America, 1990), p. 1-2.

it is in part through our projects that we draw together the elements of our practical field, giving them meaning. In other words, it is through engaging with the world that meaning is produced. At the same time, the world touches us and has qualities which both inspire meaning conferrals and make it amenable to the meanings conferred.

As we have seen, Roquentin does recognize both of these elements. However, these two sources of meaning are inextricably linked and can really only be discussed as distinct in abstraction. One cannot describe the subject and his intentions without reference to the world he is in, nor can one describe the world without reference to the subject for whom the world is. That is why, were one to attempt to accord distinct roles to either subject or world, as Roquentin appears to do, one is faced not with clarity but ambiguity. For Roquentin, in the grip of an expectation of purity and security of meaning, these elements pull apart from each other, leaving a meaning vacuum. But, in fact, these elements are the necessary aspects of meaning, reinforcing and making each other, and meaning itself, possible at all. This does result in meaning being ambiguous; but it is still meaning.

Others

An important element in our engaging with the world is intersubjectivity. We do things with others, for others, despite others or against others. Roquentin's nausea is, at bottom, about his *disengagement* as a subject in the world of objects and others – the suspension of his projects and his participation in intersubjective meaning. It is through this disengagement that the world loses its meaning for him, that language ceases to perform its function,[5] and that his body, otherwise his subjective presence in the world, becomes an object mired in the in-itself. On several occasions, it is Roquentin's lack of a project that propels him into nausea. For example:

> I had come for a fuck, but I had scarcely opened the door before Madeleine, the waitress, called out to me:
>
> 'The *patronne* isn't here, she's gone shopping in town.'

---

[5] "Words had disappeared, and with them the meaning of things, the methods of using them, the feeble landmarks which men have traced on their surface" (182).

> I felt a sharp disappointment in my prick, a long disagreeable tickling. At the
> same time I felt my shirt rubbing against my nipples and I was surrounded, seized
> by a slow, coloured whirlpool, a whirlpool of fog, of lights in the smoke, in the
> mirrors, with the benches shining at the back, and I couldn't see why it was there
> or why it was like that. (33)

The nausea — with its characteristics of disorientation and the feeling
that the body is a mere object — sets in following the lack of a project
that would otherwise give sense to things. But perhaps a more telling
example of the connection between the lack of a project and nausea is
the moment that Roquentin gives up on writing the biography of
Rollebon. Earlier, he realised that he, as narrator, was constructing
Rollebon's history. He gives up on the biography because he no
longer has faith in capturing the past. But what is he going to do with
his life now? This throws him into a reflection on the sheer
'presentness' of things (the paper, the writing, etc.). Without a project
there is, in a sense, no future, no past. He has no project - he is stuck
in the present:

> The true nature of the present revealed itself: it was that which exists, and all that
> was not present did not exist. The past did not exist. Not at all. Neither in things
> nor even in my thoughts. (139)

What makes this example so interesting is that it reveals the spiraling,
(non-Hegelian) dialectical nature of Roquentin's nauseous worldview.
In the earlier example of the patronne, external forces stymie
Roquentin's project: she is just not there. In this example, however, it
is Roquentin's worldview itself that brings about the cessation of the
project. Because of his view that there is no past, only existence, he
gives up as pointless a project which has hitherto taken him beyond
sheer existence, and this in turn makes sheer existence more evident to
him:

> Monsieur de Rollebon was my partner: he needed me in order to be and I needed
> him in order not to feel my being. [...] [I]t was for him that I ate, for him that I
> breathed, each of my movements had its significance outside, there, just in front
> of me, in him. (142-43)

What is more, this example points to a way in which others can be
implicated in our projects. They can provide (or be) the goals *for
which* we act, such that we have paths to tread, obstacles to negotiate,

instruments to use. In short, such that the world is bestowed and has meaning.

Apart from abandoning projects to do with others, Roquentin disengages himself from the 'backdrop' of meaning that others provide through pursuing their own projects. In several places in the diary (though less and less frequently as it progresses), we see others (as flesh and blood others, or in terms of the practico-inert ensembles they create and in which they participate) as providing a refuge from meaninglessness.

> The Paris train has just come in. People are coming out of the old station and dispersing in the streets. I can hear footsteps and voices. A lot of people are waiting for the last tram. [...] Well, they will have to wait a few minutes more: the tram won't come before a quarter to eleven. [...] [W]hat is there to fear from such a regular world? (11)

Others, through coordinating their activities with each other, do provide regularity and predictability. Others also make things for each other with the intention of those things being used by others in their projects. The social and intentional imbuement of these objects enables them to exert a centripetal *Sinngebung*, which is to say, they strongly suggest a significance to the subject, calling for him to recognize them within a range of meanings. Some objects (such as towns, libraries, and cafés), more than others, are quite 'humanized' and Roquentin initially finds refuge and comfort in these less alien places.

However, this comfort cannot last, as it relies on recognizing value in the web of meanings in which others participate. Having encountered superfluity, absurdity, and contingency, having seen the terrible truth of the world, Roquentin becomes increasingly unable to respect others and their worlds. At times this disrespect takes the form of pity. Others simply do not know the truth, and perhaps for them it is just as well. For example, there is the incident in the Boulevard Noir. It is cold, dark, pure (Roquentin likes it), the nausea is over there, under the lamplight. He spots Lucie, who has just fought with her husband:

> She needs to be taken by the shoulders and led to the lights, among people, into the pink, gentle streets: over there you can't suffer so acutely; she would soften up, she would recover her positive look and return to the ordinary level of her suffering. (45)

Others can provide you with comfort — so long as you are a dupe.
    But more typically, Roquentin is less sympathetic to others, instead
holding them up for ridicule and contempt. *Their* meaning is no
meaning at all. For example, there is the parade of 'gentlemen of
substance'. Here Roquentin describes the Bouvilleans' Sunday ritual
as if from the perspective of complete outsider or, perhaps, curious
scientist. The participants in the ritual are not given subjectivity,
intentionality, or purpose. They are comically objectified.

> I advance slowly. I stand a whole head higher than both columns and I see hats, a
> sea of hats. Most of them are black and hard. Now and then you see one fly off at
> the end of an arm, revealing the soft gleam of a skull; then, after a few moments
> of clumsy flight, it settles again. [...] A group has just formed [...] It's over now:
> the group has broken up, we start moving again. Another group has just collected,
> but it takes up less space. (67-68)

Here Roquentin works hard to de-mean the proceedings, describing
them almost as an entomologist might describe the behaviour of ants.
His distance from the social world of Bouville is underscored in a
further description of Sunday.[6]

> I could feel the afternoon all through my heavy body. Not my afternoon, but
> theirs, the one a hundred thousand citizens of Bouville were going to live in
> common. At this same moment, after their copious Sunday dinner, they were
> getting up from table and for them something had died. Sunday had spent its
> light-hearted youth. (76-77)

But others, with their 'meaningful' lives, are not only fools; some of
them — the 'great citizens of the past' — are bastards. These are the
figures that do most to keep alive the myths of progress, purpose and
value. In doing so, they obfuscate reality from the citizens of the town.
    I said earlier that we can think of nausea in terms of
disengagement, and have already mentioned some examples in which
Roquentin sees himself as separate to others. Roquentin expresses his
feeling of solitude several times, and it plays an important role in his
nausea. For example:

---

[6] Actually, Roquentin does allow himself to participate in the adventure of Sunday,
which makes him happy (84), only for him to berate himself the next day:
"[Yesterday] I got worked up like a fool. I need to clean myself up with abstract
thoughts, as transparent as water" (85).

> I for my part live alone, entirely alone. I never speak to anybody, I receive nothing, I give nothing. (16)

> I was neither a grandfather, nor father, nor even a husband. I didn't vote, I scarcely paid any taxes; I couldn't lay claim to the rights of a tax-payer, nor to those of an elector, nor even to the humble right to honour which twenty years of obedience confer on an employee. My existence was beginning to cause me serious concern. Was I a mere figment of the imagination? (126-127)

> I haven't any troubles, I have some money like a gentleman of leisure, no boss, no wife, no children; I exist, that's all. (153)

That he has so little intimacy with others and that he has so few commitments to his community make it easier for him to cut himself loose from society and to look down on it from his great height.[7] As with his turning away from projects, there is something of a dialectical, positive feedback loop at play in his isolation from others. Given his isolation from others he is able to see beyond their 'stable' world, which now appears less worthwhile, such that he distances himself from them further… And so it goes on.

What are we to make of Roquentin's reactions to others? If he believes that they are wrong about the world and their place in it, then it makes sense to see them as ignorant and unreflective, if not purveyors of inauthentic falsehoods. But one gets the impression that there is more going on here than just this. Roquentin desperately wants meaning and he sees that others at least think that they have it. And on some level he envies them. He wants something like (though not exactly like) what they have, but he cannot have it. Hence the derision and the petulance. The meaning that is lost for Roquentin is, at least in part, intersubjective meaning. This is why much of his ire is directed at others. He had been given the hope of direction and stability, yet what he finds is instability and ambiguity. His is the anger accompanying disappointment at a broken promise.

Is he right to condemn others as he does? That, at least some, others unthinkingly live their lives, as if there were no question about the value of their pursuits is worthy of criticism. It is false and inauthentic. Their mistake is to see things in terms of unquestionable

---

[7] Interestingly, Roquentin's scathing attack on the bourgeoisie notwithstanding, there is something of the 'bourgeois brat' about him and his lifestyle. I am not sure that a single parent of three would often have the luxury of nausea.

clarity, perfect, stable meaning. This is the kind of meaning that Roquentin had expected but found to be illusory. However, Roquentin's mistake is to swing to the other extreme. Having sought perfection and received something less, he sees things in terms of utter chaos and absurdity. The truth lies between these two extremes. The paths of our lives are not laid out for us, we have a role in constituting our world through our projects, which, relying as they do on our freedom, do not have the character of necessity. However, in conducting a project, the world does have meaning for us. This makes meaning 'local' and contingent. It is not at all clear to me why 'locality' and 'contingency' should be incompatible with 'meaning' (as Roquentin seems to think). Through relations with others we find that meaning is not *so* local as to make us meaning-solipsists, nor is it *so* contingent as to be just a matter of caprice. As with the centripetal *Sinngebung* from the world, there is a centripetal *Sinngebung* exerted on the self by others and intersubjective life. We grow up in and into cultures with shared systems of value and meaning, which carry us along and provide us with direction. As free beings, we may critically engage with these systems, questioning and subverting them. But even in criticism there is still direction provided by those systems, though the path followed might be subversive. To say this is not to champion conservatism. The questioning, critical attitude is a hallmark of human subjectivity and its results can be radical. It does suggest, however, that, despite the room to move that freedom affords us, we are not as cast adrift as Roquentin claims we are. We do have reference points and launching pads, which are neither fixed nor evanescent. While this is a far remove from fixed, universal meaning, it also seems a long way from the stultifying chaos of nausea. Nauseous thoughts may well serve as useful correctives to the complacency that we are prone to slip into, but they do not exhaust the possibilities of meaning.[8]

---

[8] I am grateful to Alistair Rolls, the convenor of a conference on *Nausea* held at the University of Newcastle, Australia, 2004, for providing me with the occasion to think more seriously about the novel and the position that the protagonist seems to advocate. I am grateful also to those who participated in that conference, and at a session of the English Department's seminar series held at Rhodes University, South Africa, for useful comments on earlier drafts of this chapter.

Peter Poiana

The Subject as Symptom in *Nausea*

While the existential meaning of nausea, a condition that reveals an inauthentic relationship with the world, has been elucidated by Sartre and other commentators, more needs to be said about how it functions in relation to the unconscious. This chapter will consider, from a Freudian and Lacanian perspective, how the subject in Sartre's novel is constituted as symptom. It will examine the narrative in order to locate the areas of resistance, compromise and substitution that prepare the scene for the return of a different subject to the voluntarist one envisaged by Sartre. In this case, the subject as symptom is modeled on the figure of the hysteric who, in letting the body speak its desire, provides a basis for establishing a different kind of relationship with the world.

* * *

The hero of Sartre's novel is a pathological condition. Its effects are first visible when Roquentin picks up a pebble with the intention of throwing it into the water. At this point he loses his physical capabilities, is overcome by a feeling of disgust, and can do no better than to turn away and suffer the jibes of the children behind his back. Thereafter, the nausea re-appears at many points of the narrative, gaining each time in amplitude and significance, such that by the end of the narrative it loses its status as anomaly and becomes Roquentin's sole mode of existence. It is a "deep, deep boredom" (224) from which he never emerges.

Sartre's narrative appears to invert the conventional structure of redemptive narratives. Instead of portraying a subject that overcomes, after a series of trials, the illness and its symptoms, Sartre offers a scenario in which the illness defeats the subject, thereby erecting the symptom in the place of, and at the expense of, the subject. Speaking of the nausea that overwhelms him in a café, Roquentin admits to abandoning himself to its rule: "The Nausea isn't inside me: I can feel it over there on the wall, [...] everywhere around me. It is one with the café, it is I who am inside it" (35).

Examining the novel from firstly a Freudian and secondly a Lacanian perspective, we shall show how the subject of the novel is constituted as symptom. The appeal to psychoanalysis may well be seen as controversial, particularly in view of the stand Sartre takes, in *Being and Nothingness*, against the notion of the unconscious. Here, he denounces the unconscious as a myth, an 'easy way out' for weak individuals who succumb to 'bad faith' rather than committing themselves to making life-forming decisions. By positing the existence of a psychic space that draws together conflicting unconscious drives, psychoanalysis, asserts Sartre, has "hypostasized and 'reified' bad faith".[1] It may be argued, however, that the very thing the existentialist philosopher denounces in his attack on psychoanalysis as a 'distraction' or a 'lie', is an essential ingredient of the novelist's craft. The illusion chased away by philosophy returns surreptitiously in the raft of images that are brought together in the narrative under the guise of phantasies, dreams, false impressions and involuntary acts. That the unconscious is ever-present in the novel can be seen from the fact that Roquentin, like a good patient of Freud, is repeatedly led to places that he clearly would prefer to avoid. All of which suggests that the realm of the unconscious and its point of contact with the real, namely the symptom, are as central to the concerns of Sartre's novel as the notion of consciousness and its point of contact with the real, namely action. That said, *how* the symptom is constituted, and *how* it determines the destiny of the subject in Sartre's narrative, are questions that demand to be solved if one is to understand the role of the unconscious in Sartre's novel.

Following Freud, we can characterise symptom as resistance. In his work *Inhibitions, Symptoms and Anxiety*, Freud explains that symptoms arise from the resistance to impulses that, were they left free to express themselves, could place the subject in danger.[2] Instances of these defensive processes appear frequently in the early parts of the narrative in the form of resistance to emotions, resistance to action, resistance to recognition, resistance to intelligibility, resistance to knowledge, and finally resistance to the pleasure of the food and sex that is on offer in the cafés and restaurants of Bouville. Resistance drives the narrative by causing it to deviate from those

---

[1] J.-P. Sartre, *Being and Nothingness*, trans. by H. Barnes (London: Methuen, 1957), p. 54.
[2] S. Freud, *Inhibitions, Symptoms and Anxiety*, trans. by A. Strachey (London: Hogarth Press, 1936), p. 33-35.

situations and settings that cannot be countenanced by an anxiety-prone subject. Such resistance is at work in the scene that introduces the "window trap" and the "mirror trap" (49). Disgusted by the view from the window, because it can only show him a predictable world that "can never take [him] by surprise" (50), Roquentin moves away from it, only to find himself in front of the mirror where he is "captured" again, this time by the false view of eternity that appears in his own reflection. He is forced to make another evasive move. "Finally, I escape from my image and I go and throw myself on my bed. I look at the ceiling, I should like to sleep" (51). The narrative consists of a series of such traps in which Roquentin recognises, then rejects violently, the avenues of human fulfilment that society offers him.

The narrative of resistance is productive of symptom when it operates not by negation, but by substitution. The Freudian subject, when faced with a dangerous impulse that demands to be satisfied, protects itself by substituting one object for another, thereby allowing the impulse to be partially satisfied while concealing its true object of desire. It is interesting to note that Freud uses this same model of substitution to account for literary and artistic production throughout the ages. Against the notion of transcendence that was widely used by Enlightenment and Romantic thinkers to account for artistic creation, Freud envisages a transfer of energy from sexual objects to so-called higher order creative pursuits, such that the libidinous energy associated with the former is re-channelled to support the sublimated ends of the latter. Freud's account of Dostoevsky's writing, for example, which he considers to emanate from the guilt the Russian writer suffered as a consequence of his gambling addiction, is a typical if not controversial application of the substitution principle.[3] A similar Freudian reading can be applied to Sartre's notion of consciousness. The negativity on which consciousness is founded in Sartre can be understood in terms of the substitution of the objects of desire, such that what results is not freedom, but symptom. Colette Soler expresses in the following terms the ontological basis of symptom:

---

[3] S. Freud, *Art and Literature*, trans. by J. Strachey (Harmondsworth: Penguin, 1987), pp. 456-57.

The result is that one seeks; that's why one speaks and why there is even satisfaction in blah blah blah, unless one finds a [...] replacement. That is what symptom does: it plugs up the "there is no such thing" of the no-relationship with the erection of a "there is".[4]

Symptom "plugs up" the nothingness that invades the sentient world the moment the Sartrean subject directs his hostile gaze towards it. Symptom is a loud "No!" that fills the space left by the abandoned object, while imposing itself noisily as a new command to fulfilment. Like the ripples caused by a pebble dropped into a pond, symptom progressively invades the subject's space, disturbing its emotional balance, undermining its verbal performance and compromising its social standing.

The mechanisms underlying symptom are revealed for the first time in the scene in which Roquentin rejects Mercier's invitation to travel with him to Bengal. Roquentin is clearly disturbed by the unwelcome proposition, going so far as to describe it as a "voluminous, insipid idea" (15). At the source of this violent reaction is the substitution of the "voluminous, insipid" invitation by the figure of the "little Khmer statuette on a card-table" (14), such that it is against the statuette, which he finds "stupid and unattractive" (15) as it stands before him, and not against Mercier, that Roquentin hurls his disgust and anger. As the product of the substitution of the objects of desire, symptom reveals its essentially ambivalent nature, ambivalence being understood here as the kind of "instinctual fusion"[5] that causes feelings of love and hate, attraction and repulsion, to be released simultaneously. Roquentin's violent but ambivalent reaction betrays an erotic interest in the phallic-looking statue, to which contribute significantly both the intoxicating effect of Mercier's bearded and perfumed head moving side to side, and his pressing insistence: "I know you'll end up by saying yes" (15). The contrasting emotions of disgust and attraction are both palpable in Roquentin's confession: "[...] It sickened me so much that I couldn't look at it" (15).

---

[4] C. Soler, 'Literature as Symptom', in *Lacan and the Subject of Language*, ed. By E. Ragland-Sullivan & M. Bracher, (New York & London: Routledge, 1991), pp. 213-19 (p. 216).
[5] S. Freud, *The Standard Edition of the Complete Psychological Works of Sigmund Freud. Vol. 19. The Ego and The Id and Other Works*, trans. by J. Strachey (London: The Hogarth Press, 1961), p. 41.

In addition to substitution and ambivalence, symptom reveals a third mechanism that Freud refers to as "conversion".[6] Conversion operates in symptom by translating a psychic tension into a physical alteration, thereby making it empirically observable and, ultimately, liable to social sanction. Roquentin reports factually his loss of motor ability — "Well, I was paralysed, I couldn't say a word" (14) — just as he acknowledges, though less directly, the anxiety that overcomes him as he contemplates the kind of destiny that symptom has reserved for him: "[...] I'm afraid of what is going to be born and shall take hold of me and carry me off — I wonder where" (15).

The substitution, ambivalence and conversion that characterise the work of the symptom in Sartre's narrative are typical of the features that Freud examines in his account of hysteria, published as *Dora: An Analysis of a Case of Hysteria*. The symptom that appears in Roquentin in the scene in Mercier's office involves a hostile emotional reaction to a "proposition" that has a definite sexual content, recalling Freud's telling assertion: "I should without question consider a person hysterical in whom an occasion of sexual excitement elicited feelings that were preponderantly or exclusively unpleasurable" (*Dora*, p. 22). Like the hysteric's, Roquentin's reaction is disturbing in its visibility, as it gives bodily expression to both the desire and its censure, such that both the acceptance and the rejection, the "yes!" and the "no!", coexist and reinforce each other.

Following Freud, symptom marks the site of a resistance. It is a disturbance, or as Freud quaintly puts it, an "unwelcome guest", which makes its appearance by way of a substitution of objects of desire. Finally, it is a release of affect that in the case of the hysteric is located in some part of the body by virtue of a principle that Freud calls "somatic compliance" (*Dora*, pp. 35, 36). This last property of symptom, that is, its bodily expression, calls for a fuller treatment in the context of Sartre's narrative.

Much has been written about the role of body parts in Sartre's novel. A quick survey shows that the hands and face are among the most common sites for Roquentin's hysterical symptoms. Unquestionably, however, the organ that is most affected by the symptom is the throat. The first appearance of the symptom in the throat occurs in Lucie who, when she recalls her bitterly unhappy marriage, points to her throat: "'It's there', she says, touching her

---

[6] S. Freud, *Dora: An Analysis of a Case of Hysteria*, trans. by A. & J. Strachey (New York: Touchstone, 1997), p. 46.

throat, 'it won't go down'" (23). Roquentin succumbs soon after to the
same symptom during his lunch with the Autodidact. When faced with
the latter's suspicious appeal to fraternal love, Roquentin's throat
seizes up, losing its ability to speak or to swallow food:

> I can't speak any more [...] I laboriously chew a piece of bread which I can't
> make up my mind to swallow [...] I feel like vomiting — and all of a sudden,
> there it is: the Nausea. (176)

In targeting the throat, the symptom affects the two vital functions
that serve to ensure the subject's autonomy, namely those of ingestion
and speech. While in the throes of nausea, the throat rejects its normal
function of ingestion, such that the food that is destined to be
swallowed is held in abeyance, poised before the orifice that refuses to
accept it. On one occasion, it is the cold chicken that Roquentin
cannot bear to contemplate eating in the company of the ravenous
Autodidact (166), and on another, the cold tea he reluctantly sips as he
realises that all possibility of renewing his relationship with Anny is
lost (218). As well as obstructing the passage of food, nausea
suffocates Roquentin, preventing him from articulating the words that
might liberate him from his anxiety. Like Lucie who cannot bring
herself to speak of her unhappy love affair, Roquentin struggles with
words that remain "stuck in the throat". When he does manage to
articulate a phrase or two under the effect of the nausea, the words are
so distorted that they lose their connection with reality. During the ill-
fated lunch, Roquentin's urge to wound the Autodidact with the
butter-knife is so distorted by the symptom that all he can offer
ultimately by way of response is a bland excuse for having to leave:
"I'm a little tired. It was very nice of you to invite me. Good-bye"
(177). By targeting the organ that enables the passage of food and the
articulation of speech, the symptom weakens the subject's autonomy
and seriously hampers its capacity to withstand the psychic pressure
emanating from the unconscious drives.

The repercussions of symptom are felt in the peculiar way it affects
the narrative's arrangement of its imaginary spaces. To understand
how this relates to the symptom's apparent predilection for the throat,
it is necessary to recall that the symptom affects not just the biological
function of the organ, but also the pleasure derived from it. It is
common knowledge that the pleasure of oral ingestion is fundamental
to the development of the infant as it explores through ingestion the
objects of the world around it, just as it aids the older child develop

socially by encouraging culinary discernment and speech, both of which are driven by oral stimulation. Given this, any blurring of the boundaries between pleasure and displeasure will seriously alter the subject's perception of the world and its place in it. Nausea afflicts Roquentin principally by abolishing the distinction between pleasure and displeasure. Where he once experienced the physical satisfaction of ingestion, he now feels the unpleasant bitter tasting digestive juices as they rise in his mouth. When displeasure is experienced in the organ of pleasure, the boundary between pleasure and displeasure becomes a shifting one, such that one can be mistaken for the other. The tension created by such confusion finds an outlet in nightmare phantasy. Phantasy, it should be recalled, is a return to "imaginary gratifications"[7] by which the individual compensates for the pleasure lost as a result of the sanction of reality. However, when the impulses associated with unpleasant or frightful memories are strong enough to break through the protective shield of phantasy, the displeasure that was previously held at bay re-invests the imaginary setting, giving rise to symptom. The invasion of unpleasant and frightening images is a constant structural feature of the narrative. The familiar world of Bouville, with its streets, bars, public parks and port activity, loses the sense of comfort and security that Roquentin seeks; and in its place is created a landscape of frightful figures. The description of the calm surface of the sea, for example, is overrun by images of sea-dwelling monsters that threaten to emerge and devour the curious bystander:

> A monster? A huge carapace, half embedded in the mud? A dozen pairs of claws slowly furrow the slime. The monster raises itself a little, every now and then. [...] I went nearer, watching for an eddy, a tiny ripple. (116)

A similar nightmare phantasy occurs when, in the place of the well-tended gardens of Bouville, there appears an army of curling, gripping and clawing plants that happily destroy their victims with their "long black pincers" (222). As symptom, nightmare phantasy is the imaginary equivalent of nausea in so far as it conflates the experience of pleasure and displeasure in line with the principle of ambivalence that marks the hysterical condition.

Turning now to the function of speech, the point has been made that nausea signals the separation of the subject from language, as a

---

[7] S. Freud, *Introductory Lectures on Psycho-analysis*, trans. by J. Riviere (London: George Allen and Unwin, 1922), p. 312.

result of which it is alienated from the world, from others and from its
future. As a lonely, displaced individual, Roquentin is deprived of the
opportunities to engage in speech; as a hesitant writer, he is unsure of
the value of what he writes and subsequently loses faith in writing.
When he gives up writing his book on Rollebon, he loses his sole
productive activity, his sole reason for living in Bouville and his
connection with language. He finds himself, at this point, on the verge
of social disintegration. In Lacanian terms, the subject loses, when
deprived of language, the exclusive vehicle of its desire. This explains
why, in the treatment of hysteria, the efforts of the clinician are solely
directed towards making the hysteric speak, for it is only through
speech that the subject constitutes itself as subject. As Lacan asserts,
"[...] the differential feature of the hysteric is precisely this — it is in
the very movement of speaking that the hysteric constitutes her
desire".[8]

Deprived of the language with which to articulate its desire, the
subject succumbs to symptom. The throat seizes up, and the hands, as
the agent of the written word, fall inert: "A feeling of immense disgust
suddenly flooded over me and the pen fell from my fingers, spitting
ink" (140). Roquentin contemplates confusedly the words that detach
themselves from him as quickly as the ink dries, leaving him with an
impression of lifelessness, while the printed characters on the page all
point to his own deficit of being. If this were a redemptive narrative,
one would expect the solution to reside in the rehabilitation of the
subject through the revival of the bodily connections to language,
specifically through the throat and the fingers. However, the narrative
does not envisage taking this path other than by alluding to it as a
distant possibility. Both the beginning and the end of the narrative
raise the question of strategies of rehabilitation, but no advance is
made in the struggle against the symptom. The first sentence carries
the suggestion that "the best thing would be to write down everything
that happens from day to day" (9), and if Roquentin remains for some
time faithful to this strategy, it is formally abandoned in the final
scene in which he envisages writing a work of fiction: "The sort of
story, for example, which could never happen, an adventure [...] A
book. A novel" (252). Between the two announced literary projects,
the narrative develops as a search for a new relationship with language
that aims to replace the one that the symptom has destroyed. However,

8 J. Lacan, *The Four Fundamental Concepts of Psychoanalysis*, trans. by A. Sheridan
(Harmondsworth: Penguin, 1979), p. 12.

the search fails in its stated goal, for its only effect is to consolidate the reign of the symptom.

Having started out as a local irritation, the symptom overwhelms the subject, forcing it to submit to the destiny that it, the symptom, imposes on it. The primacy of the symptom is evident in the way it informs the narrative, by means of the figures of substitution, ambivalence and conversion that have been identified previously as being characteristic of the condition of hysteria. Indeed, symptom drives the action of the novel by forcing Roquentin to search constantly for ways to counter its effects. Examples include: getting lost in the Sunday crowd in the hope of discovering a sense of oneness with others; sitting in restaurants and looking at people around him consume their orders, in the hope that some of their pleasure will come his way; visits to the library where he can immerse himself in the universe of knowledge; the research project he devotes his time and energy to, in the belief that he will arrive by this means at a historical truth that will resist all questioning; listening to his favourite piece of music in the bar; thinking about the fulfilment that awaits him, should he and Anny manage to renew their interrupted relationship. All these attempts to defend himself against the symptom prove to be fruitless because they depend on outside circumstances over which he has no control. If there is a lesson to be learned from these failed attempts to overcome the symptom, it is this: one can only attack it by attacking its corporal envelope, that is, by seizing it *by the throat*.

Giving the throat up to the action of the symptom, Roquentin accedes to the symptom's wish to speak on his behalf, which it does with the aid of the libidinous energy stored in the unconscious. Lacan explains how the hysteric achieves this by positing, through the symptom, its desire "as an unsatisfied desire" (Lacan, 1979, p. 12). The subject's lack is thus turned into the symptom's gain. Among all the characters of the novel, the Autodidact has the most success in causing this kind of transfer of power to the symptom in Roquentin. In the Autodidact, the separation between language and desire is so great that it creates in Roquentin an interpretative frenzy that ends in the hysteric's cry of anguish:

> I must be ill: there is no other way of explaining that terrible rage which has just overwhelmed me. Yes, a sick man's rage: my hands were shaking, the blood rushed to my head, and finally my lips too started trembling. (165)

In response to what appears to Roquentin as a superbly hypocritical discourse, the body speaks its resistance with an intensity and purity that prevent it from being assimilated into structured forms of verbal communication. When the body speaks its desire as an unsatisfied desire, the subject loses its formal identity and is emptied of its volitional unity, leaving the symptom to fill the space it has evacuated.

The question might be asked whether, from a Lacanian perspective, this scenario does not amount to enabling the symptom to propagate itself endlessly, establishing itself as law. Might it not give rise to the same kind of infinite extensibility as that suffered by the ill-fated 'ego', the 'I' that Anny complains about, when she says that "it is always the same thing, a dough which goes on stretching and stretching" (214)? And might it not exhaust itself by reproducing itself indefinitely in this fashion? Lacan again provides an insight into these questions when, notably in his later writings, he insists that symptom can never be reduced to an abstract signifier. Because of its irreducible corporality, symptom properly belongs to the Order of the Real as the realm of the unsymbolisable since, as Gueguen reminds us, the Real "abolishes meaning, it is lawless".[9]

Symptom is not a signifier whose value is wholly derived from the signifying chain in which it appears. Because of its organic consistency, it escapes being assimilated into a pre-determined system of representations. Rather, symptom is "unpredictable, uncodable". As Lacan scholar Mikkel Borch-Jacobsen points out, it heralds a system where "anything can refer to anything else" according to how it manifests itself at any particular instant.[10] The irreducible contingency of the symptom is revealed to Roquentin when he contemplates firstly his hand hanging limply from the end of his arm, then, as an extension of the hand, the heavy mass of his body that resists all attempts to understand its function. As he bewilderingly states: "wherever I put it, it will go on existing; I can't suppress it" (144). And later: "The body lives all by itself, once it has started" (145). One might suspect, here, that the concept of contingency puts an end almost too conveniently to the philosopher's search for an ontological foundation, blinding him

---

[9] P.-G. Gueguen, "Elements pour l'analyse du symptôme", *Ornicar?* (on line) http://www.wapol.org/ornicar/articles/164gue.htm (consulted November 5th, 2003), p. 2.

[10] M. Borch-Jacobsen, *Lacan: The Absolute Master*, trans. by D. Brick (Stanford (CA): Stanford University Press, 1991), p. 184.

to the reality of the symptom that marks out for the subject a clearly bounded, corporally thick space.

As Freud acknowledged, a striking characteristic of symptom in the clinical situation is that it does not disappear when the subject is made conscious of its cause. That the symptom survives the cure suggests that the subject desires the symptom more than the cure. This is a discovery that opens new perspectives for psychoanalysis inasmuch as it provides an insight into what might become the destiny of the subject when it has exhausted its possibilities within the Symbolic Order. In his work on James Joyce, published under the title *Joyce le symptôme I* (Joyce-the-Symptom I),[11] Lacan envisages an end to the psychoanalytic cure that, paradoxically, consists in acknowledging the primacy of the relationship between the subject and the Real. The finality of the cure is no longer assimilation into the law of the Other that is the guarantee of paternal authority, but the experience of *jouissance*, sometimes translated unconvincingly by the English term *enjoyment*, in which this law is both recognised and systematically transgressed. In *jouissance*, the subject is identified with a lack of being that is experienced here as a positive entity, as a body that possesses mass and consistency, and endowed with an erotic attraction that is heightened by its inherent defectiveness. *Jouissance*, in other words, properly belongs to the nether regions of Being where the languishing subject 'bumps against' its lack.

'I' am in the place from which a voice is heard clamouring 'the universe is a defect in the purity of Non-Being'. And not without reason, for by protecting itself this place makes Being itself languish... This place is called *Jouissance*, and it is the absence of this that makes the universe vain.[12]

Following Lacan's account of the destiny of Being, the subject in Sartre's novel exists only to the extent that it embraces the reality of the symptom as *jouissance*. As a form of resistance, symptom defies all attempts to incorporate it into a network of conventional meanings. Rather, it remains riveted to the body, which gives it a sensual and affective density and makes its impenetrable to rational thought. At the same time, through being knotted (*noué*) to the body, the symptom

---

[11] J. Lacan, 'Joyce-le-symptôme', Lecture given on June 16th, from notes taken by E. Laurent and edited by J.-A. Miller (on line), http://www.ecole-lacanienne.net/documents/1975-06-16.doc.

[12] J. Lacan, *Ecrits: A Selection*, trans. by A. Sheridan (London: Tavistock Publications, 1977), p. 317.

constrains the subject, forcing it to consume itself in the ecstatic experience of *jouissance*. For Lacan, such an experience is one that occurs on the other side of the discourse of the Other, when the process of symbolisation has exhausted its possibilities.

Symptom appears to Roquentin in the form of a man sitting opposite him in the tram, whom he notices, curiously, the moment he interrupts the train of vain thoughts that were absorbing him. Symptom appears, in other words, when Roquentin gives up on himself, admitting: "the best thing you can do is turn your eyes away and think about something else" (180). Having noted the psychic resistance that marks the entry of symptom, it is worth examining more closely the features of the passenger. Firstly, he is eroticised in his pose, "half-lying of the seat", and in his "terracotta face with its blue eyes" (180-81) Roquentin notices a sedimented form of life that cannot survive outside its mineral prison. His ravaged face is furthermore divided into a right side that is paralysed, and a left side that is covered with a parasitic growth that proliferates, suggesting that between the deficit of being that Freud explains controversially in terms of the death drive, and the overdetermination of being that results from the action of the unrestrained libido, there is no intermediary that can mark out the domain of the human. Instead, in the frightening physiognomy of the deformed man, the limits of the symptom are traced out with the accuracy and brutality of a sculptor's chisel.

The subject submits to the symptom when the latter claims its autonomy as a place of *jouissance*. In this episode, the symptom appears as a physical anomaly that exalts in its defectiveness, such that it becomes the exclusive site of erotic election. The symptom is no longer a consequence of a mysterious destructive force, nor is it to be equated with a noxious object that must be destroyed to preserve the integrity of the individual. Rather, it is a mode of being in which the subject loses itself to pleasure, while remaining indifferent towards the rule of the other. Symptom reveals itself in the moves performed by the passenger, as his arm slowly moves up: "[W]hen it reached the height of the skull, a finger stretched out and started scratching the scalp with the nail. A sort of voluptuous grimace came and inhabited the right side of the mouth" (181). The finger that under its own impulsion attaches itself to a skull, independently of all extraneous volitional force, and remains locked to it as if by a natural affinity, suggests an erotic satisfaction that goes beyond the pleasure principle, prompting Lacan to state that *jouissance* belongs to a totally different plane to that of pleasure (Lacan, 1979, p. 184). A similar scene will occur later in the novel, when Roquentin observes the Autodidact's face melt in pleasure, as his "brown hairy" finger (234) strokes the upturned palm of a boy in the library. This time, however, it has disastrous consequences for the Autodidact, who is violently evicted from the library. In both scenes, symptom seizes the subject, causing it to languish and to abandon itself to its reign. For his part, Roquentin cannot countenance the sight of *jouissance*, and it is no surprise, then, that he jumps off the bus, claiming that he cannot stand things being "so close any more" (181), in the same way that, in the scene in the library, he instinctively tries to avoid witnessing the seduction of the boy: "I bent my head over my newspaper and I pretended to read" (234). As the trigger of symptom, resistance causes Roquentin to become progressively more entrapped in its mechanisms, such that the more he attempts to avoid symptom, the more he submits to its power. The inevitability of the process finally strikes home to Roquentin in the scene in the municipal park, when he encounters symptom in the form of the large shapeless root of the chestnut tree emerging from the ground.

The scene in the park marks the moment when the final identification with symptom occurs. That the root appears as a "black nail" (181) gives it the same narrative function as the tram passenger's fingernail and the Autodidact's brown hairy finger, but whereas in the other episodes Roquentin could not countenance the sight of the offending organ, he is now won over by it. More than this, Roquentin now accepts the likeness between it and himself. His pose in front of the root suggests that he has become one with it, sharing in its substance: "I was sitting, slightly bent, my head bowed, alone in front of that black, knotty mass" (182). Here, he is colonised by the symptom that takes up residence in the place of his being, as *jouissance*. Roquentin gives it another name — existence — which he says "is penetrating me all over, through the eyes, through the nose, through the mouth" (181). Existence is the preferred term for Roquentin who takes great pains to highlight symptom's contingency, that is, its rejection of the logic of cause and effect and indeed of all meaningful connection with its surroundings. However, it is the ambivalence in evidence in Roquentin's violent reactions that ensures his identification with the symptom. Although fearful of its "frightening, obscene nakedness" (182), he admits to being attracted by the root that "fascinated me, filled my eyes, repeatedly brought me back to its own existence" (186); and although he is calmly accepting of its "perfect gratuitousness" (188), Roquentin cannot prevent hostile sentiments from overcoming him and causing him to lose his countenance. Speaking of the existence that, like a fog, envelops him and everything else in the vicinity, he shouts:

> 'What filth! What filth!' and I shook myself to get rid of that sticky dirt, but it held fast and there was so much of it, tons and tons of existence, indefinitely: I was suffocating at the bottom of that huge boredom. (193)

Caught between the positive and negative emotions, between the life-enhancing impulses and the death wish, Roquentin is immobilised in a manner that imitates the inert root in the ground.

In this physically inert state, Roquentin becomes a receptacle for the conflicting drives that tear at him from all sides. Transfixed before the root which he now resembles, Roquentin gives himself up to a *jouissance* that, like the nausea, is "born behind my head" (145), since it has no visible source other than his Being. Roquentin freely admits: "I should have liked to tear myself away from that atrocious pleasure, but I didn't even imagine that that was possible; I was inside" (188). Having identified with the symptom, Roquentin turns away from the scene just as he will shortly thereafter calmly leave Bouville, not in fear or disgust this time, but with the calm determination that comes with having submitted to the destiny of the symptom. He becomes a model of *jouissance*: "My body turns very gently towards the east, wobbles slightly and starts walking" (227).

CONTEXT

Elizabeth Rechniewski

Avatars of Contingency: Suarès and Sartre

André Suarès was a leading figure in the literary field of the 1920s and 1930s: he published widely in the best-known journals including in the same critically important journal, the NRF, as Sartre, in the late thirties. Though little known today, this second-generation symbolist writer gave powerful expression to a vision of man, contingency and transcendence which had developed amongst artists of the 'restricted field of production' in the nineteenth century. This chapter argues that the fundamental concepts and relationships which structure Sartre's early writings, most notably La Nausée *and* L'Etre et le néant, *correspond to the broad lines of this artistic vision of the world which was firmly rooted in certain of his literary predecessors and had been brought to a high point of refinement in the early twentieth century by Suarès.*

* * *

A recent collection of articles, *La Naissance du phénomène Sartre : Raisons d'un succès, 1938-45*[1] brings together the latest research on the question of the influences on Sartre and the factors that help explain his evolution as a writer in this early period. It is striking, however, that although the contributions cover an extensive range of possible influences, not a single reference is made to the work of André Suarès. And yet Suarès was one of the dominant figures of the literary field in the 1920s and 1930s, he published widely in all the leading journals including in the same, critically important journal, the *Nouvelle Revue Française*, as Sartre himself did in the late thirties. As Malraux declared of his generation: "pour nous, au lendemain de la guerre, les trois grands écrivains français, c'étaient Claudel, Gide et Suarès [For us, after the war, the three great French writers were Claudel, Gide and Suarès]".[2]

---

[1] I. Galster (ed.), *La Naissance du phénomème Sartre: Raisons d'un succès 1938-45* (Paris: Seuil, 2001).
[2] J. Lacouture, *Malraux, une vie dans le siècle* (Paris: Seuil, 1973), p. 22 (author's own translation).

This chapter attempts to reconstruct this relatively ignored aspect of the intellectual framework within which Sartre undertook his early work in literature and philosophy. It argues that the fundamental concepts and relationships which structure his early works, and most notably *Nausea* and *Being and Nothingness* correspond to the broad lines of an artistic vision of the world which was firmly rooted in certain of his literary predecessors.

When seeking to explain the development of Sartre's philosophy, critics have often attached importance to the influence of the philosophers, particularly Husserl, whom he studied in Berlin in the thirties. This chapter does not attempt to deny the importance of these studies in the elaboration of his philosophy. However, the German philosophers exercised this influence, it could be argued, because Sartre 'recognised' in certain aspects of their work a conceptual framework within which he could elaborate a philosophy whose basic structures corresponded to a prior vision. As Vincent Descombes argues: "le texte dont on tombe amoureux est celui dans lequel on ne cesse d'apprendre ce que l'on sait déjà' [the text with which one falls in love is the one in which one never stops learning what one already knows]".[3] Descombes quotes, in relation to the generation of Sartre, the comments of Merleau-Ponty who wrote: "en lisant Husserl ou Heidegger plusieurs de nos contemporains ont eu le sentiment bien moins de rencontrer une philosophie nouvelle que de reconnaître ce qu'ils attendaient [on reading Husserl and Heidegger several of our contemporaries had the feeling much less of meeting a new philosophy than of recognising what they were waiting for]" (Descombes, p. 15).

What was the nature and origin of this vision which underlay, I would argue, both *Nausea* and *Being and Nothingness*? Fundamental to both texts is a vision of man, contingency and transcendence which had developed amongst artists of the restricted field of production in the nineteenth century, and which had been brought to a high point of refinement in the early twentieth century by a writer of whom it will in particular be question here: André Suarès.

It is not possible in this chapter to do more than sketch the stages in the evolution of this vision through the nineteenth century, an evolution which, I suggest elsewhere, results from a hardening and darkening of Romanticism as a result both of social and political events and of

---

[3] V. Descombes, *Le Même et l'autre* (Paris: Minuit, 1979), p. 14 (author's own translation).

changes in the structure of the field of artistic production. [4] This hardening of the romantic vision can already be identified in movements such as the Jeune France — the second generation of romantic writers — in the 1830s. From this period on, the increasing autonomisation of the artistic field sees the avant-garde writers, caught up in a relationship of mutual rejection and incomprehension with the public, turn away from their society, seeking to distinguish themselves at all costs from the tastes of the common man. This 'recherche de la distinction' [5] fosters an ideology of separatism, elitism, solipsism and idealism, and a preoccupation with form over content, ideas that were to be fully elaborated in the artistic programme of the Symbolist movement in the late nineteenth century. It is significant in relation to the argument of this chapter that Sartre showed great interest in the acknowledged leader of the movement, Mallarmé, claiming to recognise in his work an exemplary search for lucidity and transcendence. [6]

It was in the writings of the following generation, however, and most notably in those of André Suarès, that the aesthetic ideals of the Symbolists were transformed into a coherent, rigorous and essentially tragic vision of the totality of the human condition. Born in 1868, Suarès belonged to the second generation of Symbolists: Mallarmé was born in 1842, Villiers de l'Isle-Adam in 1836; Symbolism was established as the 'official' avant-garde by the mid 1880s. Although Suarès never openly declared that he belonged to this or indeed to any movement — for such allegiance would have contradicted the solitary and independent cast of his mind — Mallarmé and Villiers de l'Isle-Adam remained throughout his life the writers whom he most passionately admired. He shared the Symbolist aesthetic project, developed it in fact to its logical and tragic conclusion, with a jansenist rigour from which Pascal's 'pari' was not absent.

Suarès was a complex, tortured, and contradictory personality. Jewish in origin, he occasionally expressed violently anti-semitic sentiments and emphasised his assimilation to the French nation and civilization through the use of French and Celtic pseudonyms ('Caerdal' was one). He rejected Romanticism as facile and

---

[4] E. Rechniewski, *Antécédents littéraires de l'existentialisme, Suarès, Malraux et Sartre* (Paris: Minard, 1996).

[5] P. Bourdieu, 'Le Marché des biens symboliques', *L'année sociologique*, 22 (1971), 49-126.

[6] J.-P. Sartre, *Mallarmé: La Lucidité et sa face d'ombre* (Paris: Gallimard, 1986).

self indulgent and yet embraced totally the Romantic image of the artist struggling in poverty and social isolation to defend his integrity. He loathed the public of his time and yet was avid for recognition. Interested in many forms of modern art he was, however, able to be generous only to those practitioners who were not his rivals. Extremely sensitive, if not paranoid, he saw affronts where none were intended and quarreled with many of his contemporaries. He understood himself to be — and was portrayed in a lithograph by Rouault as being — a Christ-like figure, whose martyrdom was necessary for the redemption of humanity through art.

The author of unperformed and unperformable plays written in the Symbolist style which he believed were his greatest creations, he in fact won fame for his numerous essays, particularly on the great French writers of the past, on the nature of art and the role of the artist. His ideas were first clearly expressed in *Voici l'homme*, written at the very end of the nineteenth century and published in 1906, whose themes he continued to elaborate throughout his life, up to the very month of his death in 1948, in a declarative and aphoristic style which allows for no nuance and brooks no opposition.

The fundamental structures of his vision can best be described as founded on a triple alienation:
— alienation from the natural world, seen as irredeemably abject, sunk in the degradation of matter, subjected to deterministic laws, the negation therefore of freedom and transcendence;
— alienation from the world of other men, from society, seen as given over to materialistic ends, corrupt, the public of the time considered the greatest enemy of the artist;
— alienation from the self, from those parts of the self that belong to the natural world: the body, instincts, physical needs and pleasures, but also from the mind itself where this is invaded by the commonplaces shared by all.
Only the creative, spiritual self rises above the universal mire.

Thus Nature is the realm of pure contingency, of instinct, where the meaningless proliferation of forms, crawling and heaving with senseless and nauseating existence, excludes thought, intelligence, reason, morality. Pungent metaphors flow from his pen to describe the universal degradation that surrounds him. Raw Nature is everywhere: it has infiltrated the cities though people do not see it because they are immersed in it, but one day the true nature of existence will be revealed in all its horror.

In 'La nuit des atomes' written in 1900 but apparently not published during his lifetime,[7] Suarès recounts a vision (or is it a prediction?) of the disintegration of matter into its primal elements. One night the inhabitants of the city are awoken by strange events and noises: the lights go out, people gather in the streets in alarm, then suddenly the trees begin to move... they adopt grotesque and disgusting forms, are transformed into a swarming, heaving mass of sticky decay:

> Ils se dénouaient lentement et rampaient sur l'air de la nuit, vipères verticales sur leur queue. Chaque arbre apparut alors comme un faisceau d'énormes vers, de boas fabuleux et de colossales chenilles. Chaque arbre et dans chaque arbre, chaque souche et chaque branche, et chaque rameau, chaque feuille, tout était ver, pieuvre, reptile. Ils grouillaient avec lenteur, ayant le temps éternel pour eux; ils se déroulaient sans hâte, ils dardaient leurs visqueuses puissances, leurs muscles gluants, gelée de la nuit bandée sur l'arc des ténèbres, et ils détendaient les ventouses engourdies de leurs bras et de leurs palpes géantes.
>
> [They slowly untied themselves and crawled over the night air, vipers standing vertically on their tail. Each tree then appeared a knot of gigantic worms, of fabulous boa constrictors, of colossal caterpillars. Each tree, and in each tree, each root and each branch, and each twig, each leaf, all was worm, octopus, reptile. A slow, crawling existence, having eternal time on their side; they unfolded themselves without haste, they pointed their sticky powers, their gummy muscles, the frost of night covering the arched shadows, and they unbent the sluggish suckers of their arms and of their enormous feelers.][8]

In their turn the monuments of the town, palaces, streets and bridges, rupture and break apart, and finally the living bodies of the inhabitants gape open to reveal "les vers rouges grouiller [a swarming mass of red worms]"; as all forms of life dissolve back into contingency, as the stars go out: "Toute la vie, tout l'univers, grouillement... [All life, the whole universe, crawling life...]" (*Bouclier du zodiaque*, p. 147 — all translations of Suarès' works are author's own; I have quoted throughout the chapter, either in the body of the text or in the footnotes, the French text, since the choice of vocabulary is significant for the argument).

As this passage suggests so strongly, men are but a part of nature, they share its basest aspects. They are likened by Suarès to ants, insects, vermin. Like Shakespeare's Caliban, chosen by Suarès as a symbol of the common man,[9] they are semi-beasts engulfed in their appetites, enslaved by their instincts, imprisoned in their flesh, without

---

[7] Robert Parienté includes it in his 1993 edition of *Bouclier du Zodiaque*.

[8] A. Suarès, *Bouclier du zodiaque* (Paris: le cherche midi, 1993), p. 146.

[9] A. Suarès, 'Baudelaire', *Sur la vie, III* (Paris: Emile-Paul, 1928).

individuality: "telles les fourmis, telles les feuilles [like ants, like leaves]".[10] Voracious, abject and depraved, but not conscious of their abjection, they lead an automatic existence. The artist cannot but view this humanity with horror and occasionally pity. Pity because of the misery and absurdity of the human condition: "L'absurdité ou la misère de l'homme, laquelle des deux passe l'autre... ? [The absurdity or the wretchedness of the human condition - which is the greater?]" (*Voici l'homme*, p. 435). Horror because the artist too is imprisoned in this nature, is confronted each day by the abjection of those who surround and oppress him by their very existence, for they remind him of what he shares with them: "l'odieuse nullité de tout : elle nous environne, elle nous presse, elle nous étouffe sous la forme de l'espèce humaine [the hateful nothingness of everything: it surrounds us, oppresses us, smothers us, in the form of the human species]" (*Voici l'homme*, p. 218).

Thus the artist must maintain an eternal vigil: an instant of weakness or inattention and he will fall back into the morass and be engulfed in mediocrity. But rising above the mass is not a slow process of ascent through the gradual accumulation of reason and learning, it is a qualitative leap by means of that spark of creative power which marks out the artist. In an essay of 1909, entitled 'L'Autodidacte', Suarès ridicules the common man who hopes through self-education to rise above his place.[11] His autodidact is a socialist orator, portrayed by Suarès as a marionette, physically deformed, ludicrous in his pretensions and his ambitions for the progress of mankind. Suarès cannot envisage the improvement of humanity, for the debased condition of mankind is unchanging. Transcendence can only be found in the moral and spiritual superiority of certain gifted individuals. What can the relationship between the crowd and the elite be if not one of envy and hostility on the one side, and fear and mistrust on the other? For the crowd seeks to drag the great man down to its level; it spies on him, judges him, strives to bring low a freedom which it cannot understand and yet resents: "C'est eux qui nous offensent en tous leurs gestes et tous leurs jugements. Leur seul regard est une calomnie, et leur présence seule une injure à la vie [It is they who offend us in all their acts and all their judgements. Their very gaze is a calumny and their very presence an affront to life.]" (*Sur la vie III*, p. 205). For Suarès, the trials of Flaubert and Baudelaire illustrate symbolically this relationship.

---

[10] A. Suarès, *Voici l'homme* (Paris: Albin Michel, 1948), p. 261.

[11] A. Suarès, *Sur la vie, I* (Paris: Emile-Paul, 1925).

At all times the writer must fear the gaze of the mob, which, filled with resentment, seeks to impose its mediocre norms on the free spirit, to confine and imprison him.

Within this vision of the human condition, the body denotes bestiality, decay, suffering and death: the final triumph of matter over the spirit and the will. The body is the jailor, the torturer and finally the executioner of the spirit. Instinctual desires and bestial appetites beset the creator and sap his will. Thus the affirmation of freedom supposes the triumph over the flesh: "Il est beau de vaincre la chair. L'homme charnel est un esclave entre esclaves [It is noble to triumph over the flesh. Carnal man is a slave amongst slaves.]" (*Voici l'homme*, p. 94).

Yet the mind is no sure refuge, no pure source of inspiration to be freely tapped: it is marred by its own weaknesses and inauthenticity, beset by dangers. On the one hand the artist must avoid the clichés of thought that are the automatic, conventional responses of the common man; on the other, he must transcend the chaos of unformed sentiments and the self-indulgent histrionics of the Romantics, where the spirit is not its own master but is submerged in the flux of its passions. The only freedom comes through the unwavering exercise of lucidity, self-discipline, asceticism, rigorous examination of the self and its motives, in order to achieve that refinement and purification of 'la conscience' or 'l'esprit créateur' which enables the superior man to rise above — for however brief a moment — the universal degradation.

This internal struggle has, however, no significance unless the fruits of victory are demonstrated in the world. Salvation can only come through action and creation, intentions prove nothing: "Le pouvoir de créer et d'agir, voilà ce qui compte [The power to create and to act, that is what counts]" (*Voici l'homme*, p. 183). Moral and spiritual force must find expression in the capacity to impose form on the chaos and meaninglessness of existence: "Sans cesse la personnalité puissante se projette. Elle tend toujours à considérer le monde comme un objet, où il s'agit pour elle de mettre sa marque [Unceasingly, the powerful personality projects itself, tending always to consider the world as an object on which to leave its mark.]"[12]

As the great man creates order in the world, so he gives his own life meaning. Among Suarès' heroes are the great conquerors — Caesar, Napoléon, Achilles — who, in imposing their own order on the world,

---

[12] This is taken from unpublished notebook 92, quoted by Yves-Alain Favre in *La Recherche de la grandeur dans l'œuvre d'André Suarès* (Paris: Klincksieck, 1978), p. 121.

give their life shape, direction and meaning. But those who are at the same time conquerors and artists (d'Annunzio, for example) are particularly admired by Suarès, for those who seek only to conquer the world see their conquests slip sooner or later from their grasp. It is the artist who is the greatest conqueror of them all, for only his creations endure. He remodels and transforms nature according to his vision, he introduces the life of the spirit into brute matter and gives it form, and in so doing he saves his own life and redeems humanity as a whole. Like God, the artist creates order from chaos. He awakens in humanity a glimmer of the divine. Is he not indeed, as Suarès frequently suggests, a god himself, able to create himself as he creates his world: "Etre Dieu ou n'être pas, voilà la véritable alternative [To be God or not to be, that is the real alternative]" writes Suarès to his friend Romain Rolland.[13]

While elements of the vision I have outlined can be found in many writers of the same generation, notably Rémy de Gourmont, Valéry and Claudel, Suarès transforms them into a coherent, rigorous, uncompromising meditation on the tragedy and the absurdity of the human condition. He is the privileged interpreter who, in Lucien Goldmann's theory, allows the researcher to identify the essential structures of the vision of a whole group.[14] However, the importance of Suarès in the literary field of the early twentieth century has been greatly underestimated by contemporary critics even though Malraux declared that for his own generation Suarès was one of the three most influential writers. We know that there was personal contact between Malraux and Suarès.[15] Though the same is not known for Sartre and Suarès, it seems impossible that Sartre was not familiar with the work of the older writer, a conclusion which I hope to demonstrate through textual and conceptual comparison with *Nausea*.

On the level of vocabulary, symbol and metaphor it will be apparent that the passages used above to illustrate Suarès' ideas show remarkable similarities with Sartre's writings. Both Suarès and Sartre use the same pool of metaphors to represent contingency as slime and stickiness, as plenitude and teeming abundance, as entrapment and decay. In *Nausea* the celebrated description of the public garden in Bouville, where the alien sub-life represented by the tree comes to symbolise the universal

---

[13] A. Suarès, *Cette âme ardente: choix de lettres d'André Suarès à Romain Rolland, 1887-1891* (Paris: Albin Michel, 1954), p. 35.

[14] L. Goldmann, *Sciences humaines et philosophie* (Paris: Editions Gonthier, 1966), p. 161.

[15] Their first meeting is described by Suarès in a letter to his mécène Jacques Doucet, written in August 1924 and published in *Le Condottière et le magicien*, p. 375-6.

reign of matter, offers a striking parallel with the passage already quoted from Suarès' 'La Nuit des atomes'. Roquentin observes: "Ça grouillait d'existences, au bout des branches, d'existences qui se renouvelaient sans cesse et qui ne naissaient jamais [There were swarms of existences at the end of the branches, existences which constantly renewed themselves and were never born]" (157; 190).[16] We have already seen the significance of the term 'grouillement' used in Suarès' essay to evoke the teeming proliferation of base matter. Roquentin feels that his flesh, too, is bursting open, as did the flesh of the watchers in the town: "[...] ma chair elle-même palpitait et s'entrouvrait, s'abandonnait au bourgeonnement universel, c'était répugnant [my very flesh was throbbing and opening, abandoning itself to the universal burgeoning, it was repulsive]" (157; 190).

In both texts the city is described as invaded by the decay and corruption of contingency; unseen by the inhabitants, nature is omnipresent and threatens at any moment to break through the facade of human constructions to reveal a repugnant, abject, rotting matter. Roquentin observes: "[...] la grande nature vague s'est glissée dans leur ville, elle s'est infiltrée, partout, dans leurs maisons, dans leurs bureaux, en eux-mêmes [vast vague Nature has slipped into their town, it has infiltrated everywhere, into their houses, into their offices, into themselves]" (187; 226). Seated on a hill high above the town, he imagines that one day Nature will break open its placid surfaces: a father will see his daughter transformed into a haunch of rotten meat; a mother will watch as her child's cheek erupts to reveal a mocking eye; a man will find that his tongue has become a centipede, and all kinds of grotesque and disgusting forms will fill the streets and invade the bodies of the inhabitants, as contingency reasserts its rights. Throughout *Nausea* people are described in terms borrowed from the realms of animal or plant life, not just the bourgeoisie, as is often said, but the ordinary workers, drinkers and card players in the cafés he frequents and the women who accompany them.[17] From a distance, the

---

[16] All references to the novel give the French page reference first followed by the English translation. The French text is the Pléiade edition, taken from J.-P. Sartre, *Œuvres romanesques* (Paris: Gallimard, 1981), pp. 1-210.

[17] The card-players in the café form "un paquet tiède [a warm packet]" (26; 34). The terms which describe this packet are taken from the animal or vegetable kingdoms: the packet is like a single animal, with its "grande échine noire [long black spine]" (26; 35); one of the players has a "tête de chien [face like a dog]" (27; 36). Adolphe at the counter "s'ébroue, jappe et se débat faiblement, comme un chien qui rêve [he snorts, yelps, and writhes feebly, like a dog having a dream]" (26; 35).

inhabitants of Bouville are seen as lines of insects or — in a passage which recalls Suarès' description of Caliban occupied by his bodily functions — "les bêtes [qui] digèrent ou dorment, dans leurs trous, derrière des amoncellements de détritus organiques [beasts which digest or sleep in their holes, behind piles of waste matter]" (184; 220). Both Sartre and Suarès take as their target an Autodidact, a socialist with humanist pretensions; both show him as a pathetic figure, physically repulsive, intellectually ridiculous.[18]

These similarities on the level of theme, vocabulary and metaphor only become truly significant if they correspond at a deeper level to a shared vision, a common interpretation of man's relation to the self, to the world, to other men, to transcendence, those structures which Goldmann identified as the defining elements of a 'vision du monde'. It is to those deeper structures of Sartre's thought that I draw attention in conclusion, arguing how closely the fundamental relationships between mind and matter, between man, the world and the self found in *Nausea* correspond to Suarès' vision: the polarisation of matter and human consciousness, matter being perceived as the dead hand of determinism and contingency, the enemy of the spirit and of freedom; the search for transcendence over contingency through an ever-renewed act of creation that is also self-creation; the problematic and essentially conflictual relationship with others, who threaten the individual through their very existence, who remind him of his own contingency.

Sartre's 'theory of contingency' is already being referred to by his friends in the mid-1920s, long before he had made a serious study of German philosophy. We have no texts surviving from that period to show the forms that his theory took then, but we have no reason to think that it was at odds with his work of the thirties, however much he may have developed and elaborated on his early ideas. We know that Sartre himself saw his early work as profoundly influenced by the literature, and particularly the nineteenth-century literature in which he was steeped. In *Words* he recounts the evolution of his ideas and character in the context of his reading and early writings, from his childhood to his adolescence, and describes ideas which are very similar to those of Suarès: art as a calling requiring sacrifice and suffering; art as redemption and the artist as redeemer of a humanity threatened with

---

[18] For the physical description of Sartre's Autodidact, see for example *Nausea*, page 48, where he is described as being like a dog with a bone and as having a "chicken–like neck". Later Roquentin refers to his "great ass's jaw-bone" (55). It is true that he is described as having wonderful eyes, but they are a blind man's eyes… (153).

annihilation.[19] Writing in 1964, Sartre looks back on his early ideas with wry irony but adds that they were not a passing childish fancy but a 'knot of vipers' which it took him thirty years to unravel - ideas which stayed with him, that is, till the 1940s and the turn towards political engagement. Elsewhere in *Words* he refers to both *Nausea* and *Being and Nothingness* as having been written while under their spell (*Words*, p. 208-9). Roquentin's reflection at the end of *Nausea* on the possibility of writing a book of the imagination, which would be as bright and hard as steel and make people ashamed of their existence, seems to involve precisely that redemptive recreation of the world and of the self which Suarès affirms to be the calling of the artist.

Words recounts the formation of Sartre's 'habitus', to use Bourdieu's term: the socially constructed set of ideas, schemes of perception and appreciation which the writer brings to the intellectual field and which orient him towards certain influences and suggest a certain trajectory. This chapter has attempted to indicate one of the components of the literary and cultural capital which Sartre would carry with him into that field. Other critics have also drawn attention to the importance of literature and artistic ideals in Sartre's thinking, notably Anna Boschetti, who, in *Sartre et les Temps Modernes*, argues for the importance of Flaubert and draws a number of parallels between the two writers. However, the parallels seem to me to be considerably closer between Sartre and Suarès, which is not to say, of course, that it is a simple question of the older writer influencing the younger — the surprising similarity of Suarès 'La Nuit des atomes' to the passage in the public garden of Bouville, for example, cannot apparently be explained by any direct influence, since Suarès' text was not published until 1993. The coincidences, then, are all the more striking and illustrative of the existence of an underlying force-field of shared references. As I suggested at the beginning of the chapter, the ideas which Suarès so forcefully articulates are in fact characteristic, in a less developed form, of many writers within the restricted field of production of the time; they constitute a rich capital on which Sartre was to draw not only, indeed, for the elaboration of his early literary work, but for *Being and Nothingness*.

---

[19] J.-P. Sartre, *Words*, trans. by I. Clephane (London: Harmondsworth Press, 1967), p. 148-9.

Chris Falzon

Sartre and Meaningful Existence

At the philosophical level, Nausea *is a text that purports to shake off all presuppositions in order to confront things as they really are - meaningless, contingent and nauseating. In this, Sartre not only enacts a kind of philosophical critique of ordinary presuppositions, but also seeks to distance himself from certain philosophical positions. However,* Nausea*'s view of the world as meaningless arguably reflects certain philosophical presuppositions of its own, notably a very demanding standard for what would count as being meaningful.* Nausea*'s meaningless world opens the way to Sartre's most important early philosophical statement,* Being and Nothingness, *but we may ask whether Sartre is entitled to strip the world of meaning in the first place.*

* * *

Ordinary presuppositions

First of all, *Nausea* appears to be inviting us to shake off our ordinary, taken-for-granted presuppositions about the world, or more precisely all the principles, categories and forms we might ordinarily appeal to in order to justify, organise, explain, give meaning, order, or point to the world and ourselves. They are the forms we try to impose on the world, the coverings or trappings that hide the world from our eyes. To abandon them is to discover the truth about the world, to confront things as they really are, to come face to face with brute existence — meaningless, contingent, superfluous, absurd, and nauseating. This at least seems to be the journey that Roquentin takes, from his first feeling of "sweet disgust" imparted to him by the pebble (22), to the climactic encounter with the chestnut tree in the park (182-3).

It is true that Roquentin is suffering from nausea, afflicted by it, rather than seeking it out. But while there is an air of passivity about him, his encounters with increasingly strange objects can also be seen as an awakening on his part, an emergence from a dream or illusion, a falling of the scales from his eyes. As Beauvoir, in a late conversation with Sartre, put it, there is "a revealing of the world" in *Nausea*.[1] The chestnut tree episode has the force of a revelation in which "existence had suddenly unveiled itself" (183), and it is also the point where Roquentin has become fully awakened to the world. And for Sartre, as with other affective states like anxiety and shame, the feeling of nausea is not only something that we suffer, but also has cognitive significance. It is a mode of apprehending the world, a way of being aware of the things around us. The feeling of nausea reflects our apprehension of the world and our selves as they really are, i.e. absolutely contingent, gratuitous, without justification.

In the light of this revelation, the principles, forms or categories, in terms of which we ordinarily view the world, become for Roquentin the "veneer" (183) that we have imposed on the world, the "feeble landmarks" we have traced on the surface of things (182), and which conceal a brute reality that in fact escapes all meaning and explanation. For the unthinking, the unreflective, this appearance of order is simply taken for reality, as in the case of the complacent, self-confident pillars of bourgeois Bouville society whose portraits Roquentin inspects in the local museum (120-138, see also 225). For them there is simply an unquestioned order of things in which they have an assured, secure place, as if the universe meant them to have their property, position and security. Later, such an attitude will be condemned by Sartre as 'bad faith', or the 'spirit of seriousness'.

Roquentin's judgement on the town worthies is equally harsh. We have to say farewell to those "Bastards" (138), and confront existence as it is, heroically, without pretence. Roquentin's discovery sets him apart from all those who have a self-deceptive belief in an orderly world. This includes the citizens of Bouville in general, who stupidly believe that "the world obeys fixed, unchangeable laws" (225), as well as the main individuals he has dealings with in the course of the novel: the pathetic Autodidact who behaves as if the world were ordered like an encyclopaedia, whose secrets can be unlocked by reading alphabetically through the books in a provincial library (48-9); and Roquentin's ex-mistress Anny who wanted to live her life as a series of 'perfect moments', in which "certain acts [...] have to be performed, certain attitudes [...] have to be assumed" (211-12), as if

---

[1] S. Beauvoir, *Adieux: A Farewell to Sartre*, trans. by P. O'Brien (Harmondsworth: Penguin, 1984), p. 207.

what happens in life really has this structure — though by the time Roquentin meets her in Paris she is making the same discovery Roquentin has about the world.

Roquentin himself, once he has started to wake up from his illusions, is also harshly dismissive of his own earlier beliefs, and relentlessly clear-sighted about the lack of order in things. Early on he realises that 'there are no adventures', for adventures are narrative organisations we impose on events in the course of retelling them. As he puts it:

> This is what fools people: a man is always a teller of tales, he lives surrounded by his stories and the stories of others, he sees everything that happens to him through them; and he tries to live his life as if he were recounting it. But you have to choose: to live or to recount. (61; see also 85)

Later, he gives up his biography of the historical figure Rollebon because he believes that in telling the story of that life, or that life as a story, he will falsify it as well (138; see also 26).

Philosophical context

Shaking off ordinary, taken-for-granted ways of thinking about or making sense of the world, as Roquentin does, suggests the first step in a process of philosophical enlightenment. Often, the philosophical critique of ordinary presuppositions is undertaken in order to make way for something positive, the construction of a new system of thinking. In so far as Roquentin is making a philosophical move, it is one that is primarily negative and critical rather than constructive. It is true that he does not make his case through argument, but rather undergoes a series of compelling and increasingly revelatory experiences, interspersed with reverie and reflection, which includes fragmentary philosophical insights. Nonetheless as the narrative unfolds he comes to find his ordinary ways of thinking about the world questionable, and he awakens from illusion to a reality they hide.

This points us towards Sartre's own philosophical agenda, which is finding expression in his novel. At the time of its writing, he tells us:

> I did not want to write books of philosophy [...] I wanted the philosophy I believed in and the truths I should attain to be expressed in my novel [...] Fundamentally I wanted to write *Nausea* (Beauvoir, p. 142-3)

What also comes into view is the philosophical background out of which his thought emerges, particularly his 'master', the German philosopher Husserl, whom Sartre discovered in the course of writing *Nausea*, and Descartes, the father-figure of French philosophy and deep influence on Sartre's work.[2] Both Husserl and Descartes start out by questioning taken-for-granted beliefs, our ordinary presuppositions about the world, a process that Sartre re-enacts in *Nausea*. At the same time, however, Sartre also seems to be calling into question aspects of their positions, and distancing himself from them in certain respects.

Husserl himself wants to escape from a certain kind of philosophy, a philosophical idealism that reduces the world to a mental construction, and subordinates reality to a spiritual principle. Sartre is sympathetic to this, for the idealist tradition from Kant onwards conceals the world in its brute contingency, claiming that reality can be brought into identity with, or subsumed under, universal, rational concepts.[3] Hegel represents the high point of this tradition, in which the whole of reality is to be comprehended in systematic form. Hegel refuses to regard the thinking subject as abandoned helplessly to the contingency of existence, to particulars that present themselves without reason or meaning. He subsumes existence to the workings of an unfolding Mind or Reason, which renders the world meaningful, while also seeking to preserve the multiplicity of things as stages of this unfolding.[4] Nonetheless, for Hegel contingency remains something ultimately to be overcome in the name of necessity. And for Sartre this overcoming of contingency also extends to Marx's thought, despite the latter's efforts to escape from idealism, to turn Hegelian idealism in a non-spiritual, 'materialist' direction. As Sartre puts it, "If you push Marxist thought right through to the end, for example, you find a necessary world; there's no contingency" (Beauvoir, p. 142).

---

[2] J. Catalano, *A Commentary on Jean-Paul Sartre's Being and Nothingness* (Chicago: Chicago University Press, 1974), pp. 1-13; A. Cohen-Solal, *Sartre: A Life* (London: Heinemann, 1988), p. 91-2.
[3] See Beauvoir, p. 142; S. Buck-Morss, *The Origin of Negative Dialectics* (Sussex: Harvester, 1977), p. 72.
[4] L. Kolakowski, *Main Currents of Marxism volume 1: The Founders*, trans. by P. Fella (Oxford: Oxford University Press, 1978), p. 57.

This brings us back to Husserl, who wants to make a definitive escape from idealism and, in his famous formula, to bring thought back into contact with 'the things themselves'. Husserl's starting point is the so-called phenomenological reduction, the 'bracketing' or suspending of our ordinary attitudes about the world. By attending only to things as they appear to us, we will have a firm basis on which to build what Husserl called a 'transcendental science', i.e., absolute knowledge, completely certain and free of presuppositions. For Sartre, Husserl offers a way out of idealism and back to the real world. And in *Nausea*, Roquentin can be seen as effecting a kind of bracketing, suspending ordinary ways of thinking about the world in order to return to the 'things themselves'.

But Sartre also breaks from Husserl, because he thinks that the latter failed to carry out fully his programme of going back to the things themselves, and in the end fell back into a form of idealism. For Husserl, to ignore what we ordinarily think about the world and confront it as given to us is to describe only the materials of consciousness itself, 'things as they appear in thought', as distinct from material objects. Having cut consciousness from the real world, he finds it hard to re-establish contact with it.[5] For Sartre's Roquentin in *Nausea*, the revelation of things themselves through the suspension of ordinary attitudes is a matter of coming face-to-face with things in their brute existence, the concrete stuff of reality, as in the encounter with the chestnut tree where the tree root reveals itself in all its alien otherness. This is the decisive break with idealism. As one commentator notes, for existentialism in general, human existence is "to be in encounter with a real world".[6]

Husserl's bracketing process is itself intended to be a version of Descartes' famous starting point in the *Meditations*, the process of methodological doubt which similarly aims to sweep away all previous beliefs and presuppositions, in order to start anew and establish absolute knowledge on a firm basis. Descartes' approach is to reject any belief that can possibly be doubted. In his case, the firm foundation that remains is that we cannot doubt without thinking, and we must exist in order to do the thinking (the 'Cogito' or 'I think' argument). From this, Descartes concludes that the I, the self, is a pure

---

[5] A. Manser, *Sartre: A Philosophic Study* (London: Athlone, 1966), p. 4-5.
[6] J. Macquarrie, *Existentialism* (Harmondsworth: Penguin, 1972), p. 30; N.F. Fox, *The New Sartre* (London: Continuum, 2003), p. 14.

mind or thinking substance, which has no corporeal or material characteristics, and which is more easily and directly known than the body or the world. By inspecting the contents of the mind, his ideas, Descartes then aims to determine which of his ideas are true representations of reality, and to re-establish knowledge of the world on a firm basis.

But while Roquentin can also be seen as re-enacting the initial Cartesian move of challenging ordinary presuppositions, Sartre also seems to be questioning the point that Descartes arrives at, the abstract idea of the self as a disembodied thinking thing. Once again Roquentin's journey takes him to something more concrete, more substantial. When Roquentin, who has just abandoned the Rollebon project, reflects on his situation (142ff) he encounters himself not as immaterial thinking thing but embodied being. As Manser (p. 11-12) points out, thoughts themselves do not give Roquentin a real sense of his existence. Only when he stabs himself in the hand does he become aware of himself in his corporeal existence. And he finds his thinking is permeated by his corporeal existence. Existence, Roquentin goes on to say, "takes my thoughts *from behind* and gently expands them *from behind*; somebody takes me from behind, they force me from behind to think, therefore to be something" (148). Hence, as Manser puts it, it is not so much I think therefore I am, as, "I am forced by my body to think and feel, therefore I am" (p. 12). Indeed, later in *Being and Nothingness*, the only substantial reference to the feeling of nausea is in relation to the body. Nausea is said to be our immediate awareness of the body, the "nauseous taste" of myself as contingent factual existence.[7]

So if Sartre in *Nausea* is enacting a kind of radical philosophical critique of existing beliefs in the tradition of Descartes and Husserl, he also wants to distance himself from the kind of philosophical critique that challenges ordinary presuppositions or ways of thinking about the world but remains insulated from concrete existence by abstractions such as 'things as they appear in thought', or the self as an immaterial thinking thing. This may also be why Sartre finds a non-philosophical, literary mode of presentation so congenial at this time. It makes it possible for him to evoke a lived, full-blooded experience of things and of us. Existence is not simply something we merely understand

---

[7] J.-P. Sartre, *Being and Nothingness*, trans. by H Barnes (London: Methuen, 1958), p. 338.

intellectually, but something we concretely encounter, taste, feel nauseated in the face of, and so on.

'Being and Nothingness'

On the face of it the picture *Nausea* presents is almost entirely negative. Manser bluntly refers to *Nausea* as the 'negative part' of Sartre's philosophy (p. 118). All the principles, categories or forms that we ordinarily use to organise, explain, justify, give meaning or point to the world and our own existence are called into question and rejected. As we have seen, Sartre also rejects philosophical idealism, which attempts to comprehend reality as rationally ordered, and those aspects of Descartes' and Husserl's positions which continue to obscure reality under philosophical abstractions. Things, and indeed we ourselves, are thereby revealed to be completely superfluous, contingent, utterly without reason or explanation, absurd. However, it would be wrong to see this rejection of ordinary and philosophical presuppositions as simply negative in character. For Sartre, it has significant positive implications in two respects. First of all, it makes it possible for thought to get back in touch with concrete existence. It allows us to rediscover and to confront the world as it really is. In particular it brings to the fore a feature of the world that Sartre thinks has been neglected, and which for him is one of the world's 'essential dimensions' — its contingency (Beauvoir, pp. 141-2, 207).

Secondly, by stripping the world of meaning in this way, revealing it in its brute reality as meaningless and contingent, *Nausea* also prepares the way for Sartre's own positive philosophical account which will emerge five years later in the form of *Being and Nothingness* (1943). In *Nausea* Sartre effectively clears the way for human beings themselves, the human being now understood as the heroic human subject, the almighty free will, to take centre stage as the sovereign creator of meaning. In *Being and Nothingness*, meaning and purpose become something we generate through our free choices. In choosing ourselves, we choose future possibilities, goals, ideals and values that we strive to realise. We thus give our lives meaning or direction; and in the light of these projected goals and values, we also confer significance on the external world and on our own facticity, our material existence. Through our subjective choices, the world is once again filled with meaning.

This is not of course the response to the world's meaninglessness that Roquentin comes up with in the last few pages of *Nausea*, as he sits in the café preparing to leave Bouville. There we find the tentative suggestion of an escape from meaninglessness through some kind of artistic production (246-53). After hearing the jazz song *Some of These Days*, Roquentin resolves to write a novel. That is, he resolves to create something, like the song, that stands apart from worldly contingency, a kind of ideal object with an internal necessity in which each of the parts is explained and supported by the structure of the whole.[8] While it is not possible to share directly in the internal necessity of an integral artwork, Roquentin imagines that producing a novel will shed a redeeming light over his past and cleanse him a little of the "sin of existing" (251; see also 252), at least in his recollection and in the eyes of others. They will say, "it was Antoine Roquentin who wrote it, he was a red-headed fellow who hung about in cafés" (252).

But Sartre has also indicated that by the time he finished *Nausea*, he no longer believed in this solution. The novel marks the end of one period of thinking (Beauvoir, p. 206). Indeed, from the later perspective of the Sartre of *Being and Nothingness*, it would be simply bad faith to imagine that one could in any way support or legitimate one's own existence through an external object, even something of one's own creation. At the same time Sartre in *Nausea* also seems to hint at the direction he will eventually take, during lunch with the Autodidact. When Roquentin says: "I was just thinking […] that here we are, all of us, eating and drinking to preserve our precious existence, and that there's […] absolutely no reason for existing", the Autodidact replies that he has read a book called *Is Life Worth Living?*, which concludes that "life has a meaning if you choose to give it one" (162). In *Being and Nothingness*, the only meaning the world and our lives have is the meaning we give to them through our prodigious choices.

Yet as is well known, and as Sartre himself came to see, there are significant problems with the picture that was developed in *Being and Nothingness*. As the sovereign creator of meaning, the heroic Sartrean subject chooses itself entirely, "without any help whatsoever" (*Being and Nothingness*, p. 440-1), and here Sartre falls back into a kind of

---

[8] H. Barnes, *Sartre* (London: Quartet Books, 1974), p. 29; Beauvoir, p. 205-6.

self-enclosed idealism. All meaning is reduced to a function of our all-embracing choices. Nothing external, nothing outside enters to help or support those choices. Indeed, we even elude the influence and support of our own choices, which fall into the past and can no longer determine us. At every moment we are required to choose ourselves anew. Without any kind of external, conditioning circumstances the Sartrean subject is strangely unlocated and abstract. This needs to be immediately qualified. It is true that for Sartre, the subject only exists embodied, in a concrete situation. That is the realist side of his account. There is a world beyond the subject, which it does not choose or create, and the subject only exists in a concrete encounter with this reality. This is the brute, meaningless existence that Roquentin encounters in *Nausea*, and which reappears in *Being and Nothingness* under the title of 'being-in-itself'.

However, none of this conditions in any positive way the imperious Sartrean subject. This subject only exists insofar as it stands apart from, 'negates', the in-itself; and all apparent influences, constraints and obstacles in its environment and factual make-up only appear as such in the light of the goals it chooses to pursue. There may be a world beyond us, which we do not create, but the meaning of the world is reduced to a product of our choices of ourselves; it is I who choose the meaning of the situation I am in.[9] Even my embodiment is effectively subordinated to choice. While my body, my primary facticity, locates me in the world, I 'exist' my body as the immediate past that I escape towards my projected goals. And it is only through my choices, through which I confer significance on the world, that the world is revealed to me as 'being from a certain point of view', indirectly referring to me located within it (*Being and Nothingness*, p. 318). This marginalising of our corporeality is perhaps why the body in *Being and Nothingness* no longer 'violates' me, no longer 'takes me from behind', as it does in *Nausea*, but registers to direct awareness as little more than the 'nauseous taste' of my contingent factual existence.

So we end up with a radically free but also problematically abstract and indeed curiously Cartesian notion of the subject, standing apart from all conditioning circumstances — not only material but also linguistic, social and historical. But the important point here is that

---

[9] *Being and Nothingness*, p. 443; C. Falzon, 'Sartre: Freedom as Imprisonment' *Philosophy Today*, 47:2 (2003) 126-37 (p. 127).

Sartre is not turning his back on the more concrete picture that emerges in *Nausea*. On the contrary, by abandoning various principles we might appeal to in order to give meaning to the world and ourselves, stripping the world of meaning, *Nausea* opens the way to the imperious subject of *Being and Nothingness*, which generates all meaning through its subjective choices. So it is useful to go back to *Nausea* and look at what allows Sartre to deprive the world of meaning in the first place.

Back to 'Nausea'

While the world is stripped of meaning in *Nausea*, this is not simply a matter of abandoning principles and categories that we ordinarily use to give meaning to the world. This abandonment is undertaken in the light of a certain philosophical requirement. That is, the world is stripped of meaning because it fails to measure up to a certain philosophical conception of what would count as meaningful. For things in the world, including ourselves, to be meaningful, they need to be there necessarily. They need to be founded or justified in some strong way, following from whatever founds them with logical or near-logical necessity. And whatever principle founds them, it presumably cannot itself be in need of justification, or the problem reappears at a higher level. It must be an absolute foundation, secure ground, a basic principle (there may of course be a hierarchy here, but the final principle at least must be basic).

We can characterise this as a 'rationalist' conception of meaningfulness. The label refers us once again to Descartes, and his approach to philosophy. For Descartes, if philosophy is to have the certainty of mathematics, it has to develop like geometry, through a clear and distinct process of deduction from axiomatic first principles (in Descartes' case, these are the first truth of his own existence and certain undeniable 'truths of reason'). For things to be justified in this strong way would be for them to be completely contained within, and to follow entirely from, all-embracing first principles of some sort. This is what Roquentin is looking for. Tellingly, he does not find a circle absurd, because all its properties are necessitated; they are neatly contained within, and follow necessarily from, its definition, with nothing left over, nothing superfluous (185-6).[10] But a circle is an ideal object, and a rationalist looking for that sort of necessity and order is bound to be disappointed by the real world.

It is because things in the real world fail to exhibit this necessity or groundedness that Sartre is able to reach his radically negative conclusions in *Nausea*. Because reality cannot be derived deductively from founding principles, Roquentin finds things to be completely without meaning or reason for being. As he puts it while standing in front of the chestnut tree in the book's climactic moment, "to exist is simply *to be there*; what exists appears, lets itself be *encountered*, but you can never *deduce* it" (188). As a result, things are superfluous, contingent, gratuitous, absurd. As Roquentin puts it: "we were [all] a heap of existents inconvenienced, embarrassed by ourselves, we hadn't the slightest reason for being there, any of us; each existent, embarrassed, vaguely ill at ease, felt superfluous" (184); and: "everything is gratuitous, that park, this town, and myself. When you realise that, it turns your stomach [...] that is the Nausea" (188).

In these terms it is possible to give a philosophical interpretation of the specific symptom, the feeling of nausea, that Roquentin feels throughout the book. As Thody points out, nausea, in the sense of the desire to vomit, is "the product of excess".[11] In other words, we feel nauseated, sick, when we have eaten too much, when we cannot digest what we have eaten. Roquentin finds that there is too much of everything in the world, "tons and tons of existence" (193) as he puts it, a profusion of particular, contingent, disorderly things. This profusion of things not only surrounds him but is within him as well, in his own corporeal existence. It cannot be swallowed, digested, assimilated, completely contained or brought to order within any conceptual system or framework of principles. So Roquentin chokes on the world, is sickened by it, feels nauseated in the face of it. The feeling of nausea is the rationalist's sickness in the face of the conceptual indigestibility of the world.

This then is the philosophical requirement that lies behind Sartre's questioning of principles we might ordinarily appeal to in order to give meaning to the world and ourselves. These principles fail to contain the world, which exceeds what they can justify. It does not follow necessarily from them, cannot be derived from them, and so is

---

[10] A. Danto, *Sartre* (Glasgow: Fontana/Collins, 1975), p. 25.
[11] P. Thody, *Introducing Sartre* (Cambridge: Icon, 1999), p. 19.

additional, superfluous and contingent. Over and over again in *Nausea* we have the image of things as failing to be contained, as escaping from or overflowing the categories or forms we try to impose on them (182; see also 178-9, 184, 186, 225-6). In the novel Sartre also interprets recourse to God, to a theological foundation, as a failed attempt to overcome contingency. People, says Roquentin, "have understood [the contingency of existence]" and "have tried to overcome this contingency by inventing a necessary, causal being" (i.e. the medieval notion of God as *causa sui*). "But", he continues, "no necessary being can explain existence"; contingency is not an outward show, an appearance: "[…] It is absolute, and consequently perfect gratuitousness" (188).

It might be thought that a God could in fact provide the kind of strong justification that Sartre requires to overcome contingency. That is, if there were a God, there would presumably be a good reason for the world and ourselves to exist, because God would have made them according to his will; and everything would have a role in the divine plan. This in fact is the conception of God that seems to come to the fore later on in the 1945 popular lecture, 'Existentialism is a Humanism', where Sartre pursues the idea that a God could provide the world with meaning and purpose, and human conduct with justifying rules. There, the problem is not that God fails to overcome worldly contingency, but that he does not exist, and as such human beings are 'abandoned', 'thrown' into a meaningless world without justification or excuse for what they do.[12]

Here we need to remember that Sartre is not simply a disappointed rationalist who looks for order and justification in the world and cannot find it. He is using the rationalist conception of meaningfulness to call into question our ordinary principles, our ordinary ways of making sense of the world. And he also rejects other candidates, like the God of 'Existentialism is a Humanism', that purport to provide foundations or justification of the required sort. This provides us with another way of reading Sartre's rejection of a number of philosophical positions in *Nausea*. He can be seen as rejecting various foundational principles that have been invoked within the philosophical tradition, starting with the Archimedean ground of Descartes' own existence as

---

[12] J.-P. Sartre, 'Existentialism is a Humanism', in *Existentialism from Dostoevsky to Sartre*, ed. by W. Kaufmann (New York: New American Library, 1975), pp. 345-69 (p. 352-3).

a thinking thing, which together with certain unquestionable principles is supposed to allow Descartes to deduce the existence of the world, and its broad features. Indeed, Sartre rejects all rationalist systems that seek to capture and subsume reality under foundationalist principles of some sort. This includes idealist philosophy from Kant onwards, which as we have seen, represents a comprehensive attempt to subsume reality under universal, rational concepts, and reaches its high point in Hegel.

Finally, Sartre rejects Husserl's attempt to escape from idealism, which seeks both to return to the 'things themselves' and at the same time to preserve philosophical foundations. Since transient, contingent things cannot be the basis for certain knowledge, Husserl distinguishes between natural objects and 'things as they appear within thought'. Stripped of their messy contingency and particularity, objects will yield their timeless essences and provide the firm foundation for a 'transcendental science'. But for Sartre, this amounts to a turn away from the things themselves and a fall back into a form of idealism. Thus Sartre abandons a range of philosophical attempts to give meaning, order, or point to the world and ourselves in terms of foundational, first principles of various sorts. And in the absence of such foundations we are faced once again with things in their brute particularity and contingency, along with our own contingent factual existence.

Alternatives

As noted earlier, the negative trajectory that Sartre pursues in *Nausea* — the questioning of the principles and categories that we might ordinarily appeal to in order to give meaning to the world, along with the rejection of various philosophical foundations — has positive implications for his thinking. In the first instance it strips the world of the veneer of meaning and brings us back in touch with the things themselves; and in particular it brings to the fore the dimension of contingency that Sartre takes to have been neglected. And it also prepares the way for Sartre's own philosophical account in *Being and Nothingness*, in which the imperious Sartrean subject enters the scene as the sovereign creator of meaning in a meaningless world. Brute reality, without meaning, order or justification, is precisely the conception of the external world that Sartre needs in order to assert his radical conception of subjectivity. Reappearing as being-in-itself, it is a key element in the later picture. As free subjects, we no longer choke on the indigestible being-in-itself, are no longer invaded or violated by it. We exist as standing apart from it, fleeing from the world and from our own material existence, towards the goals we project through our undetermined choices. The Sartrean subject thus reigns supreme — but it is also wholly unsupported, strangely unlocated, problematically abstract.

But we can now ask whether we should have come to this point in the first place, where we have to regard the world and ourselves as being without meaning, order and justification. After all, this presupposes a very specific, rationalistic conception of what is required for meaningful existence, in terms of something's only being meaningful if it follows with logical or near logical necessity from some absolute foundational principle. If we accept that, then we are placed in an either-or situation: either we are able to satisfy that standard for meaningfulness, or we cannot speak of meaning at all. But we might wonder if this is not in fact an impossibly high requirement for meaningfulness in the first place.

First of all, with respect to there needing to be an absolute, foundational principle, any principle we invoke as our ultimate justification is going to be itself unfounded, and hence contingent and arbitrary. The problem with demanding a firm foundation is that you end up making the paradoxical claim that everything must be grounded, except that which is the ground. Hence the dubious medieval attempt to make God into a principle that somehow justifies itself, a strategy that cannot be pursued without falling into circularity. The only alternative seems to be an infinite regress, in which every ground has to be itself founded through a further principle, and so on *ad infinitum*. The proper response here is not to suppose then that no justifications are possible at all, which continues to presuppose the impossible demand for absolute foundations. The real answer seems to be that we need to get used to the idea that while we can justify things to a certain extent, at a certain point, justifications are simply going to run out; and indeed, that it is only because justifications run out at a certain point that we are able to provide justifications.

In relation to our own conduct, for example, we can function meaningfully as agents because we adhere to certain principles, values and commitments, a framework of guiding principles, in terms of which we are able to weigh up choices and actions, and choose between alternative paths. We can justify what we decide and do, even if only retrospectively, in terms of a basic framework that constitutes 'who we are' and 'where we stand'. If we lose touch with these basic values and commitments, we will be crippled as agents, unsure what we stand for; and if we are forced to act in ways that violate our basic values and commitments, we can be entirely destroyed as coherent agents. Yet, as Nagel puts it, when we step back and reflect, we are likely to find that this whole system of justification "rests on responses and habits that we can never question, that we should not know how to defend without circularity, and to which we shall continue to adhere even after they are called into question".[13] This does not mean that all that we do is meaningless, but simply that there are limits to what we can rationally justify in our existence.

Secondly, it is also asking too much to hold that things can be meaningful only if they follow necessarily or with near logical necessity from some principle, only if reality can be contained or comprehended within a conceptual system or set of principles. The problem with this demand is that things can only follow necessarily from principles if they lack all independence from them, if they are no more than functions of those principles. They will then only follow 'by definition', and will only reflect what is already contained in those principles. We will not be saying anything about reality, about the world, only about our initial principles. Once again, the proper response is not to say that reality is in consequence completely meaningless, lacking any sense or order at all. That continues to presuppose the impossible requirement that matters of fact somehow follow necessarily from first principles.[14] A better alternative, to restate a point made by Tom Martin in his chapter in this volume, is that real meaning depends on an interplay between two things, an organising principle that we impose on reality, and something 'out there', something independent of it, to which we are answerable.

---

[13] T. Nagel, 'The Absurd', in *Mortal Questions* (Cambridge: Cambridge University Press, 1979), pp. 11-23 (p. 15) and C. Taylor, 'What is Human Agency', in *The Self: Psychological and Philosophical Issues*, ed. by T. Mischel (Oxford: Blackwell, 1977), pp. 103-35 (p. 124-5).
[14] A. McIntyre, 'Existentialism', in *The Encyclopedia of Philosophy* (London: Macmillan, 1967), p. 147.

On this view, the circumstance Roquentin encounters in *Nausea*, that things fail to be contained by the categories or forms we impose on them, but escape or overflow them, and thus have a degree of independence, is in fact necessary for meaningfulness. Meaning emerges out of the self's interplay with, its involvement in, the wider world. And this involvement can be extended by suggesting that the wider world here also includes the social context in which we find ourselves. This social context brings with it the processes of nurturing, training and shaping by other people which provide us with the basic principles, commitments, and values that we bring to bear on the world. In other words, on this view, the principles, commitments, and values which Nagel suggests we ordinarily take for granted and do not question, are acquired, at least in the first instance, through our training, our upbringing, through the shaping influence of our social environment.

So to summarise the argument, *Nausea*'s vision of the world as meaningless is not a revelation of the world as it really is, stripped of a deceptive veneer of forms that we try to impose on it. That vision presupposes a specific philosophical conception of what would count as meaningful, a rationalistic standard for meaningfulness that turns out to be impossibly demanding. If we abandon this demand, we never get to the point where we have to regard the world and ourselves as lacking all meaning, order or justification. Moreover, we do not have to then go on and posit a self standing outside the world, an unlocated, sovereign self that creates all meaning *ex nihilo*, entirely out of its own prodigious activity. In the alternative account of meaning that has been briefly sketched here, we are beings who are always involved in the world, and with others, with meaning emerging out of the interplay between the self and the wider world. To adopt this view is to arrive at a more plausible conception of meaningfulness; but it is also to take our leave of *Nausea*.

Amanda Crawley-Jackson

La Nausée des Fins de Voyage ?

This chapter takes as its starting point the only reference to nausea in Sartre's juvenilia: namely, "the nausea that comes at the end of a journey". By focusing on the importance (and disappointments, or anti-conclusions) of travel in the Sartrean corpus, it seeks first to open up a space in which to consider a variety of novel intertexts (including the Greek katabatic narrative), before focusing more specifically on Bouville as a site of spatial organization and practice. Noting the shared topographies and cultural histories of Bouville and Le Havre (the town which Beauvoir claims inspired Sartre's fiction), it will argue that the spatial tensions inherent in the novel (linear/circular, enclosed/disrupted, bounded/unbounded, monumental/fissured) echo and illuminate Sartre's ontological dynamic of perpetual becoming.

* * *

In both *Les Carnets de la drôle de guerre* and the juvenilia, Sartre makes a connection between nausea and travel.[1] In *Jésus la Chouette*, written in 1922, we discover the first use of the word 'nausée' in the phrase: 'la nausée des fins de voyage'.[2] This is, of course, consonant with the etymology of the word *nausea*, deriving from the Greek *naus* — ship. However, little work has been done specifically on the travel/nausea link, and even less so on the relationship between nausea and the *end* of travel, and it is thus the aim of this chapter to go some way towards remedying that lacuna. A second (and related) aspect of this chapter will be Sartre's attention to urban space, which has also

---

[1] In *Les Carnets de la drôle de guerre*, Sartre's explanation of his aim in *Nausea* ("to capture the secret smiles of things seen absolutely in the absence of men" [J.-P. Sartre, *Les Carnets de la drôle de guerre, novembre 1939-mars 1940* (Paris: Gallimard, 1983), p. 182 – author's translation]) is prompted by a three-page disquisition on Valéry Larbaud's *Barnabooth* and travel writing more generally. He goes on to make a further connection between the narrative of *Nausea* and travel: "Roquentin, confronted with the jardin public, was like I am in front of a street in Naples: things called out to him in signs, and he had to decipher them" (*Les Carnets de la drôle de guerre*, p. 182).
[2] J.-P. Sartre, *Les Ecrits de jeunesse* (Paris: Gallimard, 1990), p. 45.

received little critical treatment to date. I shall make the case, with particular reference to *Nausea*, that there is a useful link to be made between urban architectonics and ontology in the Sartrean text, and that recurring fissures perceived in the urban landscape are a reflection of contingency and human ontological processes more generally. As many critics have noted, Bouville — the end of Roquentin's journey — is a context topographically and climatically suited to the nauseating revelation of contingency. Focusing on the town's topographical and architectural specificities, we will show how its liminality, which manifests itself in the tensions between the chthonic and the constructed aspects of the town, mirrors the structure of the Sartrean self and tells us something of the drive behind both being and travel. Finally, an understanding of that richly evocative, mythological space, 'the journey's end', and its unusual treatment in the Sartrean corpus will shed light on the 'agoraphile diktat' (a term I adopt from Michel de Certeau) which governs both the ontological and textual Sartrean dynamic.

Writing in 1955, Claude Lévi-Strauss posited the end of travel or, more precisely, the end of the *dream* of travel. He argued (like later critics of Orientalism) that the 'elsewhere' was simply an exotic corner of the European imaginary. In fact, the reality of the elsewhere — thanks to the intrusive, hegemonic presence of the West — was tending towards globalised homogeneity. Lévi-Strauss also decried the tokenistic narratives ('impressions') which were brought back from 'elsewhere': "Amazonia, Tibet and Africa fill the bookshops in the form of travelogues, accounts of expeditions and collections of photographs."[3] Apparently moveable feasts, they articulated a version of the elsewhere which would satisfy a market hungry for a paradoxically already familiar exotic. Thus commodified, travel narratives — according to Lévi-Strauss' terms — reduced the elsewhere to a discursive, verbal fact which had little to do with its reality:

> [...] Interspersed among the anecdotes, are scraps of hackneyed information which have appeared in every textbook during the past [hundred] years and [which] have been presented with remarkable effrontery (an effrontery nevertheless perfectly in

---

[3] C. Lévi-Strauss, *Tristes Tropiques*, trans. by J. and D. Weightman (London: Jonathan Cape, 1973), p. 17.

keeping with the naivety and ignorance of the audience) as valid evidence or even original discoveries. (Lévi-Strauss, p. 18)

The 'elsewhere', he concludes, exists only in the mode of representation. Beneath the tightly corseted metalanguage of travel and discovery is a reality few of us are equipped, or willing, to confront.

Roquentin's journal describes a similar disenchantment with the dream of the elsewhere. Having travelled for six years across four continents (and notably in the French colonial territories), this seasoned globetrotter comes to the following conclusion:

It seems to me as if everything I know about life I have learnt from books. The palace of Benares, the terrace of the Leper King, the temples of Java with their great broken staircases, have been reflected for a moment in my eyes, but they have remained yonder, on the spot. (95)

This revelation is profoundly destabilising in that it causes him to reassess both the experiences he has had in the past, and his representations (or memories) of those experiences in the present. Both past and present encounters with the elsewhere seem to him to have been filtered through what Rana Kabbani has called, "the limitations of the inherited language,"[4] and *reality* remains elsewhere, ineffable:

As for that square in Meknès, although I used to go there every day, it's even simpler: I can't see it at all now. All that remains is the vague feeling that it was charming, and these five words indissolubly linked together: a charming square at Meknès. No doubt if I close my eyes or stare vaguely at the ceiling I can reconstruct the scene: a tree in the distance, a short dark figure running towards me. But I am inventing all that for the sake of the thing. [...] I can't *see* anything any more: however much I search the past I can only retrieve scraps of images and I am not sure what they represent, nor whether they are remembered or invented. (52)

Scraps they might be; but articulated within the parameters of the metalanguage of the exotic, they become both authoritative and attractive in the eyes of an audience desiring (and expecting) confirmation of a pre-existing imaginary:

---

[4] R. Kabbani, *Europe's Myths of Orient* (Bloomington: Indiana Univeristy Press, 1986), p. 11.

> At this rate, I could get myself invited to people's houses and they would tell one another that I was a great traveller in the sight of Eternity. Yes: the Moslems squat to pass water; instead of ergotine, Hindu midwives use ground glass in cow dung; in Borneo, when a girl has her period, she spends three days and nights on the roof of her house. I have seen burials in gondolas in Venice, the Holy Week festivities in Seville, the Passion play at Oberammergau. Naturally, that's just a tiny sample of my experience... (102)

In this sense, the typical narratives of seasoned travellers like Roquentin differ little from the dreams of armchair travellers such as the sedentary Autodidact:

> Under this skull Samoyeds, Nyam-nyams, Madagascans, and Fuegians are celebrating the strangest solemnities, eating their aged fathers, and their children, spinning to the sound of tom-toms until they faint, giving themselves up to the frenzy of the amuck, burning their dead, exposing them on the rooftops, abandoning them to the river current in a boat lighted by a torch, copulating at random, mother with son, father with daughter, brother with sister, mutilating themselves, castrating themselves, distending their lips with plates and having monstrous animals carved on their backs. (55)

All of this is brought home to Roquentin when, in the colonial office (located in Hanoi or Saigon — there is an inconsistency in the text which only underscores the point we are about to make), he contemplates the absurd juxtaposition of a Khmer figurine and the trappings of French bourgeois bureaucracy:

> The statue struck me as stupid and unattractive and I felt I was terribly bored. I couldn't understand why I was in Indo-China. What was I doing here? Why was I talking to those people? Why was I dressed so oddly? My passion was dead. For years it had submerged me and swept me along; now I felt empty. But that wasn't the worst of it: installed in front of me with a sort of indolence there was a voluminous, insipid idea. I don't know exactly what it was, but it sickened me so much I couldn't look at it. (15)

It seems that the decontextualised figurine, like the photograph, postcard and other fetishes of the elsewhere, has been required to *stand in for* the real. What is more, like other emblems of the elsewhere, it has aphrodisiacal properties which blind the consumer to its actual emptiness. This is why Roquentin is able to satisfy the Autodidact "by stuffing his pockets with postcards, prints and photos" (57); it also explains why the Autodidact is so unsettled when the veracity of existing images and narratives (in other words, the metalanguage) is questioned or denied. We see this when he examines a photograph of the carving of St. Jerôme in Burgos; familiar only with the Burgos of books, he asks: "Have you seen that Christ made of animal skin at Burgos? There's a very curious book, Monsieur, about those statues made of animal skin and even human skin" (54). Only that which is *known of the unknown* passes muster; and that which is known tends to be that which marks the 'elsewhere' out as being so radically (and, paradoxically, *reassuringly*) different from 'here'. If the Autodidact chooses not to face up to the reality which lies behind the screen of myth, Roquentin confronts it. Slavoj Zizek's account of the breakdown of fantasy seems then particularly pertinent to a reading of Roquentin's journal as an encounter with the *real*:

> [F]antasy is on the side of reality [...] it sustains the subject's 'sense of reality': when the phantasmic frame disintegrates, the subject undergoes a 'loss of reality' and starts to perceive reality as an 'irreal' nightmarish universe...; this nightmarish universe is not 'pure fantasy' but, on the contrary, *that which remains of reality after reality is deprived of its support in fantasy.*[5]

The dream of the 'journey's end' (to which Sartre elsewhere — in his letters, for example — admits to being susceptible) sustains its own kind of (discursive) reality, but one which dissipates upon contact with the *real*, prompting the great sense of *unreality* which besets Roquentin in the colonial office. If, as in a dream, the strangest concatenation of circumstances, events, people and apparel appears 'normal' when closeted behind the mythical screen, an awakening into the real — as we can see from Roquentin's journal (What am I doing here? Who are these people? Why am I dressed so oddly?) — prompts a feverish and bewildered reassessment.

This disaggregating of the real and the imaginary underpins Sartre's discourse of travel and, more specifically, his understanding of the *destination*. In *Being and Nothingness*, Sartre describes how the perceived qualities of the viscous are derived from human perceptions of (and indeed engagements with) it, rather than being inherent to it. The same might be said of the nature of the destination, whose characteristics in the Sartrean text derive in large part from the nature of the motivations which prompted the journey towards it. Because

---

[5] S. Zizek, *The Plague of Fantasies* (London: Verso, 1997), p. 66.

Nausea ostensibly begins already with the *end* of Roquentin's travels,
I should like to turn first to the narratives of the juvenilia — replete as
they are with journeys both real and mythological — in order to do so.
     Early narratives such as *Jésus la Chouette* (1922) and *Er
l'Arménien* (1927) have an element of pastiche about them, as is
perhaps the wont of juvenilia. Simone de Beauvoir criticizes Sartre,
particularly with regard to *Er l'Arménien*, for having mimicked the
classical style and having produced as a result a rather awkward and
clumsily expressed narrative. It is certainly the case that the journey
described in this philosophical essay-cum-mythological parable
closely resembles the *Katabasis* of classical Greek narrative.
Katabasis describes the classical hero's descent into the underworld to
seek something which is lost (usually a friend or family member) or
desired (spiritual or material wealth). The most obvious examples are
to be found in Book 11 of Homer's *Odyssey*, and Book 6 of Virgil's
Aeneid. Erling B. Holtsmark, in his work on the katabic narrative in
contemporary cinematography, describes a purgatorial, underworld
topography which is typically characterized by the dark, damp and
labyrinthine. If the hero is able to successfully navigate his way
through this riverine landscape, he will return to assume "roles of
increased responsibility and leadership" on the basis of "his harrowing
in hell". Moreover, he will have acquired a certain sense of his own
self, or an identity which was lacking or deficient before his descent.
The katabasis is thus, according to Holtsmark, "a journey of self-
discovery, a quest for a lost self."[6]
     The questions which arise in our reading of the juvenilia are: what
motivates the protagonists to embark on such journeys? What do they
hope to find at the journey's end, and what is the *reality* of their
destination? In *Er l'Arménien*, the eponymous hero yearns to
rediscover the ambition and dynamism which characterized his early
years. His embarkation upon a katabic journey derives principally
from that condition which, according to Dennis Porter, prompted
many a journey in the modernist period: satiety.[7] Listless because

---

[6] E. B. Holtsmark, 'The *Katabasis* Theme in Modern Cinema' in *Classical Myth and
Culture in the Cinema*, ed. by M. M. Winkler (Oxford: Oxford University Press,
2001), pp. 23-50 (p. 26).
[7] D. Porter, '*Orientalism* and Its Problem', in *Colonial Discourse and Post-Colonial
Theory: A Reader*, ed. by P. Williams and L. Chrisman (New York; London:
Harvester Wheatsheaf, 1993), pp. 150-61.

materially secure, indolent because wealthy and influential, Er has the bourgeois privilege of being able to turn his thoughts to the meaninglessness of his existence: "I was fully aware that I had lost that privileged situation which I had had as an adolescent, and which had lent my actions a superb harmony" (*EJ*, p. 300).[8] Life, stripped of its goals and absolutes, becomes intolerable for him: "all objects dominate and crush me / All earthly objects are too big for me" (*EJ*, p. 305). To a large extent, it is the teleological nature of adventure itself which entices the subject away from his desperate and disaggregated reality. Sartre explains: "Definition of adventure: the sense of a fatal liaison between past, present and future, which implies a simultaneous knowledge of all three and of their liaison. The sense of time passing as in a piece of music."[9] However, it is also about that sense of *meaning* and clarity with which the subject seeks to reimpregnate his existence. Er imagines an elsewhere, "Where, as the sun's celestial companion, all terrestrial things are illuminated and without mystery; where the earth finally appears as flat as the moon" (*EJ*, p. 306). Thus, Er hastens his own death in the hope of discovering from the gods the meaning of life on earth. At first, it seems as though his wishes have been granted:

> What a delicious awakening. [...] I was no longer alone. Nature, mute on earth, here proclaimed the existence of the Gods. I bathed in their will as I did the night, the only mortal admitted to the realm of the Hyperphysical. A powerful gust had extinguished the ardent flame which consumed me: all was night, silence, renewal. (*EJ*, pp. 306-7)

In fact, this celestial kingdom of ends is quickly revealed as an illusion ('it was a moment of respite'; 'the calm enjoyed by my soul could not be [*deleted*: but precarious]' [*EJ*, p. 308]):

> I cannot tell you just how disappointed I was: all my muscles, taut with enthusiasm, relaxed suddenly. My whole being, which had reached out to external objects, curled back up into itself, like a shell. Humidity and Melancholy fell at the same time upon me. (*EJ*, pp. 308-9)

---

[8] For the sake of clarity, *Les Ecrits de jeunesse* (Sartre, 1990) will be referred to as *EJ* in the body of the text. (All translations of *Les Ecrits de jeunesse* are the author's own.)

[9] J.-P. Sartre, *Œuvres romanesques* (Paris: Bibliothèque de la Pléiade, 1981), p. 1681 (author's translation).

What is immediately striking in the description of this purgatorial space is the use of the terms 'Mélancolie' and 'Humidité' to describe Er's sensations and impressions as he arrives at this disappointing journey's end. *Melancolia*, as we know, was the original title of *Nausea*, and 'Humidité' resonates with the viscous, cloying mud and fog of Bouville. Topographically, it has more in common with the foggy underground depths of classical purgatory than the celestial heights of Mount Olympus:

> My soul, which had prepared itself for marble palaces, the incomparable prairies of Helicon, the inestimable parks of Hesperides, was dumbfounded. I was in a huge, abandoned garden. The paths and lawns had disappeared beneath swathes of weeds, like boats which had sunk to the bottom of the sea. When the wind stopped blowing, you could, for a moment, just about make out their pure and austere shapes beneath the tips of the weeds. An entire, austere and classical order had been inflected and relaxed, as a proud soul weakens in adversity. (*EJ*, p. 309)

This other world is markedly liminal in character. As is the case with existence itself, order and disorder, immanence and transcendence, nature and civilization co-exist in an impossible tension. Images of earth, fog and night — all of which convey the same sense of distance from, and yet awareness of the celestial (a cosmological echo of the human condition?) — can also be found in Homer's description of the place at which Odysseus enters the underworld. However, if this frontier marks the *beginning* of Odysseus' journey, for Er it marks the end. A space which is transitional and transformative in the classical text becomes a sticky trap for Er. He finds none of the wisdom which vivifies and enriches his classical counterpart, and returns to earth with little to impart other than the fact that the 'elsewhere' closely resembles the 'here', or the terrestrial.

A similarly disappointing journey is staged in *Jésus la Chouette*. Paul, the narrator, is freed from the maternal bond and leaves for La Rochelle in search of love and (masculine) maturity. Like Er, he finds a place which is profoundly liminal in character and seems designed to thwart his every intention. It is unpleasantly hermaphroditic ("We went to sit on the jetty, at the place where a stone break-water, like a dribbling grey slug, pushes itself bit by bit into the sea" [*EJ*, p. 71]) and ambivalent. Introduced as 'a crepuscular town' (*perpetually* neither night nor day), La Rochelle epitomises the *flou* (haziness) and the dissipation of boundaries:

> The street lamps cast expanses of light which merge a little into each other, as in a painting by Monet. The pale colours of the sky encroach upon the old watchtowers of the Anse, turning their hard forms blue and softening their rigidity. In the port, a thick body of water dozes, plated with white like those black puddles of oil left on the road by cars. (*EJ*, p. 63)

Here, then, all rigidity becomes soft and pliable; white becomes black; distinct melodies emerging from cafés become vague and unidentifiable from one another. The divine is but a distant memory; confusion and indistinctness reign. Temporal distinctions are eroded: Paul's usual intuitions of the future dissolve as he enters his new lodgings, the "villa 'Remember'" (*EJ*, p. 64). The maid who answers the door does so "With a grimace of lassitude, standing in a sluggish pose of abandon, with everything about her breathing negligence" (*EJ*, p. 65). The glorious past of the house has given way to a proliferation of unruly vegetation (a frequent metaphor in the pre-war corpus), and the panorama is one where intention, project and all trace of the human will have been submerged. The house and its gardens are an exotic travesty of human civilization and represent the return to a primitive and unruly state:

> Thus I remembered the 'Villa Remember' as a white building in the Greek style, as white as the terraces of Ithaca and Mycene were supposed to be. But, an exception to an almost universal rule, the house had the heaviness of a Jewish casbah and the tacky inconsistency of a Swiss chalet. Exotic, hothouse plants, heavy cacti and disgraceful yuccas, gave the front garden the appearance of an overfilled greenhouse; two placid lion cubs, covered in moss, masterpieces of bad taste, framed in their symmetry the three grey stone steps which led to the front door. [...] This house, deprived of light by the tall chestnut trees on the main street, lost in the exuberant foliage of its own garden, had all the unhealthy humidity and awful sadness common to cheap romanticism. (*EJ*, p. 64)

The return to this state of fundamental ambiguity (or, perhaps, *contingency*) reveals the worrying porosity between the two worlds of reason and ambiguity. These, then, are "the barriers we have set up between the objects and ourselves, all the refuges we have built – the walls, the towns, the physical laws, the framework of time and space, the libraries with the reassuring certainty they convey to us that everything which happens — even miracles — happens according to certain laws."[10] However, while it appears relatively easy to cross into the liminal space, it is very difficult to leave once the subject is there. Loosdreck, Paul's unfortunate and eventually doomed host, is caught in its horror and thus refers to the viscous qualities of its water: "You can't wash in water from La Rochelle. Look, I washed my hands twice this morning; you can't get clean with this water" (*EJ*, p. 76).[11] Unsurprisingly, given this context, Paul finds neither the love nor the chivalrous identity he had initially hoped to discover. As Sartre will write in *Nausea*: "the idea of transition was another idea of man. An idea which was too clear" (189).

What both these texts have in common is a search for an absolute, be that meaning or identity. The journey – or katabasis – is inflected, however, finishing in an absorptive and perpetual threshold. The journey's end reflects an intensification of the very condition which the subject had sought to escape: ambiguity, incompleteness and that sense of unending becoming which fissures identity, plenitude and complacency. There is a kind of pathetic fallacy at play in Sartre's use of the *limen* as an ironic and inflected backdrop to the protagonists' desires. For this reason, all destinations become, in their deficiency, another starting point. Whether this results in a destructive, annular dynamic or something more akin to the pyrrhic ethics advocated by Simone de Beauvoir in response to a similar realisation remains to be seen. However, what is clear is that the liminal space which describes the disappointing ambiguity of the 'journey's end' is articulated as a locational contradiction. When, in *L'Ange du Morbide* (1922), Louis Gaillard travels to Altweier, in the Alsace region, in search of a coherent identity, he discovers rather a place which is neither French nor German, Catholic nor Protestant, but *both* at the same time. In fact, Altweier epitomizes the *in-betweenness* of the destinations arrived at by the characters in the juvenilia. Gaillard's search for an absolute has brought him to this site of ambiguity and ambivalence which he will be able to flee only by seeking refuge in bad faith. The spatial discourse of *Nausea* is, on the other hand, more complex in that it posits not a juxtaposition of existing plenitudes, but rather a

---

[10] C.-E. Magny, 'The Duplicity of Being' in *Sartre: A Collection of Critical Essays*, ed. by E. Kern (Englewood Cliffs, NJ: Prentice Hall, 1962), pp. 21-30 (p. 24).
[11] Cf. "I open my hands, I want to let go of the slimy and it sticks to me, it draws me, it sucks at me" (J.-P. Sartre, *Being and Nothingness: An Essay on Phenomenological Ontology*, trans. by H. Barnes (London: Routledge, 1989), p. 609).

disjunction between an imaginary utopia and a *real* heterotopia. Furthermore, it reinserts the subject (or consciousness) into the spatialising process, thereby deconstructing the homogeneity of space and the possibility of a journey's end (as both destination and project).

'On the map of history, perhaps the water stain is memory.'
(Anne Michaels)

Bouville, like La Rochelle and Alsace, represents the 'end of travel' for Roquentin. The name — Mudtown — is suggestive of the liminality we have come to expect, and — in its viscosity — epitomises for Sartre "compromise" (*Being and Nothingness*, p. 605), the "essentially ambiguous" and "fixed instability", "between two states" (*Being and Nothingness*, p. 607). The mud also reminds us of the riverine underworld visited by the classical hero, and is now supplemented with the ice and fog of Dante's *Inferno*. It seems that if — as Holtsmark argues — the classical hero is typically re-birthed in slime following his katabasis, then the mud of Bouville will be an eternal caul for the protagonist of the Sartrean text. It represents a kind of perpetual *in-betweenness*, a threshold or *limen* in which one will be caught in the process of *becoming*, forever.

Bouville, however, emerges not from a juxtaposition of *a priori* locational binaries (clean/dirty, bourgeois/working class, centre/suburbs), but from process and flux: a *dialectical* relationship between subject and space, transcendence and immanence, construct and practice. This is made immediately clear in the 'Undated sheet', when space as inflexible Euclidean geometry, independent of human consciousness, is deconstructed as a (reassuring) bourgeois fiction:

> This evening I am quite at ease, with my feet firmly on the ground. This is my room, which faces north-east. Down below is the rue des Mutilés and the shunting yard of the new station. From my window I can see the red and white flame of the Rendez-vous des Cheminots at the corner of the boulevard Victor-Noir. The Paris train has just come in. (10-11)

Roquentin's measurement and narration of this space resembles what Gerald Prince has called "a description of a block of pre-fabricated space, in the manner of Balzac."[12] The narrative refers to points of the compass; it resembles a "system of spatial coordinates"[13] in which space is a topology or *metric* – rather than a spatial relation with the self. It is non-directional; proximity derives from the measurement of distances (or "the observational measurement of space"[14]) with no sense of a spatialising human consciousness. Objects are organized not as instruments or obstacles, but there is rather "a multiplicity of positions for random Things" (Heidegger, p. 147). This space is also situated temporally according to external (and ostensibly non-human) markers. Roquentin accepts as a given that the last tram will pass beneath his window at precisely 10.45pm and depends on the clock to regulate and confirm this. However, in *Being and Nothingness* Sartre claims that only because there is *néantisation*, is there temporality and, by extension, space: "the For-itself dispersing its being in three dimensions is temporal; due to the very fact that it nihilates itself" (*Being and Nothingness*, p. 142). The present is "the mould of indispensable non-being for the total synthetic form of Temporality" (*Being and Nothingness*, p. 142). However, Roquentin's ability to understand space in these Euclidean terms falters as the narrative progresses. This culminates in a scene reminiscent of Dürer's *Melancolia*: he, like the angel of the woodcut which initially lent the novel its name, contemplates a range of instruments wholly inadequate to the task of quantifying immense and ineffable reality:

> *Superfluous*: that was the only connexion I could establish between those trees, those gates, those pebbles. It was in vain that I tried to *count* the chestnut trees, to *situate* them in relation to the Velleda, to compare their height with the height of the plane trees: each of them escaped from the relationship in which I tried to enclose it, isolated itself, overflowed. I was aware of the arbitrary nature of these relationships, which I insisted on maintaining in order to delay the collapse of the human world of measures, of quantities, of bearings; they no longer held any grip on things. (184)

---

[12] G. Prince, *Métaphysique et technique dans l'œuvre romanesque de Sartre* (Geneva: Droz, 1968), p. 87 (author's translation).
[13] Y. Arisaka, 'Spatiality, Temporality, and the Problem of Foundation in Being and Time' *Philosophy Today*, 40: 1 (1996), 36-46 (p. 38).
[14] M. Heidegger, *Being and Time*, trans. by J. Macquarrie and E. Robinson (Oxford and Cambridge, MA: Blackwell, 1995), p. 135-37.

It is typically documented[15] that Le Havre – in which Sartre taught in the early 1930s – provided the inspiration for Bouville.[16] Beauvoir notes that Sartre quite liked the city (Beauvoir, p. 93), and that together they shared happy times discovering its streets and cafés. Her own description of the port is lyrical and focuses on the atmosphere which derived from the city's divergent populations:

> The crowd we encountered in its streets and public spaces was livelier and more colourful than the one in Rouen; it's because Le Havre was a large port; its population was made up of people from all over the place; people were doing big business there, using modern methods; everyone was living in the present, rather than stagnating in the past. [...] In Rouen, I came up against walls wherever I looked; here, I could see as far as the horizon and a fresh wind, which came from the ends of the world, blew in my face. (Beauvoir, p. 233 – author's translation)

This description gives us nothing of the grey, foggy claustrophobia of Bouville, but it does convey — very clearly — the startling heterogeneity of the place, and as such constitutes a way into an appraisal of Bouville as an open, 'flawed' and limitless metropolis. While she condemns Sartre's attempt to 'synthesise' (or systematise) London when they visit the English capital in 1933 (see Beauvoir, pp. 164-168), she finds something authentic in his fragmented, *situated* and thus partial rendering of Le Havre in *Nausea*: "j'avais alors l'impression qu'il m'en révélait la vérité" (Beauvoir, p. 168).

In order to better illustrate the fallaciousness of Roquentin's initial apprehension of space and the emerging spatial dialectic of Bouville, it will be useful to say something briefly about the history (and popular historical knowledge) of Le Havre, for there exists a rich stream of subtexts (geographical and literary) to inform the reader's topographical imagination. This will enable us to open up an account of Bouville's heterogeneity and the tension (between transience and

---

[15] See for example, S. Beauvoir, *La Force de l'âge* (Paris: Gallimard, 1960), p. 168.

[16] There are also references in *Nausea* to topographical and other features which appear to suggest a clear link. The most telling example is Sartre's reference to Bouville's old and new railway stations. Le Havre's new railway station was officially opened – amid great pomp and circumstance – just before Sartre took up his teaching post there and was, presumably, still the subject of much local talk. Other links – such as shared street names and churches – are also in evidence. Gerald Prince argues, however, that while Bouville resembles Le Havre, it is not supposed to *be* Le Havre. He quotes from a scene in the Maison Bottanet, in which a young man recounts his team's recent victory over the Le Havre football team (cf. Prince, p. 84, note 3).

permanence, volatility and immanence) which characterises it. It was in the sixteenth century that the beginnings of Le Havre were built – at great financial and human cost – upon the most unsuitable and resisting of Norman terrains. While the topographical features of the coastline (such as sheltered estuaries and maximal high tides) were well suited to shipping needs, the surrounding landscape of waterlogged marshes was hostile to the construction of a port and indeed any kind of urban settlement. Construction was nonetheless pursued, due in no small part to the political and economic interests of local dignitaries and also François 1er, who, in an attempt to encourage an influx of population into the emerging city, granted settlers an exemption from certain taxes in 1520. The Italian architect Girolamo Bellarmato, commissioned by the King to design this unlikely city, chose Venice as a model and began by fortifying the terrain in order to prevent subsequent flooding. The marshes were apparently conquered; the city expanded in the face of the threat that one day, the sea might reclaim the land on which it was built.

I have taken the time to mention this history because a similar one occurs in *Nausea* and also elsewhere in the Sartrean text, particularly in *La Reine Albemarle ou le dernier touriste* (which Beauvoir claims was the *Nausea* of Sartre's maturity). Bouville was created, against the odds, through human effort: "lengthening and widening", "necessary extensions", "constant dredging" all played a vital part (122). Referring explicitly to the watery origins of Venice, and more obliquely to the St Petersburg of Pushkin's *Bronze Horseman* (1837), Sartre later reveals a preoccupation with such a stubborn stitching of urban structures onto a watery and hence unstable ground. We see this when he writes to Olga Kosakiewicz in the 1930s, describing a Naples harrassed by an obstinate sea, a city in which watery chance erodes intention and design.[17] Pushkin's description of the revenge of the River Neva on Peter the Great's city summarises the fantasmal obsession of primal return which cuts through Sartre's urban and textual imaginary:

> Harried by the gale / Out of the gulf, the Neva turned back, angry, / Turbulent, and swamped the islands. The weather / Raged more fiercely, Neva swelled up and roared, / Bubbling like a cauldron; suddenly / Hurled herself on the city like a beast.

---

[17] J.-P. Sartre, *Lettres au Castor, 1926-1939* (Paris: Gallimard, 1983), p. 71.

This extract stages the vengeful upsurge of an element (or memory) repressed in a space constituted by autocratic power, and it is precisely this which the mud of Bouville represents.

We can use the example of the rue Tournebride to illustrate this point. Authorities including the church, the municipal council and leaders of industry transformed a lubricious tract of land ("[in 1847] it must have been a dark, stinking alley with a gutter along which fishes' heads and entrails floated between the paving stones" [65]) into "the meeting place of fashionable and distinguished people" (66). As Sacré-Cœur was erected in Paris to commemorate victory over the Commune, so, in Bouville, a new church — Sainte-Cécile-de-la-Mer, a "monstrous edifice" to industrial success (66) — is built by a group of men who wish to "hold in check the parties of disorder" (122); it is erected on the former site of the Halle-aux-Morues (*morue* means both cod and prostitute). Designed to enable the separation of middle-class worshippers from "the shopkeepers" (65), of clean from dirty, orderly from disorderly, the rue Tournebride, "which was dirty and ill-famed, had to be entirely rebuilt and its inhabitants were driven firmly back behind the place Sainte-Cécile" (66). Segregation, repression and strict hierarchism between high (the Coteau Vert, home of the rich) and low (the aptly named boulevard Maritime, home of the less wealthy) appear to have contained the chthonic, original element, represented by the water. Indeed, the apparent victory of force over the sea is celebrated in specially commissioned artworks, art itself of course being a symbol of the civilization of the chthonic:

> [The bourgeoisie] had entrusted themselves to a celebrated painter so that he should discreetly carry out on their faces the dredging, drilling, and irrigation by which, all around Bouville, they had transformed the sea and the fields. Thus, with the help of Renaudas and Bordurin, they had enslaved the whole of nature: outside themselves and in themselves. (131)

There are many aspects of Bouville which remind us of Haussmann's project to cleanse, control and organise Paris: the axial system of boulevards and avenues which cut communicative lines across its flesh ("behind me the boulevard leads to the heart of the town, to the big fiery jewels of the central streets, to the Palais Paramount, the Imperial, the Grands Magasins Jahan" [41]); a concern with the monumental and the monumental perspective (the statue of Impétraz stands imperiously at the centre of the town square; Sainte-Cécile is constructed on a site which allows an unfettered view); the clearance of slum areas and the appearance in their place of libraries, museums and parks. This colonisation of urban space reproduces the model described by William Curtis: "the splendid city centres with their monuments to consumption and cultural display, and the squalid factories, slums and tenements on the fringes".[18] Such was the project of Haussmann, to create a "great consumer's market, a vast workshop, an arena of ambitions" (Curtis, p.23), a disciplined urban space, organised around the principles of light, circulation and surveillance. J.J. Honeger, writing in 1874, notes: "Haussmann's urban works are a wholly appropriate representation of the absolute governing principles of the Empire: repression of every individual formation, every organic self-development, 'fundamental' hatred of all individuality".[19] The desired effect of this urban politic of apotropaic and efficient rectilinearity is what Le Corbusier — whose work was very much in the public eye at the time Sartre was researching and writing *Nausea*, and was indeed implemented by the city planners of Le Havre — called a 'hygienic space'; in French, *le propre* — the clean and the self-same. The rue Tournebride, in its ritualised homogeneity and banishment of what Adrian Rifkin has called (with reference particularly to the 1920s and '30s) the "fantasmagoric margins",[20] appears also to exemplify this aspect of urban policy.

However, architectural and urban historians have been quick to point out that this process of what Walter Benjamin called "strategic beautification",[21] designed to quell revolutionary and disruptive forces, projected a "city of finite form" (Curtis, p. 35) onto what was very clearly a city in tremendous process. There was anxiety as the urban fabric was "ripped, patched, extended, holed" (Curtis, p. 35). Curtis also notes that "industrialisation changed the size, shape and relationship of buildings in the cityscape, disturbing pre-existing conventions of representation and exacerbating uncertainties about the

---

[18] W.J.R. Curtis, *Modern Architecture Since 1900*, 3rd ed. (London: Phaidon, 1996), p. 23.
[19] Quoted in W. Benjamin, *The Arcades Project*, trans. by H. Eiland and K. McLaughlin (London: The Belknap Press of Harvard University Press, 2003), p. 122.
[20] A. Rifkin, *Street Noises: Parisian Pleasure, 1900-1940* (Manchester: Manchester University Press, 1993), p. 28.
[21] Quoted in S. Buck-Morss, *The Dialectics of Seeing: Walter Benjamin and the Arcades Project* (Cambridge, Massachusetts; London: The MIT Press, 1989), p. 90.

basis of style" (p. 34). Railways, for example, (and of which Bouville has two) "epitomized the semantic confusion" of a city which had "a utilitarian shed on one side, an urban façade of uncertain form on the other" (Curtis, p. 34). In *Nausea*, this is most clearly visible around the boulevard Noir, where two zones meet and implacably confront each other: "The asphalt ribbon breaks off sharply. On the other side of the street there is darkness and mud" (41); "The three saw-works of the Soleil Brothers [...] open on the west, with all their doors and windows, on to the quiet rue Jeanne-Berthe-Cœuroy, which they fill with purring sounds. On the boulevard Victor-Noir they turn their three backs, joined by walls" (41-42).

Additionally, Susan Buck-Morss makes the valuable point that these urban 'renewal' projects

> attempted to create social utopia by changing the arrangement of buildings and streets – objects in space – while leaving social relations intact. Under Haussmann, schools and hospitals were built, and air and light were brought into the city, but class antagonisms were thereby covered up, not eliminated. Haussmann's slum 'clearance' simply broke up working-class neighbourhoods and moved the eyesores and health hazards of poverty out of central Paris and into the suburbs. (Buck-Morss, p. 89)

We are confronted, then, with the unhealing scar of process and change in the model (or planned) city, and a series of 'other spaces' which are provisionally concealed but whose very existence threatens the stability of the dominant centre. Earlier, we made mention of the way in which the industrialists of Bouville had transformed themselves, with the help of renowned artists, into an imposing portrait. This transformation was expressed in the same terms used to articulate the construction of the city. As we know, however, one of Roquentin's functions is to undermine the spirit of seriousness which underpins the portraits in the municipal gallery; equally, as we shall now go on to show, he will reveal the internal inconsistencies and 'other spaces' (or 'heterotopias') of the urban topos. As such, and as his experience in the town square reveals, he represents a force of unwelcome disruption: "A vague power emanates from [the statue of Impétraz], like a wind pushing me away. Impétraz would like to drive me out of the cour des Hypothèques. I shan't go before I have finished this pipe" (47).

"The memories we elude catch up to us, overtake us like a shadow. A truth appears suddenly in the middle of a thought, a hair on a lens."
(Anne Michaels)

It is Roquentin who first reveals the mud which lies scarcely concealed beneath the surface of Bouville. At one level, his primal experience with the pebble reveals a shift from a topological account of space to one which derives from the encounter of the self with objects, in other words, the spatial *relation*: "It was a flat pebble, completely dry on one side, wet and muddy on the other" (10). The viscosity of the mud can be read as representing a mucoid *entre-deux*: the lubrication between the self and the world; a promoter of unwelcome porosity, boundary dissolution and intersubjectivity. Thus, as Roquentin contemplates the monstrous pebble, we register his fear of contamination: "I held it by the edges, with my fingers wide apart to avoid getting them dirty" (10). Unfortunately for Roquentin, this is the nature of the self's position in the world. The narrative will go on to reveal that space is constituted in its relation with human consciousness, a notion to which we shall return presently. At another level, the mud represents the unwelcome irruption (or prehistoric reminder) of chthonic reality in civilization: the encounter between disruptive water and the model city. When the dry pebble described in the 'Undated Sheet' slyly reveals its slimy underbelly to Roquentin, this marks the beginning of the inexorable slide of the *immaculate* (or architectonic) city and subject towards their fantasmal, primal and unspoken origins.

The intrusion of the mud can be linked via Balzac's *Le Père Goriot* (whose protagonist — Rastignac — is mentioned by name in *Nausea*)[22] to the *impropre* which Haussmann and, later, Le Corbusier sought to erase from the model city. Completed in 1834, *Le Père Goriot* constitutes a kind of *pre-history* of both modern (post-Haussmannian) Paris and the fragile urban carapace described in

---

[22] Allusions to this work can also be detected in Sartre's juvenilia. For example, both Frédéric (*Une Défaite*) and Rastignac undergo a painful 'éducation sentimentale', which culminates in their contemplation of the city beneath them. In *Andrée* the narrator's mission on behalf of a friend to retrieve compromising letters from a former lover reminds us of Rastignac's role in retrieving letters written by Mme de Beauséant to Count Ajuda. One might suggest that Loosdreck, the unfortunate provincial teacher of *Jésus la Chouette*, bears – in his (misguided) devotion to his family and his miserable death – great similarities to Goriot.

Nausea. The Paris of Balzac — "an ocean of mud in which a man might drown if he so much as stepped in it"[23] — is a fragmented space which, with the exception of occasional clusters of propriety, is a medieval, vermin-ridden space clogged with effluence and mud, and clouded by deep, disorienting fogs. It is a city settled precariously on a welter of mud that serves not only to inhibit and frustrate Parisians in their daily encounters with the city, but also as a metaphor for the *bassesses* (baseness) upon which cosmopolitan and polite society is hypocritically — and unsteadily — erected. Vautrin describes the city as a quagmire (Balzac, p. 101) across which the young Rastignac must tread "with a thousand precautions in order not to dirty himself" (Balzac, p. 108). "Come on kid, you need at least twenty-five thousand in your pocket if you don't want to land in the shit..." (Balzac, p. 215). Mme de Langeais, a wealthy aristocrat and friend of Rastignac's cousin, echoes his opinion: "The world is a quagmire. Let us endeavour to remain above it" (Balzac, p. 134). Inescapably, it seems, traces of the *bourbier* – in the form of mud on his frequently polished shoes – cling obstinately to Rastignac as he attempts to make his way in the upper echelons of Parisian society, reminding him of the depths he seeks to escape.

The mud which clogs Balzac's Paris is thematically and metaphorically similar to the mud of Sartre's Bouville. This view is supported by clear intertextual resonances, for example in a scene in the Café Mably when Roquentin observes the behaviour of a couple at a neighbouring table. As they are about to leave, he notes:

> I lowered my eyes so as not to seem to be staring at them. After a few moments I heard a creaking noise and I saw the hem of a skirt and two boots stained with dry mud appear. The man's shoes followed, polished and pointed. They came towards me, stopped and turned around: he was putting on his coat. At that moment a hand started moving down the skirt at the end of a stiff arm; it hesitated slightly and then scratched the skirt.
> 'Are you ready?' asked the man.
> The hand opened and touched a large splash of mud on the right boot, then disappeared. (106)

---

[23] H. Balzac, *Le Père Goriot* (Paris: Livre de Poche, 1995), p. 320 (all translations for this book are the author's own).

There are self-evident similarities between this and Rastignac's unfortunate predicament as he crosses the city to visit his cousin, Madame de Beauséant: "The student got dirty and was forced to have his boots polished and his trousers brushed at the Palais-Royal" (Balzac, p. 108). Like the boots of the young woman in the café, his shoes — despite all polishing — retain an indelible "faint mud stain" (Balzac, p. 102).

What, then, is the significance of mud in the mythology of the urban space? On the one hand, it serves as a persistent, archaeological intrusion, a reminder of the city's origins and the repressions which have been effectuated in order to constitute it. A similar disturbance — repressed but ever present — is described by Sartre in *La Reine Albemarle*. He recounts how the Altieri palace in Rome – while prompting the demolition of innumerable dwellings which stood in its path — was eventually built around a hovel belonging to an old lady, who refused to give way to the builders and sell them the land. As a result, and because the Pope finally gave in: "it seems that the edifice still bears on its flank the mark of papal moderation: a little window which disrupts the harmony of its lines".[24] What is interesting, Sartre notes, is that the same story can be found one hundred years later, in the Prussia of Frederick II. In fact, "this same story reappears every time big business decides to ruin its smallest competitors..." (*La Reine Albemarle*, p. 28). It seems, then, that for Sartre all construction carries the indelible trace of its other. What, then, *is* the viscosity of Bouville? A rich, inescapable and sometimes fantasmagorical substratum of the ordered town, like the people who had been *refoulés* when the new church was built, it represents the return of the repressed, an otherness which is all the more disturbing for having been repressed.

Le Corbusier writes that the elimination of "this mould which eats away at the pavements" and "the primitive hut", a focus on "cleanliness" and the "recuperation" of squalid parts of the city are vital to "the architectural symphony we must create".[25] Like mud, the recurring eruption of the colour *black* in the city alludes to the chthonic elements which the model city seeks to repress. It also acts as

[24] J.-P. Sartre, *La Reine Albemarle ou le dernier touriste* (Paris: Gallimard, 1991), p. 28 (author's translation).
[25] Quoted in F. Choay (ed.), *L'Urbanisme: utopies et réalités, une anthologie* (Paris: Seuil, 1965), pp. 241-242.

another marker of the city in process, when by process we mean either burgeoning life forms ("I've seen enough of living things, of dogs, of men, of all the flabby masses which move about spontaneously" [41]) or an inherent tendency towards decay. There are frequent references to the pink urban tissue which veils the body of the city: "the pink gentle streets" (45), "a square paved with pink bricks" (45), "its pink bricks and its houses" (46). However, black and green, the colours of decomposition and decay, threaten the pink façade much like the flies, fungi and other *memento mori* that haunt the fruits and flowers of *vanitas* paintings. Roquentin muses that the pink-bricked town square might once have been "a cheerful place", but now "there is something dry and evil about it, a delicate touch of horror" (46). Dr Rogé's cheeks are pink, as befits an exemplary citizen, yet they are "a horrible pink colour" (103) and cannot conceal from Roquentin the death which lies just beneath the surface. Similarly, old ladies dressed in black swarm like flies around the pink paved square, congregating at the feet of the statue (or corpse?) of Gustav Impétraz, which itself is slowly rotting. Even bronze, it seems, is susceptible to the disfigurements of time:

> I look Impétraz full in the face. He has no eyes, scarcely any nose, a beard eaten away by that strange leprosy which sometimes descends, like an epidemic, on all the statues in a particular district. He bows; his waistcoat has a big bright-green stain over his heart. He looks sickly and evil. (47)

This colour scheme of urban decay finds its parallel in embodied human existence: "If you existed, you had to exist *to that extent*, to the point of mildew, blisters, obscenity" (183-184). The blemishes and rottenness of the city reveal to us that to be in the world is to begin to decay and die; existence disintegrates from the inside.

Black plays a second and important function in that it denotes a space *beyond* the city, a heterotopia. The boulevard Victor-Noir is constituted by "layers of black", at the end of which Roquentin is able to "make out a pale patch of pink: it is the avenue Galvani" (42). Other than registering a sensation of dark, icy coldness (40-43), Roquentin undergoes a kind of sensory deprivation in this tunnel-like space. He notes: "The air does me good: it hasn't got the taste of sugar nor the winey smell of vermouth" (40). The noise from the saw mills is muted in this part of town (41) and "familiar noises, the roar of motor-cars, shouts, and the barking of dogs scarcely stir from the lighted streets, they stay where it is warm" (42-43). The boulevard Noir is abiotic: all signs of life ("nobody *lives*" here [41]), and thus process, are distinguished as the requisites for life — light and warmth — are extinguished. To this end, the blackness of the boulevard finds its counterpart in *light*: the Nausea stays "over there, in the yellow light" (43); ordinary mortals are drawn away from the boulevard, "led to the lights" (45). The processual nature of the space beyond the boulevard is framed in metaphors of female sexuality and fecundity. At its extremities, the boulevard is impure: the presence of the railway station has, for example, "fertilised the first hundred yards", and "spawned' a series of street lamps and cafés" (41). However, moving along the boulevard, Roquentin notes: "I have gone out of the range of the street lamp; I enter the black hole" (42). The hole, "this canal" (44) is unwelcoming to life: "I have the impression of plunging into icy water" (42). This space is "the reverse side of the rue Jeanne-Berthe-Cœuroy, of the avenue Galvani" (43), and the reverse side of the female sex. It has an austerity which challenges "the indecent look of bourgeois streets, which try to charm the passers-by" (43). In fact, Roquentin believes he has found in this blackness something refreshingly inhuman, beyond process ("Like a mineral") and sex ("Like a triangle") (43).

Utopia and heterotopia

In *La Force de l'âge*, Simone de Beauvoir describes the influence of Kafka's *Metamorphosis* and *The Trial* on *Nausea*. She writes: "in both cases, the hero distances himself from his familiar surroundings; the result for him is that the human order collapses and he falls alone into a strange, shadowy place" (Beauvoir, p. 214 — author's translation). This marks a significant transition from the katabatic narratives of the juvenilia, in which the protagonist arrives at a pre-constituted, albeit ambiguous space. What Beauvoir is suggesting is that for Sartre, like Kafka, *another space* — and one which is at some remove from 'normal' societal space — is created by the protagonist himself. In this sense, the purgatorial space is no longer one in which 'relentless opposites'[26] co-exist; rather, it is something akin to what

---

[26] M. Foucault, 'Of other spaces, heterotopias', 1967, http://foucault.info/documents/heteroTopia/foucault.heteroTopia.en.html (accessed on the 29th of September 2004).

Foucault has called a *heterotopia*: 'un espace autre'. For Lefebvre, who adopted the term from Foucault, Bouville counts as a heterotopia by dint of its being a port, and thus open and heterogeneous: "places devoted to exchange and commerce are unmistakably marked with the signs of heterotopia".[27] Beyond this, however, the spaces which Roquentin inhabits and creates might also be categorised as being somehow 'other'. The Boulevard Noir, as we have just described it, resembles what Foucault calls a heterotopia of crisis; a space in which a subject in the throes of change or calamity can seek refuge or distance from others.

Foucault also posits a heterotopia of deviance, which I would like to think of, in the context of *Nausea*, as a verminous space practised synchronously with — and at the heart of — bourgeois utopia. A panoply of verminous creatures — "headstrong characters and eccentrics" (103) — inhabit Bouville: rats (M. Achille), slugs (the Autodidact), cockroaches (the old woman) and insects (the man who exposes his body from beneath his shiny, purple cloak). Roquentin himself, like Baudelaire's *flâneur*, is excluded from the city centre (the centre of production), due to his status as parasitical *rentier*. These characters haunt the marginal and transient spaces of the city: cafés, reading rooms, and the industrial wastelands around the Boulevard Noir (where, we are told, the 'normal' inhabitants of Bouville refuse to live [41]). However, it is the propensity of vermin to inhabit also the interstices of organised space: the Autodidact uses the library (a feature of the Haussmannian city) to admire and flirt with boys; Roquentin saunters with his critical gaze down the rue Tournebride, his existence unacknowledged by the *habitués* such as Coffier; and the old woman, whose presence serves little function in the narrative other than to recur and thus disrupt, faces up to the fearful statue of Impétraz:

> I see an old lady timidly emerge from the arcade and look at Impétraz with a shrewd, stubborn expression. She suddenly plucks up her courage, crosses the courtyard as fast as her legs can carry her, and stops for a moment in front of the statue with her jaws working. Then she runs away again, black against the pink pavement, and disappears through a crack in the wall. (46)

---

[27] H. Lefebvre, *La Révolution urbaine* (Paris: Gallimard, coll. Idées. 1970), p. 17 (author's translation).

These disruptions serve to undermine the propriety of the urban space; they also reveal how that space is purposefully constituted and aggressively defended. The character of the rue Tournebride, for example, has been developed by its bourgeois inhabitants and is maintained by a series of prescriptive (and exclusive) rituals which are, moreover, virtually impenetrable to the uninitiated. The draughtsman and his wife, while attempting to make their "first communion" in this sacred space, are marked out as deviant by their dress, accents, values and demeanour (70). However, Roquentin notes that while the centre is a fortress of bourgeois propriety, the extremities of the street are more heterogeneous, escaping the surveillance of the centre. Equally, should one stroll along the rue Tournebride at an unprescribed hour, one notices that "nothing distinguishes it any more from the neighbouring streets" (81). Roquentin's choice to live adrift — in the temporal sense — from the other inhabitants of Bouville constitutes another kind of heterotopia. A good example is when he chooses to walk along the jetty rather than visit family members or the cemetery, as is the custom: "Not my afternoon, but theirs, the one a hundred thousand citizens of Bouville were going to live in common" (76), thus creating an *other* (real) space within (utopian) space. In addition, this temporal shift can take the form of impudent memory. Again in the rue Tournebride, Roquentin remembers *another time*, and thus creates another space. Significantly, his memory is of

> an impudent little shop [which] still displayed an advertisement for the Tu-pu-nez insecticide. It had flourished at the time when codfish was hawked on the Place Sainte-Cécile, it was a hundred years old. The display windows were rarely washed: you had to make an effort in order to distinguish, through the dust and mist, a crowd of little wax figures dressed in flame-coloured doublets, representing mice and rats. [...] I was very fond of this shop, it had a cynical, obstinate look, it insolently recalled the rights of vermin and dirt a stone's throw from the most costly church in France. (66-67)

Although the new owners had done their best to destroy this memory of pestilence by rebranding the shop as 'La Bonbonnière', the sweet pinkness of its façade is not enough to prevent Roquentin from remembering and uncovering that which was repressed.

Roquentin's engagement with Bouville, and his creation and revelation of heterotopic spaces within it, brings us to a preliminary conclusion. Roquentin notes: "in another world, circles and melodies kept their pure and rigid lines. But existence is a curve" (184). However, as the end of *Nausea* and indeed *Being and Nothingness* both suggest, the human subject will strive, by whatever means, to reimpose that rectilinearity (or organisation) upon chthonic existence. Such is the ontological pro-ject which underpins Sartrean thought. In this sense, he is not so different from Le Corbusier, who wrote that "the human animal is like the bee, a constructor of geometrical cells";[28] "man, by reason of his very nature, practises order; that his actions and his thoughts are dictated by the straight line and the right angle, that the straight line is instinctive in him and that his mind apprehends it as a lofty objective" (Le Corbusier, p. 23). However, when Le Corbusier castigates the disruptive and chthonic element — the *curve* of existence, or the 'pack-donkey's way' — Sartre parts company from him. At this point, rather, his dialectical ontology brings him closer to the urban theory of Henri Lefebvre who, while acknowledging that "the non-city and the anti-city will conquer the city, make it explode" (Lefebvre, p. 25), also believes that the effect of this process is urban *reality*.

Earlier, we applied Slavoj Zizek's theory of fantasy to account for the nightmarish return of the real in *Nausea*. To conclude, I should like to return to his work now, noting how he construes identity as a "*phantasmic* promise", "alternately compelling and disappointing".[29] Judith Butler summarises:

> the 'subject' is produced in language through an act of foreclosure (*Verwerfung*). What is refused or repudiated in the formation of the subject continues to determine that subject. What remains outside this subject, set outside by the act of foreclosure which founds the subject, persists as a kind of defining negativity. The subject is, as a result, never coherent and never self-identical precisely because it is founded and, indeed, continually refounded, through a set of defining foreclosures and repressions that constitute the discontinuity and incompletion of the subject. (Butler, p. 189-90)

The mud of Bouville, the traces of decay, and heterotopic spaces amount to the fundamental 'defining negativity' of dialectical urban thought. As a heterotopic space, Bouville resists the appellation,

---

[28] Le Corbusier, *The City of Tomorrow and its Planning*, trans. by F. Etchells (London: Rodker, 1929), p. 31.
[29] J. Butler, *Bodies that Matter: On the discursive limits of sex* (London: Routledge, 1993), p. 188.

'journey's end', defying as it does all notions of fixity, the absolute and absolution. Its incompleteness and liminality prompts Roquentin to leave the city for Paris, although (and this is entirely in keeping with the dialectical/ontological process) the *patronne* of the Rendez-vous des Cheminots predicts that he will, sooner or later, return (244). The fact that there is no journey's end seems to annul, of course, the validity of travel; heterotopia discloses the illusory nature of utopia. The real (in other words, *process*) displaces the imaginary. Equally, if space — like existence — is a process without end, then "everything is like everything else: Shanghai, Moscow, Algiers are all the same after a couple of weeks" (62). However, travel — like transcendence (the line, the project) — is an ontological necessity in the face of the immanence and immobility represented by the Home: "A mausoleum, a house, they're one and the same thing", Sartre writes in *Er* (*EJ*: 298). If Sartre finds a solution in terms of the urban, finding authenticity in the deliberately provisional and processual nature of American cities ("they remain in fusion, they never reach the internal temperature of solidification"[30]), it nonetheless remains to be seen what form travel might take when deprived of the illusory, teleological seduction of narrative, 'adventure' and the journey's end.

---

[30] J.-P. Sartre, *Situations III* (Paris: Gallimard, 1949), p. 97.

INTERTEXT

Keryn Stewart

'I Have Finished Travelling': Travel, Displacement and Intertextuality in Jean-Paul Sartre's *Nausea*

Employing a Riffaterrian model of intertextuality, this chapter explores the ways in which later intertexts inform and transform Jean-Paul Sartre's Nausea, *revealing its investments not only in the Existentialism traditionally attributed to the text, but also in Surrealism. The relationship between these two seemingly oppositional forces is paralleled by the novel's wider concern with the processes of displacement, which, as the intertexts* Love and Nausea *and* Paris, Texas *expose, is figured by the recurrent metaphor of travel. In this sense, the concept of Nausea can be viewed as a kind of travel sickness, in which anxieties about travel and its analogues act as a means for Sartre to play out similar anxieties about existence.*

* * *

> *TRAVIS: I knew these two people…*
> *JANE: What people?….*
> *TRAVIS: They were in love with each other…*
> *Together, they turned everything into a kind of adventure, and she*
> *liked that.*
> *Just an ordinary trip down to the grocery store was full of*
> *adventure…*
> Paris, Texas, *directed by Wim Wenders*

> *Robert decided to treat the book as a manual for his life.*
> *If he followed the basic injunctions, the rest would follow –*
> *the philosophical insights, the women, the travel.*
> Love and Nausea, *David Wilson*

Jean-Paul Sartre's *Nausea* is a work uneasily balanced between two competing (although not mutually exclusive) forces, with the tension between the novel's status as literature and the philosophical tenets it expresses resonating throughout its narrative of alienation. This tension, however, is usually resolved in favour of a philosophical reading of the text, which foregrounds the metaphysical, and specifically existential, elements of the novel. However, there are several troubling gaps and inconsistencies that result from interpreting the novel through the lens of Sartre's later philosophical writings, in particular how to interpret its apparently 'bad-faith' ending. Using a Riffaterrian model of intertextuality, which posits relevant intertexts as the keys to interpreting these inconsistencies, it is possible to see that this ending participates in a process within the novel in which travel, and specifically nausea as a kind of travel sickness, becomes the dominant system of reference.

The first text which has a bearing on *Nausea*'s negotiation of the problem of travel is, in fact, not an intertext at all, but a paratext: the 'Editor's Note', which prefixes the body of the novel. This text, although short, encodes a preoccupation with travel as well as a recognition of the text's uneasy assimilation of philosophical and literary forms, and in particular the problem presented by the novel's necessary fictitiousness. Although it is tempting, in the wake of post-modernism, to read the supposedly authenticating Note as an ironic pointer to the work's fictive nature, its context within the French literary tradition, as Nicholas Hewitt notes, suggests the opposite, moving the text towards realism rather than self-conscious metafictionality.[1] Despite this, however, the Note's position as the introduction to an obviously creative work means that it necessarily participates in the shifting relationship between *Nausea*'s novelistic and didactic tendencies.

This already uneasy relationship is furthermore complicated by the Note's reference to Roquentin's time spent "travelling in Central Europe, North Africa, and the Far East" (8). In such a compressed space, the inclusion of any information must be significant: why tell the reader, in such detail, of the author's travels? Although consistent with the biographical information likely to be provided in such a note, the scantness of any other extra-textual description of Roquentin begs the question of its inclusion. Critical response to this problem has been unsatisfactory: James Wood, in his introduction to the Penguin translation of *Nausea,* raises the matter only to express scepticism about the "unlikely number of places" (viii) that Roquentin claims to have visited, opining that "[w]e hardly believe that Roquentin was ever

---

[1] N. Hewitt, '"Looking for Annie": Sartre's *La Nausée* and the Inter-War Years', *The Journal of European Studies*, 12 (1982), 96-112 (p. 101).

in Hanoi" (viii). His conclusion, that Sartre "flourishes this fictive quality [...] to let us know that Roquentin is a thoroughly unstable invention who has no real past outside the words of his creator" (viii), fails to do justice to the interplay between travel (and its corollaries of transport, transition and motion) and the philosophical elements of the text. Roquentin's adventures, we feel, *are* significant, and while a reading of this initial paratext can alert us to the workings of travel within *Nausea*, we need to look further.

Love and Nausea, by British author David Wilson, is a novel that postdates *Nausea* by some fifty years; however, it both critiques and expands upon the central preoccupations of Sartre's novel to an extent that makes it an exceptionally useful tool of analysis. Michael Riffaterre, in his model of intertextuality, does not exclude later texts from the status of intertexts;[2] the important factor is that they make explicable an unresolved element in the primary text. Here, *Love and Nausea*'s examination of the unsuccessful transplantation of French Existentialism to a British context expands upon the connection with travel flagged by the Editor's Note. *Nausea,* here, is revealed to be above all a kind of travel sickness, in which the wrenching of its philosophy from its geographic and cultural setting produces a profound displacement.

David Wilson's protagonist, Robert, is deeply impressed by *Nausea,* one of "the first books he'd read voluntarily since Biggles",[3] and "decide[s] to treat the book as a manual for his life" (Wilson, p. 17). In doing so, he thus puts into practice the problem of treating a creative text as a philosophical treatise. His attempts at achieving a state of Nausea are hilariously unsuccessful, with most of the comedy deriving from the incongruous transposition of existentialist tenets to Robert's suburban London locale. Robert, desperate to experience "the Mystery of Being" (Wilson, p. 31), decides that this can only take place in a different world, "the world of Left Bank cafés" (Wilson, p. 31). Unfortunately, the North London analogues of the quintessentially French café culture are laughably unsatisfactory: in desperation, Robert runs through the possibilities, coming up finally

[2] M. Riffaterre, 'Compulsory Reader Response: The Intertextual Drive', in *Intertextuality: Theories and Practices,* ed. by M. Worton and J. Still, (Manchester: Manchester University Press, 1990), pp. 56-78 (p. 75).
[3] D. Wilson, *Love and Nausea* (London: Abacus, 1995), p. 12.

with the pitiful options of the East Finchley Wimpy Bar and the Hampstead Garden Suburb Cake Shop (Wilson, p. 31). The sense of cultural displacement that this reveals, however, cuts to the core of *Nausea*'s structuring paradox, exposing the flaw inherent in treating the novel purely as a philosophical tract. Existentialism, as its unsuccessful transposition to North London would seem to indicate, does not travel well. The philosophical treatise depends for its power on the illusion that its principles are universally applicable; a philosophy so geographically and culturally delimited as the one Roquentin stands for in *Nausea* thus radically undercuts this illusion.

The importance of locale in this balancing of philosophy and literature is emphasised in Wilson's text. Robert persistently links ideology to specific places — feminism to Calabria, Existentialism to Paris, the 'Middle Class Myth of Love and Marriage' to his own milieu in suburban London — but this drive to particularise, to localise, and to map is antithetical to that required to 'read' ideological texts successfully. In order to accept Roquentin's existential experiences as universal, Robert must read them outside of place and time, both Roquentin's and his own. The psychological and cultural disorientation this act engenders is not, in the relevant sense, a specifically Sartrean Nausea; but, in artificially wrenching the 'philosophy' of *Nausea* from its complex matrix of geographical and cultural referents, Robert experiences *Nausea* as a kind of travel sickness. Once again, Existentialism is revealed not to travel well.

Once this preoccupation with travel and travel sickness is uncovered, a whole hidden system of referents to travel resurfaces in the primary text. The most telling of these are the multiple, anxious references to the sea. Gripped by a bad bout of Nausea, Roquentin rushes to the sea-shore to seek respite from another symbol of transition and movement, the doors:

> I suddenly came out on the quai des Bassins du Nord. Fishing boats, small yachts. I put my foot on a ring set in the stone. Here, far from the doors, I was going to know a moment's respite. On the calm water, speckled with black spots, a cork was floating. (115)

However, the comfort the sea provides is fleeting, as Roquentin contemplates the horrifying disparity between its appearance and reality:

'And under the water? Haven't you thought about what there may be under the water?' A monster? A huge carapace, half-embedded in the mud? A dozen pairs of claws slowly furrow the slime. (115-6)

Now, the sea-shore, in existentialist terms, threatens because of its very liminality, with the division between the liquid ocean and the solid land being in a state of continual slippage and flux which is deeply disturbing. For Roquentin, however, an extra element of disgust is triggered by the sea's unacceptable false surface, the sheer meretriciousness of its "thin green film" (179), constituting a nauseating experience in itself.

If we shift the focus to the sea, thus reclaiming the term 'nausea' from the accumulations of existential philosophy with which it has become encumbered, we remember that its root meaning encodes a link with travel: 'nausea' is derived from the Greek word for ship, *naus*. Ships and the sea feature strongly in *Nausea*, although in contrasting and often puzzling ways. That they form part of the text's overall concern with the ramifications of travel, however, is confirmed by Roquentin's undeniably ambivalent relationship with the sea.

As he makes clear in his description of his travels, Roquentin's territory — his sphere of operation — traverses but does not encompass the sea:

I have crossed the seas, I have left cities behind me, and I have followed the course of rivers towards their source or else plunged into forests, always making for other cities. (39)

While the text abounds with references not only to travel but the geographical specificity of Bouville, this literary marking-out of territory relies upon primarily terrestrial sites such as cafés, public gardens, libraries, and squares. Cafés, however, function not simply as Roquentin's "only refuge" (33) from the Nausea; for Roquentin, they are "aquariums, ships, stars, or big wide eyes" (27). The binding element in these descriptions is their reference to the marine world, whether in the sense of its physical containment (as in the aquarium) or its metaphorical control (with the image of "stars" suggesting navigation). Even the "big wide eyes", when read as the lights they in fact are, link metonymically with the benignly controlling gaze of the "Caillebotte lighthouse" (81).

In contrast, images of the sea in which these elements of human containment and control are absent both threaten and repulse Roquentin. This ambivalent relationship with the ocean is a function of its relationship to travel, which is a persistent source of anxiety and conflict within the text. That the deep psychic disquiet produced by the experience of travel is obscured in the text by a 'philosophical' reading becomes evident in a re-examination of one of its most famous scenes. Watching some children play ducks and drakes by the seashore, Roquentin experiences a sense of disgusting contingency, which he relates to the pebble he has picked up: "What happened inside me didn't leave any clear traces. There was something which I saw which disgusted me, but I no longer knew whether I was looking at the sea or the pebble" (10). Traditional analysis of this scene has focused upon the latter, and especially on the disturbing viscosity of the pebble, "completely dry on one side, wet and muddy on the other" (10). This position is seemingly supported by Roquentin's later assertions about the event:

> I remember better what I felt the other day on the sea-shore when I was holding that pebble. It was a sort of sweet disgust. How unpleasant it was! And it came from the pebble, I'm sure of that, it passed from the pebble into my hands. (22)

However, Roquentin's repetition of his belief that the pebble, not the seashore locale, is the source of the Nausea smacks of anxious self-persuasion; although he terms it a "sort of nausea in the hands" (22), thus implicating the pebble in its transmission, his subsequent references to this type of nausea employ the language of the threatening sea and its inhabitants. References to hands abound in the text, but it is striking how persistently they are figured in terms of horrifyingly unfamiliar marine animals. From the "crab-like or lobster-like thoughts" (20) of the suspected paedophile "holding out his arms to him from a distance" (20), to the "fishy-eyed men" in cafés (19), to Roquentin's horrified vision of his hand as "a crab which has fallen on its back" (144), marine creatures (and particularly crustaceans) feature strongly in the nightmare imagery of the Nausea. As Roquentin later disgustedly notes, reinscribing his concern with treacherous appearances, "[t]he real sea is cold and black, full of animals; it crawls underneath this thin green film which is designed to deceive people" (179).

Interestingly, the sea is carefully constructed not simply as the cause of the Nausea but also its projected end; in Roquentin's words, "I am gently slipping into the water's depths, towards fear" (19). Even the Nausea which grips Roquentin in the Rendez-vous des Cheminots, in which he is "surrounded, seized by a slow, coloured whirlpool, a whirlpool of fog, of lights in the smoke" (33), suggests the disorientation of a ship lost at sea. To experience Nausea, then, is to lose one's bearings, to drift and float and perhaps become engulfed by an ocean imbued with an obscure menace. Travel, with its sense of carefully written beginnings and endings, can overcome the Nausea for a while. However, as *Love and Nausea* shows, travel can also be deeply disorienting.

Towards the start of *Love and Nausea*, Robert makes a declaration central to the novel: he decides that he will "treat the book as a manual for his life. If he followed the basic injunctions, the rest would follow — the philosophical insights, the women, the travel" (Wilson, p. 17). As this quote shows, philosophy, travel, and sex are, in Robert's conception, crucially interlinked; he "memorise[s] quotations from existential literature and philosophy in the knowledge that it was essential to him ever being truly loved or desired" (Wilson, p. 48), and imagines himself, as he loiters at "the isolated far end of tube-train platforms, as a doomed existential hero struggling to find meaning in an alien world" (Wilson, p. 49). Thus the experience of travel, for Robert, is not merely preliminary to, but correspondent with, the longed-for experience of sex, bounded by the overarching structure of (existential) philosophy. The comedy of Wilson's novel depends in part on the reader's assimilation of this co-identification, and on the recognition that, for Robert, sex may be "a definable place or territory, like France or Spain" (Wilson, p. 58), but is as distant and inaccessible to him as any foreign country.

Wilson brings these concerns to a point in the description of Robert's first real experience of Nausea, which is produced by accidentally seeing his friends having sex in the park in which he has been unsuccessfully attempting to induce the Nausea: "Fiona started to gasp and groan. Right on cue, a tube train plunged into the tunnel, and the tree roots trembled beneath them. Robert felt shocked, giddy, slightly ill even" (Wilson, p. 36).

The linking of trains and tunnels with the sexual act may seem an overdetermined relation (indeed, it is this expected association which generates the scene's humour), but the concentration of both texts on travel (and in particular trains and train stations) transforms the clichéd sexual symbolism into something more by revealing the structures that underlie its deployment. Robert, by collapsing into one three objects of desire (sex, travel/transport and the type of philosophical experience *Nausea* has taught us to associate with the tree root), exposes the dependency (obscured in *Nausea*) of each of these terms upon the other. Philosophy, far from being the dominant mode of explanation an 'existentialist' reading would assume, is in fact only one element in a tripartite structure that underpins the text.

This conflation is expressed in *Nausea* by various means. Françoise, the patronne with whom Roquentin shares an occasional sexual encounter, symbolises desire temporarily slaked, but she is also linked with images of transition and travel. The patronne caters (in both a business and sexual sense) to "commercial travelers" (6), even breaking off one of her meetings with Roquentin because she has "to go down and attend to the customers from the Paris train" (89); furthermore, she is linked to sailors whose freedom of movement between "Brazil or New York or... Bordeaux" (244) contrasts with her own immobilisation in Bouville.

Desire, travel and the experience of Nausea are similarly linked, although through less obvious pathways, in the text's employment of the recurring jazz refrain, *Some of These Days*. Present only in truncated form within the text, *Some of These Days* represents for Roquentin an escape from the crushing realisation of contingency, forming the musical equivalent to the "hard, brilliant" adventure novel that he proposes (controversially) to write at the end of the text. However, *Some of These Days*, although obviously linked to Roquentin's experience of Nausea, seems to present another of those puzzling lacunae within the text which resist closure. Deborah Evans has amply demonstrated the 'Americanness' of the tune, noting its foreignness — the words "belong to another world, another continent"[4] — but the reader feels that its significance within the text extends beyond its place of origin. Interestingly, the song is also linked ambiguously to another emblem of travel, the sea, in a puzzling reversal of movement and stasis: "it flings itself forward, like a cliff against the sea" (36). But it remains unclear why the song is imbued

---

[4] D. Evans, '"Some of These Days": Roquentin's American Adventure', *Sartre Studies International*, 8 (2002), 58-74 (p. 64).

with such importance. This apprehension of a gap in the text brings into play Riffaterre's theory of intertextuality, in which a text external to the original helps to explicate what is missing from the text. Noting that "Intertextuality [...] [is] the one trope that modifies a whole text rather than a sentence or a phrase" (Riffaterre, p. 76), Riffaterre outlines a process by which a specific term, repressed within the primary text, "become[s] a connective when readers become aware that the whole tale narrated at or hinted at is but the long periphrasis for the repressed word" (Riffaterre, p. 64-5). This term, although repressed, thus structures the entire text through its absence, and its reinsertion into the text through intertextual relations recuperates the disturbing gaps that led the reader originally to search for intertexts at all. If, however, one constitutes this repressed term as an object of desire, synecdochically representing the system in which it is the final, explanatory piece, this process begins to resemble that which constitutes the fetish, a crucial operation in *Nausea*.

In light of the general focus of the text upon travel, it is perhaps not surprising that the repressed text here is a place. *Nausea* is set, not in Paris, as might be expected from its status as an existentialist text, but in Bouville, an imaginary composite of French provincial towns. Its repressed intertext, however, is clearly Paris. Not simply a geographical location, Paris encodes a system of signs and cultural referents which, although disparate, unite in the novel into a text, or more specifically an intertext of Nausea. This conception of city as text is not a new one; for the Surrealists, Paris was a giant text, a dazzling chain of signifiers that only the surrealist consciousness could read. Significantly, this type of reading is also linked to travel; one achieved this consciousness by physically wandering the streets of Paris, or by accessing privileged locations such as train stations or gateways. In some ways, surrealist Paris resembled nothing more than a network of fantastical railways, with apparently random links in fact constituting a complex matrix of meaning — no less valid for all it was dreamlike.

Nausea evokes this sense of the city as a surrealist text in a key scene; wandering through the deserted Boulevard Noir, Roquentin observes "scraps of old posters", between which, although they are torn and disconnected, "another unity has established itself of its own accord between the twisted mouth and the drops of blood, the white letters, and the termination *âtre*" (42). This reconciliation of disparate

objects is followed by the apparently incongruous statement that
"between the planks you can see the lights from the railway shining"
(42). However, if we recognise the preceding as a reference to the
Surrealists, the introduction of the railway, which combines both the
sense of motion crucial to travel and the privileging of trains in
surrealist thinking, exposes the unspoken geographical referent: the
train, of course, is going to Paris.

Nausea represses Paris; but *Love and Nausea* redresses the
balance by making Paris an object of almost obsessive concern within
the novel. Robert's tendency to attach a specific place marker to
particular ideologies reaches its apogee in his treatment of Paris. He,
crucially, links Existentialism squarely to Paris, rather than the
provincial setting of Bouville; but Paris also represents the qualities of
intellectualism and philosophical freedom which Robert associated
with Jean-Paul Sartre, and indeed, with French culture itself. Paris, in
Wilson's text, becomes a sort of fetish for France itself, and in
particular the brand of Sartrean Existentialism that Robert reveres.
Much of the text's humour, as we have seen, derives from the
incongruous comparison of Robert's suburban British locale with a
specifically Parisian setting. Robert himself makes obsessive
comparisons to Paris; distracted by an ice-cream van in the local park
when trying to experience Nausea, he wonders "whether ice-cream
vans in Paris play Greensleeves" (Wilson, p. 38), and there are many
more examples of this sort. When we realise how important Paris is as
a repressed term within the text of *Nausea,* operating as the opposing
term to the crushing provincialism of Bouville (but also, crucially, to
the multitude of foreign destinations mentioned in the text), it is
difficult to ignore David Wilson's explicit referencing to the city.

The most important sign that attaches itself to Paris in Wilson's
novel, however, is the relationship of Jean-Paul Sartre and Simone de
Beauvoir, which Robert links both to his own relationship with Eva
and to Roquentin's unfulfilled quest for Anny. The iconic image for
Robert, which he seeks over and over again to replicate, is that of
Sartre and Beauvoir seated across from one another in a Parisian café.
Cafés, as we have seen, signify as specifically French markers in both
texts; however, *Love and Nausea* cleverly parodies the importance of
these symbolic markers in constituting the milieu of the novel.
Robert's idealistic conception of Paris as his spiritual or intellectual
home — and one that he will share with a similarly idealised Eva —

founders spectacularly when he is actually present in the city. Every attempt he makes to recreate the café scene is sabotaged by his solitude, the presence of his hopelessly English parents, or unbridgeable cultural differences. Arriving in Paris, the fictive nature of Robert's attachment — and the gap between the fetishised object and its actual experience — is revealed in the form of a disorienting culture shock:

> Within a few minutes of getting [to Paris], the main experience is humiliation [...] I realise that to the French people in this café, I am different in only a few irrelevant details to the fat Englishwoman in the tight pink t-shirt with 'Très Chic' emblazoned across the bust. (Wilson, p. 120)

This perpetual disappointment, however, does not dent Robert's confidence in Paris as the realisation of his café fantasy. Again, the elements of travel, philosophy and desire are interlinked when Eva sends him a postcard which combines the iconic scene with its appropriate text: "Inside was a postcard of two lovers sitting across a Parisian café table, and on it was written 'De Beauvoir needs Sartre.' Love Eva" (Wilson, p. 268). By taking up the offer in the postcard, Robert takes Roquentin's statement that he is "going to live in Paris. On Friday [I shall] take the 5 o'clock train, on Saturday I shall see Anny" (194) and actualises it. Crucially, however, Roquentin's desire to write an adventure story (a story, in other words, about travel) is reinterpreted by Robert as a love story; by following the "dream" of "De Beauvoir seeks Sartre", he can "confirm his existence and create a certain kind of love story, about equality, spirit, humour and intelligence" (Wilson, p. 270).

Thus, for Robert, Paris operates not only as a portal to this hoped-for experience, but also as its mythical fulfilment. Within *Love and Nausea,* then, Paris comes to occupy a curious position as both the journey and the destination. The final reference to Paris within the text cleverly encapsulates this sense of transition; in transit from London to Bombay, on his way to complete the reunion with the beloved, which *Nausea* left unfulfilled, Robert watches a film entitled *Paris, Texas.* Although its textual presence is fleeting, it is the last time that the crucial term Paris appears in the text. This confers upon it a significance that is borne out by the startling correspondences with Nausea that it reveals. Embedded within *Love and Nausea,* the filmic text *Paris, Texas* encodes an ethos of displacement and loss, and in rejecting the 'romance' endings of both *Nausea* and *Love and Nausea*, in some ways operates as a more successful existential text than either novel.

In discussing the explication of a repressed (but crucial) term, Michael Riffaterre notes that "it takes a whole text to compensate for the disappearance of the repressed intertext, and at the same time to transfer to that text a significance issuing from the intertext" (Riffaterre, p. 76). This description parallels the process at work here; it takes all of *Love and Nausea* to reveal the Parisian intertext that *Paris, Texas* finally explicates.

A film by Wim Wenders, a European director noted for his "existential road movies",[5] *Paris, Texas* is set in the parched heart of modern America. Despite its distance from *Nausea*, both in terms of medium and geography, *Paris, Texas* echoes its themes. Like Sartre's novel, the film features an isolated, alienated protagonist, Travis (Harry Dean Stanton), who is first seen wandering, sunburnt, speechless and bedraggled, from the Texas desert. Like Roquentin and Robert, Travis is searching for a woman he has lost: Jane, the mother of his child, now working in a peepshow parlour. The film also replicates the text's concern with travel, although reducing the almost surrealist aimlessness of *Nausea* to the relentless linearity of the road trip. However, *Paris, Texas* is in some ways a more 'successful' existentialist text than *Nausea*; Travis, too, has had 'adventures' — in one of the film's crucial scenes, he declares that "Together, they [he and Jane] turned everything into a kind of adventure" — but, ultimately, rejects them as factitious.

As an important text of reference in a text (Wilson's novel) which itself works through the problems of reading *Nausea*, *Paris, Texas* encodes within its title a displacement analogous to that which occurs in *Love and Nausea*. Even without specific knowledge of the film's content or context (fuller discussion of which would take us beyond the parameters of this chapter) the compression of the two disparate terms 'Paris' and 'Texas' into an incongruous relation indicates an inbuilt geographical and cultural joke. Wenders thus internalises, in the figure of Travis, the existentialist dilemma regarding both place

---

[5] R. Ebert, "*Paris, Texas.*" *Chicago Sun Times* Dec 8 2002 (on line), http://www.suntimes.com/ebert/greatmovies/paris_texas.html (consulted 15th of September 2003), p. 6.

and history that Roquentin summarises near the end of the novel: "I am between two towns. One knows nothing of me, the other knows me no longer" (240).

A final note on the workings of this intertetxual operation will perhaps provide an explanation for the puzzling primacy of *Some of These Days* within the text. Just before leaving for Paris, Roquentin visits the Rendez-vous des Cheminots to listen to *Some of These Days* one last time. He declares, however, that it is: "a very old record; too old, even, for the provinces; I shall look for it in vain in Paris" (247). *Some of These Days*, is itself a fetishised emblem of Roquentin's relationship with Anny, and by linking it with another repressed and synecdochic object of desire, Paris, Sartre unites irrevocably the elements of travel and desire in the text. Paris is the geographical embodiment of both the desired-for relationship and the achievement of the "metallic transparency" (38) that the song represents. This desire, however, is destined to be frustrated; Roquentin "shall look for it (whether "it" is Anny, Paris, or something "beautiful and hard as steel") in vain", even if he does succeed in writing down (and containing) adventures in a novel.

In addition, the Wenders intertext highlights (once again) the surrealist sympathies of *Nausea*, which are obscured by the persistent categorisation of the text as Existentialism. In juxtaposing the opposing systems represented by the words 'Paris' (which, as we have seen, resonates through all three texts) and 'Texas', Wenders sets up a unity-in-opposition in the film's title that has a distinctly surrealist quality. Mary Ann Caws, in her analysis of André Breton's poetic practice, notes that his surrealist texts hinge upon the "hope, always present, [...] [of] the reconciliation of opposites. If that optimism is lost, then all surrealist hope is gone".[6] Viewed from the perspective of reconciling opposites, of striving to bring the antithetical together, to which *Paris, Texas* alerts us, the jostling relation of Existentialism and Surrealism within *Nausea* — which produces one of the text's most fundamental lacunae — may itself be viewed as an example of surrealist poetics. The dismantling, through intertextuality, of Existentialism's monolithic status as an interpretive tool allows other

---

[6] M. A. Caws, "Reading André Breton" (on line) http://www.centerforbookculture.org/context/no11/Caws.html (consulted 16th of September 2003), p. 3.

paradigms to be entertained in the context of the novel as a creative, rather than didactic, endeavour.

An example of this type of rereading is evident in the representation of the various destinations to which Roquentin has travelled. James Wood's objection to this has been noted above; however, his attack upon the objective 'reality' of Roquentin's travels fails to recognise the text's surrealist influence. Most importantly, the sense of Saigon in particular as a reference point — the end, in Roquentin's terms, of his particular 'adventure' — is an important facet of the text's ambivalent relationship with travel. Although Saigon is only one of a myriad of exotic destinations listed, it is privileged as the locale in which Roquentin first experienced the Nausea, and is thus a hub to which the text constantly returns, albeit along different pathways. The function of the multiple foreign referents (Meknes, Tokyo, Djibouti, Canterbury, Barcelona, etc.) thus becomes explicable: they are not, as Wood asserts, ironic pointers to Roquentin's instability; they are points on a network of gateways and portals between which Roquentin is constantly shuttled. Significantly, it is the Khmer statuette which triggers (along with Mercier's "perfumed beard" [15]) the overwhelming sense of Nausea for Roquentin. When he recounts the experience later, the statuette seems to operate, for him, as an imaginative portal back to the "voluminous, insipid idea" (15) that keeps threatening to overwhelm him. Statues, of course, occupied a privileged position in surrealist thinking, where, encompassing both a sense of arrested motion and dreamlike superfluity, they functioned as markers or signposts to the world of the fantastic. The objective 'reality' of Roquentin's travels is thus irrelevant, rendered nugatory by the destabilising presence of the surreal.

This concept of the surrealist matrix recurs to a degree in *Love and Nausea*, triggered once again by material referents: in this case, the presence of postcards. Irrevocably linked to travel, and explicitly referenced in Nausea by Roquentin's "thick packet of photos and postcards" (54), these images operate both as the proof and the symbol of travel experiences; however, in a surrealist sense, they can act as important gateways. After receiving the final postcard from Eva, which states simply "De Beauvoir needs Sartre" (Wilson, p. 268), Robert imagines the words as a kind of privileged pathway through this matrix, asking himself what it would "be like for two people to come towards each other along the ley-lines of those phrases?" (Wilson, p. 270). This concept of ley-lines, of travel magically initiated by words, is strengthened by the postcard that Robert sends back; in response to the Parisian scene depicted, Robert sends back "a postcard of the London Underground" (Wilson, p. 270), with trains another network privileged in surrealist thinking. This linking of words and travel is symbolically equivalent to that which concludes *Nausea*: Roquentin's desire to write a story about adventures.

The departure from existentialist tenets is thus clear in this ending. Not only is Roquentin proposing to write an adventure novel, the "sort of story that could never happen, an adventure" (252); he is proposing to move to Paris, thus replicating the supposedly 'bad-faith' immersion in adventures of his past. Although, appropriately enough, these adventures are to be transfigured by the act of writing, specifically the creative process of writing a novel; moving to Paris is, in a sense, writing its own adventure. The tension between reading *Nausea* as a philosophical treatise and as a creative work is therefore explicated to a degree, through the complex interweaving within the text of travel, philosophy and desire. Words and travel, travel and desire: *Nausea* ends with the hope that they will be transfigured into something beyond existence, something "beautiful and hard as steel".

Debra Hely

Fact or Fiction? Reading Through the Nothingness Behind *Nausea*

Sartre plays with truths, half-truths and fiction throughout Nausea.
*Roquentin, a fictional historian is an unstable narrator and a perfect
metaphor for Sartre's existentialist view of existence. The space-time
continuum that society relies on as being predictable and stable is as
flighty as Roquentin's grasp on reality. The reader is often left
wondering what is truth and, even, when is truth. A little research
reveals an abundance of purposeful indiscretions. These apparent
indiscretions give the reader an over-abundance of choices as to their
relevant meaning within the context of the novel. But which meaning
should the reader pursue? Is meaning as fluid and ungraspable as a
song floating through the air? Or is meaning found in the unwritten,
in the nothingness behind the words?*

* * *

*First of all the beginnings would have to be real beginnings.
Alas! Now I can see so clearly what I wanted. Real beginnings... (58)*

Nausea was first published in 1938, some thirty years before
Roland Barthes' famous declaration, yet in many ways Jean-Paul
Sartre's novel pre-empted the age of multiplicities. When Barthes
declared the death of the author, he not only gave life to the reader, he
gave the reader responsibilities:

> Thus is revealed the total existence of writing: a text is made of multiple writings,
> drawn from many cultures and entering into mutual relations of dialogue, parody,
> contestation, but there is one place where this multiplicity is focused and that
> place is the reader, not, as was hitherto said, the author. The reader is the space on
> which all the quotations that make up a writing are inscribed without any of them
> being lost; a text's unity lies not in its origin but in its destination.[1]

---

[1] R. Barthes, 'The Death of the Author' in *Image, Music, Text*, trans. by S. Heath
(New York: Hill & Wang, 1977) pp. 142-48 (p. 148).

The multiple meanings that *Nausea* proliferates are such that the reader is challenged throughout the act of reading, with the entire weight of extracting meaning from authorial duplicity on her shoulders. Her individual life experiences and background will colour both her interpretation and insights into *Nausea*. Hence, an English-speaking reader with no linguistic skills in French, but who comes to the novel already familiar with the music of Sophie Tucker, who dabbles in creative writing and who once taught science, is bound to question its very foundations.

There is more to *Nausea* than a single reading can reveal; it has layers, inversions and beneath it all, the unwritten — the nothingness that underpins the novel from start to finish. For that same nothingness that Sartre describes as being secreted by consciousness — the void that mediates between the cogito and the external world, the infinitesimal gap that both separates us from the world and binds us to it, making consciousness intentional — is shifted to a textual level in the novel; just as the truth of the world depends on our relation to it, here the meaning of the text hinges upon the reader's interaction with it. And Sartre uses deliberate distortion of 'objective truth' throughout *Nausea* in order to highlight this reality, this worldliness, of the text. Throughout the novel there are many layers of revelation of truths, half-truths and untruths (the text is, after all, a novel setting itself as a diary that is based, in turn, on novelistic strategies). We shall aim to reveal the historical truths 'lying' behind some of *Nausea*'s references in order to expose a strategy of inverting the facts: inversion is a leitmotiv in *Nausea*; one of the key strategies driving the novel. In this way, it will become clear that behind the surface text there lies an essential nothingness, without which the reading experience of *Nausea* would be a simple matter of noting down statements: in short, Sartre is drawing our attention to the fact that, without nothingness, we should all read blindly, like so many Autodidacts. As Roquentin states so eloquently: "Things are entirely what they appear to be and behind them... there is nothing" (40).

Roquentin's status as a credible narrator is immediately undermined by Sartre; his authenticity is called into question with the obviously bogus 'Editors' Note' that begins *Nausea*; this is not the real beginning that Roquentin pines for in the opening quote. As soon as Roquentin's voice is allowed, he warns the reader that although his aim in writing a diary is "to neglect no nuances or little details", there is a danger that "you exaggerate everything, you are on the look-out and you continually stretch the truth" (9). Only eleven pages of writing later he confesses: "It's odd: I have just filled up ten pages and I haven't told the truth, at least, not the whole truth" (20). However, if the reader is anticipating a contrite apology for such omissions, Roquentin has other ideas entirely, as deception seems to impress him: "I admire the way we can lie, putting reason on our side" (20). Surely this is a caveat for the reader: Sartre is playing with the first-person narrative. Roquentin may or may not be telling truths or he may or may not be deliberately omitting them. Either way, nothing is assured.

Roquentin claims to be an historian, purposely living in Bouville in order to pursue leads for his biography of the Marquis de Rollebon. According to Roquentin, Rollebon was an instrumental character who took an active role in both the assassination of Tsar Paul I and the French Revolution. But Roquentin's initial enthusiasm begins to wane, as does the ink with which he has made his notes; even the Marquis' face "has grown much paler since I started taking an interest in him" (25). Does this allude to the fact that the Marquis will soon fade to nothing as far as Roquentin is concerned? Or should we infer that he never existed?

Sartre appears to be playing with the past, with history itself, which is consistent with his existential philosophy and view of history. In his book on Sartre, Neil Levy says:

> Historians have often been puzzled by the fact that the less harshly oppressed will frequently be quicker to revolt than the more. It is, Sartre thinks, a difference in ability to nihilate the situation which explains this apparent anomaly. [...] In order for us to revolt against our historical situation, first we must nihilate it. But for us to nihilate it, it is necessary that we be able to conceive of a different state of affairs – not as an impossible dream, but as a real possibility. As soon as we are able to do this, we can transcend the objective situation...[2]

Seen in this light, it is possible to view Sartre's distortion of facts as an invitation to the reader to make her reading experience a 'transcendental' act; with so many different possibilities on display, the reader is almost forced to read in good faith. Indeed, Sartre warns the reader straightaway that Roquentin is no ordinary historian:

---

[2] N. Levy, *Sartre* (Oxford: Oneworld Publications, 2002), p. 90-91.

> I don't think the profession of historian fits a man for psychological analysis. In our work, we have to deal only with simple feelings to which we give generic names such as Ambition and Interest. Yet if I had an iota of self-knowledge, now is the time when I ought to use it. (13)

Traditionally, a reader expects authenticity from an historian, even if he is a fictional character. Sartre's interest, on the other hand, seems to lie in transcending any idea of an objective truth and its place in time. History itself is to be nihilated. In a moment of angst, Roquentin realises he is unable to write anything further about Rollebon. The present overwhelms him, forcing an insight, an insight that negates history, or at the very least, questions its being. Nothingness, it seems, although hard to imagine, is at the core of everything, even our past.

> The true nature of the present revealed itself: it was that which exists, and all that was not present did not exist. The past did not exist. Not at all. Neither in things nor even in my thoughts. True, I had realized a long time before that my past had escaped me. But until then I had believed that it had simply gone out of my range. For me the past was only a pensioning off: it was another way of existing, a state of holiday and inactivity: each event, when it played its part, dutifully packed itself away in a box and became an honorary event: we find it so difficult to imagine nothingness. (139-140)

When Roquentin complains that Rollebon irritates him (87), the reader questions whether or not this is a device for Sartre, and whether he, Sartre, is also complaining that Roquentin is annoying him. Answers do not come readily to the reader questioning Sartre, Roquentin or *Nausea*, as the text often sits uneasily, even when at its most ironic. For example, Roquentin is more than annoyed when he catches Rollebon lying:

> I feel full of ill-will towards that lying little fop. Perhaps this is injured vanity: I was delighted to find him lying to others, but I would have liked him to make an exception of me: I thought that we were as thick as thieves and that he would be sure to end up telling me the truth. He has told me nothing, nothing at all... (87)

This use of *mise en abyme*, using Rollebon to stand in for the unreliable diarist that is Roquentin, calls the awareness of *Nausea*'s reader into question. At the same time, Sartre anticipates and cleverly diffuses his reader's annoyance with his own literary deceptions: possibly even creating an ironic in-joke for the more informed reader. No doubt the references to the mud and sticky dirt Roquentin constantly encounters must have provided a source of amusement for the French reader, as James Wood points out in his introduction to Robert Baldick's translation: Bouville translates into Mudtown (viii). By using such humour and irony, Sartre again alerts the reader to the possible instability of the facts within the novel and Roquentin's character. Nothing is more or less trustworthy than the existing text.

Sartre continues to play with truths and half-truths and fiction throughout the novel; he includes both fictional and non-fictional characters from French history. For example, the Parrottin brothers never existed but Diderot and Renan did. Anny adds to the instability when she recounts how she acted opposite "Thorndyke", going on to use the male pronoun, "him" (217). But it was a woman, Sybil Thorndike, who acted on the English stage in that era. Anny's world is the theatre, a place of make-believe that ultimately fails to provide her perfect moments, her happiness. Roquentin fails to interest Anny when he brings up the subject of the "old rag-time" and "the strange happiness it gives" him (216). This song or rather the voice that sings it, which only comes to life on a gramophone, is an important refrain throughout the novel.

Roquentin constantly praises the Negress who sings *Some of These Days,* and momentarily contemplates the life of its male Jewish composer. But Sartre has purposely inversed the attributes of the female Jewish singer, Sophie Tucker, and the black composer, Shelton Brooks. He never names the singer, but leaves clues as to who she is. Sophie Tucker is the perfect singer with whom Sartre can further increase uncertainty in *Nausea*.

In his essay, '"This Lovely, Sweet Refrain": Reading the Fiction back into *Nausea*', Alistair Rolls investigates the thematic content of *Some of These Days*. He proposes that "the ubiquity of the image within the novel, coupled with the fact that Roquentin only ever quotes the refrain of the song, serves to veil the reading that the lyrics contain".[3] He then cites the lyrics as follows:

> The little girlie feeling blue said I'll go too
> And show him two can play this game
> When her honey heard this melancholy news
> Why he quickly came back home again
> But when he reached the house he found his girl had gone
> So down he rushes to the train

---

[3] A. Rolls, '"This Lovely Sweet Refrain": Reading the Fiction back into *Nausea*', *Literature and Aesthetics*, 13: 2 (2003), 57-72 (p. 62).

While it was pulling out
He heard his girlie shout
This lovely, sweet refrain.... (Rolls, p. 63)

However, there is more than one recording of *Some of These Days* that can be attributed to Sophie Tucker. The version that Rolls transcribes matches the recording she released in 1911. And yet it is not this recording that Roquentin listens to, but a later one, as he explains when he begins to listen:

Madeline turns the handle of the gramophone. [...] But no, that's it, I recognise the tune from the very first bars. It's an old rag-time tune with a vocal refrain. I heard some American soldiers whistle it in 1917 in the streets of La Rochelle. It must date from before the War. But the recording is much more recent. (36)

In 1926, Sophie Tucker released a newer, slimmer version, with these lyrics:

Some of these days, you'll miss me Honey
Some of these days, you're gonna be so lonely
You'll miss my hugging
You're gonna miss my kissing
You're gonna miss me Honey, when I'm far away
I feel so lonely, for you only
'Cause you know Honey, you've always had your way
And when you leave me
You know it's gonna grieve me
Gonna miss your big fat momma, your momma
Some of these days[4]

Before Roquentin's favourite part, the refrain, starts, he describes what he hears:

For the moment it's the jazz that's playing; there's no melody, only notes, an unchanging order gives birth to them and destroys them, without ever giving them time to recover, to exist for themselves... (37)

It is another page before Roquentin is able to write:

---

[4] Author's own transcription. Modern readers, unlike Roquentin, have access to the internet and, by following the links at the following website, can hear both versions for themselves. The site is: http://www.sfmuseum.org/hist2/days.html (consulted 15th of June 2003).

Silence.
Some of these days
You'll miss me honey! (38)

Tucker's 1926 version of the song has an approximately thirty-four second musical introduction, whereas the 1911 version begins after some nine seconds with the line:

Two sweethearts courted happily for quite a while.[5]

That there could be any confusion over which version Tucker is singing, was no doubt part of the appeal for choosing it in the novel. Sartre does not confine his fascinating use of Sophie Tucker to *Some of These Days*; in all likelihood, she is the voice Roquentin hears singing from a brothel's gramophone:

When the yellow moon begins to beam
Every night I dream my little dream. (149)

The song is easy enough to trace: *The Man I Love* with music by George Gershwin and lyrics by his brother Ira - two white Jewish males. Research reveals that *The Man I Love* has two different lyric versions. The first (and original), which Sophie Tucker recorded in 1928, begins like this:

When the mellow moon begins to beam,
Ev'ry night I dream a little dream[6]

The second, more popular and shorter version begins thus:

Someday he'll come along, The man I love
And he'll be big and strong, The man I love[7]

In 1928 Sophie Tucker was not alone in releasing a recording of *The Man I Love*; four other female singers joined her, one of whom

---

[5] http://www.leonredbone.com/wwwboard/messages/618.html (consulted 12th of June 2003).

[6] http://lyricsplayground.com/alpha/songs/t/themanilove.shtml (consulted 12th of June 2003).

[7] http://www.bluesforpeace.com/lyrics/man-i-love.html (consulted 12th of June 2003).

was Bessie Brown, a Negress.[8] Sartre's inverted circle is complete if it was Brown's recording and not Tucker's. According to another source, the two women could be confused by a novice listener:

> Bessie Brown was a solo act and worked for a time as a male impersonator. She had a deep voice, and belted out her blues in a manner similar to that of "Red Hot Mama" Sophie Tucker.[9]

This evidence points to one of two things: either an amazing coincidence occurred for Sartre; or the man was a genius, and far more painstaking with his research than his literary creation, Roquentin. Roquentin at one stage laments "I don't have a high enough regard for historical research to waste time over [Rollebon]" (87). Be it Sophie Tucker or Bessie Brown singing, the experience of hearing her voice affects him powerfully:

> The voice, deep and husky, suddenly appears and the world vanishes, the world of existences. A woman of flesh had that voice, she sang in front of a record, in her best dress and they recorded her voice. A woman: bah, she existed like me, like Rollebon, I don't want to know her. But there it is. You can't say that that exists. The spinning record exists, the air struck by the vibrating voice exists, the voice which made an impression on the record existed. I am listening, I exist. Everything is full, existence everywhere, dense and heavy and sweet. But, beyond all this sweetness, inaccessible, quite close, so far away alas, young, merciless, and serene, there is this… this rigour. (149)

It seems appropriate that this voice should affect Roquentin so profoundly at this stage in the novel, because at the end of it, listening to Sophie Tucker sing *Some of These Days* for the last time, he finds a new direction for his life, writing a novel, in all likelihood the one the reader has just read.

That Roquentin decides to write a novel comes as no surprise, as he has already considered this option on several occasions. The first being whilst he was still fixated on completing his biography of Rollebon.

---

[8] http://lyricsplayground.com/alpha/songs/t/themanilove.shtml (consulted 12th of June 2003).

[9] http://ubl.artistdirect.com/music/artist/bio/html?artist=Bessie+Brown (consulted 15th of June 2003).

I am beginning to believe that nothing can ever be proved [...] I have the impression of doing a work of poor imagination. And even so, I am certain that characters in a novel would appear more realistic... (26)

Then later, when annoyed with Rollebon's deceit, he asserts that "I would have been better off writing a novel about the Marquis de Rollebon" (88). The journey Roquentin undertakes in order to write this novel is a painful one, as he first has to deal with his own existence, something Rollebon had been protecting him from doing:

Monsieur de Rollebon was my partner: he needed me in order to be and I needed him in order not to feel my being. I furnished the raw material, that material of which I had far too much, which I didn't know what to do with: existence, my existence. (142-143)

Roquentin seems to be on the verge of another encounter with the Nausea, so consumed is he with the angst of his own existence:

My thought is me: that is why I can't stop. I exist by what I think... and I can't prevent myself from thinking. At this very moment – this is terrible – if I exist, it is because I hate existing. It is I, it is I who pull myself from the nothingness to which I aspire... (145)

If history and the memory of an historian, albeit a fictional historian, can be so easily brought into doubt by Sartre, then it follows that the temporal world is also going to be called into question. The fact that Roquentin is keeping a diary constantly draws attention to time, and little errors keep cropping up, particularly with regards to Anny's involvement in Roquentin's life. When he first receives her letter on Shrove Tuesday, he claims that it is five years since he last heard from her (90). Yet, only thirty pages later, he wonders what she has been doing these past six years: the obvious implication being that it is six years since they have last spoken to each other. Then, when he finally gets to meet with her, he twice comments that it has been four years since they have seen each other (196, 218). The reader has no way of determining if one or any of these time frames are correct; Anny neither confirms nor denies Roquentin's recollections.

The timing of their meeting is also dubious. It is clearly a Thursday when Roquentin states, "A week from today I am going to see Anny" (105). But nearly a week later, on the following Wednesday morning he declares he will see her on a Saturday (194). According to

Roquentin's diary entry, he does indeed see her on that Saturday, but can he be believed? A reader who consults a source such as the Collins 100 Year Calendar (as found on the back inside pages of the red Collins 3880 Account Book) to verify something as innocuous as the date of Shrove Tuesday as recorded by Roquentin in his diary, discovers how inaccurate an historian Roquentin is, beginning with the very first date, "Monday, 29 January 1932" (13). In 1932, the date was either Friday, 29 January or Monday, 25 January. Monday, 29 January did occur, but not until 1934, two years later. Moreover, when a reader calculates the dates that are consequently omitted from the diary entries (the days are usually included, but not always), it transpires that Roquentin's last day in Bouville is Wednesday, 28 February. Normally this would be the last day of February, neatly confining the journal to a four-week calendar month, but 1932 happened to be a leap year. Roquentin's last day in Bouville is not therefore the last day of February as the reader might easily assume.[10] The following is a breakdown of the dates and events as given in *Nausea*:

Page	Diary entry	Calculated date
9	Undated sheet	A few weeks before the diary started
10	10.30	Following day
13	Monday 29, January 1932	Monday 29, January 1932
16	Tuesday, 30 January	Tuesday, 30 January
22	Thursday morning, at the library	1 February
24	Thursday afternoon	1 February
27	Friday	2 February
32	5.30	2 February
45	Thursday, 11.30	8 February
48	3 p.m.	8 February
49	Friday, 3 p.m.	9 February
60	Saturday, noon	10 February
63	Sunday	11 February

---

[10] In their notes to Gallimard's 'Bibliothèque de le Pléiade' edition of Sartre's *Œuvres romanesques* Michel Contat and Michel Rybalka seek to re-establish the truth of Roquentin's departure from Bouville; they indicate that the Monday that begins the story must be January 25 and not 29 (the story thus ending on February 24). They note that Sartre had admitted to them that he had had "no intention of altering the chronology of his story", and that it is with his permission that they have chosen to change the date in this French edition of the text [J.-P. Sartre, *Œuvres romanesques* (Paris: Gallimard, 1981), p. 1724 — our translation]. This pursuit of the truth, coupled with the need to ask the author's consent, seems to contradict the novel's status as fiction; it is our intention here not to seek to correct the original but to explore the textual possibilities of the very corruption of truth.

85	Monday	12 February
86	Seven o'clock in the evening	12 February
88	Eleven o'clock in the evening	12 February
89	Shrove Tuesday	13 February
104	Wednesday	14 February
	Thursday	15 February
105	Friday	16 February
119	Saturday morning	17 February
120	Saturday afternoon	17 February
138	Monday	19 February
149	Tuesday	20 February
	Wednesday	21 February
182	Six o'clock in the evening	21 February
194	In the night	21 February
	Friday	23 February
	Saturday	24 February
220	Sunday	25 February
222	Tuesday at Bouville	27 February
228	Wednesday. My last day at Bouville	28 February
239	One hour later	28 February

The calendar is a human invention, a means of measuring time, and Sartre appears to treat it with contempt. We should argue, however, that this is merely another way of demonstrating that only the present exists and that the past is nothing. If this is so, a contradiction arises: if Roquentin was keeping a daily journal, surely at the moment of actually writing he was always in his present, as it existed for him. Or is Sartre making a point, proving that there is "a sort of unsubstantiality of things" (112) even with time itself? As Roquentin writes, "after all, you have to kill time" (161). Once again the answers are as elusive as meaning itself is in *Nausea*.

Truth is a concept that Roquentin struggles to understand, unlike the Autodidact, who somehow believes that truth lies in its own pre-existence. This comes to light when he discusses with Roquentin, an idea he has written. He is disappointed that Roquentin has not read this idea anywhere else prior to hearing it from the Autodidact.

> 'Really, you haven't read it anywhere? Then, Monsieur,' he says, his face falling, 'that means it isn't true. If it were true, somebody would have thought of it already.' (158)

The reader, of course, does not hold much faith with the Autodidact or his beliefs. Even though Roquentin is most sympathetic whenever he describes the latter, he has been dismissed as a humanist, and not a very bright one at that. Further, his disgrace in the library, when his paedophilic tendencies are laid bare, only serves to confirm that he is not a man to be trusted. Still, Roquentin's sympathies again raise more questions for the reader: questions about Roquentin himself. He is so outraged when the Corsican assaults the Autodidact that he acts:

> I grabbed the little Corsican by the neck, and I lifted him up, with his arms and legs waving in the air: I should have liked to smash him on the table. He had turned blue in the face and was struggling, trying to scratch me; but his short arms didn't reach my face. I didn't say a word, but I wanted to hit him on the nose and disfigure him. He realized this, he raised his elbow to protect his face: I was glad because I saw he was afraid. Suddenly he started gasping:
> 'Let go of me, you brute. Are you a fairy too?'
> I still wonder why I let him go. Was I afraid of complications? (238)

The reader cannot help but marvel at this sudden surge of violence from Roquentin, and wonder if other aspects of his character have thus far been veiled. What are the complications that he fears? These complications are the very means of ensuring that Roquentin's 'truth' (be it sexual or otherwise) is negotiated between the text and the reader. Ostensibly, the only sexual relationship he has is with a consenting adult woman, but there is nothing romantic about it, it is merely an *au pair* arrangement for mutual relief. His relationship with Anny seems to be platonic, or even asexual, rather than anything romantic. The only woman that seems to arouse his passions does not exist physically but as a voice in space: his Negress singer.

A careful reading of *Nausea* uncovers many sexually ambiguous incidents in the novel. Nothing is said that would directly implicate paedophilia or homosexual behaviours in Roquentin's character; likewise, nothing is said explicitly to negate these possibilities either. But, as Lawrence Schehr points out in this volume, suspicions are aroused, constantly, starting with the first mild attack of the Nausea. Roquentin determines that something disgusts him, "but I no longer know whether I was looking at the sea or at the pebble. It was a flat pebble, completely dry on one side, wet and muddy on the other. I held it by the edges, with my fingers wide apart to avoid getting them dirty" (10). Is the pebble possibly a metaphor for Roquentin: a man who appears clean or normal on the exterior but is really dirty or corrupt internally? Is this what motivates his inability to settle down in the one place?

When he reveals snippets from his past, he is nearly always on the move, but the reasons for moving are vague at best, he often refers to awakening from dreams of some sort. Other cryptic comments he writes about himself explain nothing, while maintaining a sense of mystery. The reader cannot help but wonder what the nothing that is not there to be read is and what it would reveal if it were.

I should like to understand myself properly before it is too late. (15)

I purge myself in this way of a certain melancholy whose cause I know only too well. (17)

I should like to talk to somebody before it is too late, before I start frightening little boys. (20)

I have been lying to myself for ten years. (58)

Occasionally – not very often – you take your bearings, you realize that you're living with a woman, mixed up in some dirty business. (62)

I am writing to understand certain circumstances. (85)

I feel ashamed for Monsieur Achille. We are of the same sort… (100)

This picture gave me a final warning… (121)

I see underneath! (179)

I started looking through the books on display in the second-hand boxes, and especially the obscene ones, because, in spite of everything, that occupies your mind… (220)

What is occupying his mind throughout these incidents? Could it be thoughts of perversion that he is trying to keep from himself — an existence he does not want to admit? Could it be that he is struggling with his own bad faith? Other attacks of the Nausea are preceded by scenes involving children, which Roquentin never seems to explain fully. For example, why did the vet's daughter (37) suddenly get so scared? Was it the way Roquentin looked at her? Then, later, on his Sunday walk, he seems struck by the number of children about (79), and shortly afterwards, a boy's comments make his "heart swell with a great feeling of adventure" (81). When he recounts the rape and murder of Lucienne (146-149), could he possibly be suggesting that he is the perpetrator of these crimes? Is this the real reason why he has to leave Bouville, or why he can no longer write about Rollebon? The murder has come to be public knowledge and he wishes to avoid being pursued by the police? As usual, nothing makes this clear for the reader.

Ultimately it is Roquentin's relationship with the Autodidact that is most problematic for the reader. Although the Autodidact's humanist views are ridiculed by Roquentin, he always treats him with a certain sympathy or gentleness. Certainly his physical features are delicately described.

> It is time for his afternoon snack; with an innocent air he eats a piece of bread and a bar of Gala Peter. His eyelids are lowered and I can study at leisure his beautiful curved lashes – a woman's eyelashes. He gives off a smell of old tobacco, mingled, when he breathes out, with the sweet scent of chocolate. (49)

Only the tobacco smell would be incongruous if Roquentin had been describing a naïve young girl rather than an adult man.

Tamsin Spargo argues "that sexuality is not a natural feature or fact of human life but a constructed category or experience which has historical, social and cultural, rather than biological origins".[11] Homosexuality is a rather recent concept in our society. As Spargo notes:

> [...] While 16th-century men and women might be urged to confess that they had indulged in shameful sexual practices against the law of God and the land, the late 19th-century man engaging in a sexual relationship with another man would be seen, and be encouraged to see himself, as 'homosexual'. (Spargo, p. 18)

She further notes that in the late nineteenth and early twentieth centuries:

> The homosexual was pathologised as a perverse or deviant type, a case of arrested development, a suitable case for treatment, in short as an aberration from a heterosexual norm. As such, he was subject to the disciplining, marginalising and subordinating effects of social control. (Spargo, 1999: 20)

Throughout most of the twentieth century, writers wishing to introduce a homosexual element into their stories had to resort to codified writing so as to reach their intended target audience without having their words censored. Sartre seems to be operating on this level when Roquentin and the Autodidact have lunch together.

---

[11] T. Spargo, *Foucault and Queer Theory* (Cambridge: Icon Books, 1999), p. 12.

'I'll have sausage,' I tell the waitress. He snatches the menu out of my hands:
'Isn't there anything better? Look, there are Burgundy snails.'
'The thing is that I'm not very fond of snails.'
'Oh! Then what about oysters?'
'They're four francs extra,' says the waitress.
'All right, oysters, Mademoiselle – and radishes for me.'
Blushing, he explains to me:
'I'm very partial to radishes.'
So am I. (152)

In 1960, when Hollywood made the movie *Spartacus*, a similar technique was used. In this case, however, it had to be omitted because of its homosexual nature.[12] The censored *Spartacus* scene was:

> [...] Between Crassius (Lawrence Olivier) and his young slave Antonius (Tony Curtis), in which the older man subtly establishes his taste for both men and women. In the climatic bathing scene, the two are talking about how to treat a woman, when suddenly Crassius seems to change the subject.
> Crassius: Do you eat oysters?
> Antonius: Yes.
> Crassius: Snails?
> Antonius: No.
> Crassius: Do you consider the eating of oysters to be moral and the eating of snails to be immoral?
> Antonius: No, master.
> Crassius: Of course not. It's all a matter of taste, isn't it?
> Antonius: Yes, master.
> Crassius: And taste is not the same as appetite and therefore not a question of morals, is it?
> Antonius: It could be argued so, master.
> Crassius: Um, that'll do. My robe, Antonius. Ah, my taste... includes both oysters and snails. (Russo, p. 119-120)

A comparison reveals a level of intertextuality that may well have pleased Sartre, whose own wilfully ambiguous passage went unnoticed by censors and critics alike. At the end of the lunch in *Nausea,* there is an implication left hanging, that even though Roquentin and the Autodidact disagree politically, they may well have similar tastes in other aspects of life, tastes not commonly discussed in polite company.

---

[12] V. Russo, *The Celluloid Closet: homosexuality in the movies* (New York: Harper & Row, 1981), p. 119.

Roquentin never makes a moral judgement about the Autodidact's behaviour around schoolboys. The first time he observes it, Roquentin notes what happens, managing to elicit some sympathy for the Autodidact when he is caught out:

> He was looking with a smile at his neighbour on the right, a filthy-looking schoolboy who often comes to the library. The schoolboy allowed himself to be looked at for a while, then suddenly put his tongue out at him and pulled a horrible face. The Autodidact blushed… (60)

Finding out that the Autodidact was a prisoner of war certainly engenders further sympathy from Roquentin and the reader. Furthermore, Roquentin's attitudes leading up to and following the Autodidact's disgrace in the library indicate that he sides with the Autodidact. Before the incident is described, Roquentin is already excusing the Autodidact in the eyes of the reader:

> […] For a long time I had felt that his gentle, timid face was positively asking scandal to strike it. He was guilty in so small a degree: his humble, contemplative love for little boys is scarcely sensuality – rather a form of humanism. (228)

In fact, Roquentin recognises their commonality: "like Monsieur Achille, like myself: he is one of my own breed, he is full of good-will" (228).

Prior to the Autodidact's fall, Roquentin maintains a positive view of him with seemingly little regard for the schoolboys. Twice, he anticipates that they will cause the coming problem which he can sense but not predict:

> 'What are they going to do to him?' I thought. I knew something horrible was going to happen. […] I felt as if some nasty brats were going to drown a cat. (233-234)

The Autodidact refuses Roquentin's help after the fall, but Roquentin is the only witness in the library to offer any kindness or to risk caring about the Autodidact's future. The reader is probably astonished to find that she, too, feels sorry for the Autodidact and has concerns about his fate. Roquentin does not encounter the Autodidact again as it is approaching the time that his train will depart from Bouville, and he has some other tasks to achieve before then.

The Autodidact has blended into the nothingness that Bouville is entering into before Roquentin's very eyes. Nothing: the nothingness that existed for the reader concerning Bouville, Roquentin and the Autodidact, before they began reading *Nausea*, perhaps, will return again, after the last sentence is read. Perhaps, or perhaps not.

Sartre does not let the reader escape easily; *Nausea* resonates within, even after the act of reading is complete. Nothingness is not so final. A keen reader will find that she needs to re-read *Nausea* if she wishes to follow all the threads of this skilfully interwoven text that Sartre has crafted. The number of re-readings is up to the individual reader, but she is still faced with a final puzzle, namely the book's ending: "[…] tomorrow it will rain over Bouville" (253).

What sort of closure did Sartre intend by this oblique comment? Is it merely a romantic ending? Or does it signify a symbolic cleansing, a new start for Bouville and Roquentin? Or is it a device to let the reader know that there will be even more mud made in Bouville again tomorrow? Or is it a combination of these possibilities?

Naturally, Sartre gives the reader no insights, he gives nothing. Yet it is this nothing, or the nothingness behind *Nausea*, its very unwritten-ness that makes it both what it is and is not.

Alistair Rolls

Seduction, Pleasure and a Laying on of Hands: A Hands-on Reading of Sartre's *Nausea*

This chapter examines the way in which philosophy and fiction intertwine in Sartre's Nausea*. A case will be made for reading* Nausea *as a powerfully self-referential fictional text that, perversely, owes its very literariness to the philosophy of* Being and Nothingness*. The relationship between the author and reader will be shown to be equally perverse, the ceding of authorial power and empowerment of the reader being shown to be a complex ontological struggle. The author will become a lover seeking to make his text 'the whole world' for the beloved. And at the centre of this erotics of writing will be the hands of both writer and reader; their communication at the interface of the text will be studied as an example of the Sartrean caress.*

* * *

> *Apparently Arab scholars, when speaking of the text, use this admirable expression: the certain body. [...] Does the text have human form, is it a figure, an anagram of the body? Yes, but of our erotic body. The pleasure of the text is irreducible to physiological need.*
> Roland Barthes, The Pleasure of the Text

As was mentioned in the introduction to this volume, there is a shift in position between the writing of the pre-War Jean-Paul Sartre and that of the more visibly existential texts, beginning, for example, with *Huis clos* in 1944.[1] This visible difference has to do with the Other; it does not, however, lie in his own visibility but in his capacity to make us truly, objectively visible. The famous mirror scene in *Nausea*, in which Roquentin's own face becomes other for him, is only revealed in its full potential when *Huis clos* is presented as a markedly, self-

---

[1] Bernard-Henri Lévy, for example, traces the shift from Sartre-Roquentin to Sartre-Autodidact in the section of *Le Siècle de Sartre* entitled 'Devenir son propre Autodidacte' (B.-H. Lévy, *Le Siècle de Sartre : Enquête philosophique* (Paris: Grasset, 2000), pp. 508-13).

consciously mirror-less space. Hell becomes other people because man's only possible being for-others is that which is frozen beyond his control by the Other's gaze. Roquentin appears to emerge at a period when Sartre's philosophical concerns hinge on contingency and the problem of the raw existence in situation of the being for-itself. Roquentin sees others and realises their destructive potential; they, for their part, are as blind to him as they are to their own superfluity. Impétraz, the imposing bronze overlord, cannot see; the mirror shows Roquentin only as he sees himself; and sex, the most dangerous act from the perspective of the struggle for ontological survival, is reduced to the level of crypto-onanism. And yet the gaze of the other is present in *Nausea*, and it is via an analysis of the erotic body of the text that we are able to intertwine satisfactorily both its existential and novelistic mechanics. For it is not the case that concrete relations with others are problematized by Sartre only as early as *Being and Nothingness* (1943); they are crucial to an understanding of *Nausea*, and, ironically, the philosophy of the later treatise can be used not, as is so often the case, to overpower the novel of 1938 but, precisely, to expose its power as fiction.

If we follow Barthes' idea of the pleasure of the text, the act of writing *Nausea* can be seen as the production of an erotic body; reading *Nausea*, by the same token, involves a sensual engagement with the text. The tension that lies at the interface of these two activities we shall label 'seduction'. As Barthes points out, to be seductive a text does not need to be ostensibly attractive or even an 'enjoyable read':

> So, we arrive at this paradox: the texts, like those by Bataille – or by others – which are written against neurosis, from the centre of madness, contain within themselves, *if they want to be read*, that bit of neurosis necessary to the seduction of their readers: these terrible texts are *all the same* flirtatious texts.[2]

Nausea is one of these terrible texts; it depends for its existence — and, for Sartre, the worst criminal act there could be is the production of an existent — upon the engagement of its reader. The reader is the Other, and it is s/he whom *Nausea* seeks to seduce.

---

[2] R. Barthes, *The Pleasure of the Text*, trans. by R. Miller (New York: Hill and Wang, 1975), p. 5-6.

Nowhere is an instance of a text desiring its reader more openly expressed than in the final lines of Toni Morrison's *Jazz*:

I envy them their public love. I myself have only known it in secret, shared it in secret and longed, aw longed to show it – to be able to say out loud what they have no need to say at all: *That I have loved only you, surrendered my whole self reckless to you and nobody else. That I want you to love me back and show it to me. That I love the way you hold me, how close you let me be to you. I like your fingers on and on, lifting, turning. I have watched your face for a long time now, and missed your eyes when you went away from me. Talking to you and hearing you answer - that's the kick.* But I can't say that aloud; I can't tell anyone that I have been waiting for this all my life and that being chosen to wait is the reason I can. If I were able I'd say it. Say make me, remake me. You are free to do it and I am free to let you because look, look. Look where your hands are. Now.[3]

This quotation highlights three elements that help us to reconfigure the role of *Nausea* as novel within Sartre's philosophy of existence: firstly, the intensely sexual nature of the bond between the reader and the text, which will be shown to correspond exactly to the dynamics of the lover/beloved relationship that Sartre puts forward in *Being and Nothingness*; secondly, the role of hands, that with which we write, read (Morrison's narrator catches us in the act, shaming us both in our impertinence and our ignorance of who it is that we have been arousing and by whom we have been being aroused) and caress the other; and thirdly, the tension between authorial power and the empowerment of the reader.

In his article 'The Ending of Sartre's *La Nausée*' Terry Keefe resumes the various arguments as to whether or not *Nausea* is, is not, could or could not be the novel that Roquentin contemplates writing at the end of the text. What is clear to the reader of *Nausea* is that s/he is pitted against an authorial power in a joust for ownership of Roquentin's textuality. The role of Rollebon seems to be more clearly as fictional presence than as historical character; and, crucially, when Roquentin listens to *Some of These Days*, whilst he imagines the salvation of the piece's composer and performer, he is at the same time seducing his own reader, reminding him/her of the power that s/he has to mould his existence as protagonist. Keefe notes how Roquentin begins to think of the composer with sympathy. This can just as easily be reversed — the whole story of the song being built

[3] T. Morrison, *Jazz* (New York: Signet, 1992), p. 264-5.

around a case of reversal (all mentions of history in *Nausea* and its claims to be a genuine diary being exposed as literary tricks)[4] — and this composer be interpreted as the reader, Roquentin prostrating himself as the composed subject.

> [And] in an undeveloped and even enigmatic form, the notions of looking at, or being aware of others, as well as being looked at *by* others are now right to the fore in the book, and are presented in a very complex way.[5]

Consciousness of the gaze of the reader causes Roquentin to revel in his role as read subject, which in turn prompts us to reread his behaviour. So tightly linked are Roquentin's actions and the gaze of the reader that the act of looking at others, in which Roquentin engages at length, comes to signify 'being looked at'; similarly to read becomes 'to be read'. In *Being and Nothingness*, Sartre himself writes of the relationship between the Other and the truth of the self:

> I am possessed by the Other; the Other's look fashions my body in its nakedness, causes it to be born, sculptures it, produces it as it *is*, sees it as I shall never see it. The Other holds a secret - the secret of what I am. He makes me be and thereby he possesses me.[6]

Roquentin, in the same way that he conjures up the singer and composer by listening to the song, is read into being by the reader of *Nausea*. But as the voice of *Jazz* reminds us, "being chosen to wait is the reason [s/he] can". The reader must be wary: what do we risk by summoning up Roquentin? Might we not lose this newly realised power in the climactic pleasure of the text? Whilst Sartre/Roquentin's motivations for seducing the reader are not clear to us, it is seduction itself that is the key, and not the expected result of this game. Understanding seduction carries the key to explaining the lack of textual climax, the *sotto voce* ending of the novel that has been so much discussed.

In *Being and Nothingness* Sartre explains that the crucial problem one faces in relation to the Other is to "make [oneself] be by acquiring

---

[4] For a more extensive analysis of the layers of inversion operating within *Nausea*, see Debra Hely's chapter in the present volume.
[5] T. Keefe, 'The Ending of Sartre's *La Nausée*', *Forum for Modern Language Studies*, 12 (1976), 217-35 (p. 233).
[6] J.-P. Sartre, *Being and Nothingness*, trans. by H. Barnes (London: Routledge, 1993), p. 364 (hereafter referred to as *BN* in the text).

the possibility of taking the Other's point of view on [oneself]" (*BN*, p. 365). In light of this, to write a diary is not enough: one would simply become one's own reader. Sartre/Roquentin needs to produce a novel that will be read by the Other; *Nausea* is such a novel, and it is for this reason that it is so markedly self-referential: "[In short,] in order to maintain before me the Other's freedom which is looking at me, I identify myself totally with my being-looked-at" (*BN*, p. 365).

An early example of a self-referential ploy in *Nausea* is the pebble scene. Christopher Prendergast reminds us of the literary heritage of stones and particularly of Socrates' pronouncement in Paul Valéry's *Eupalinos* that a stone cannot reflect the perfection of a work of art. He goes on to suggest that Sartre's desire is to produce the very opposite of art:

> What Sartre has in mind is neither Ponge's ambiguous interlacing of the referential and self-reflexive, nor Valéry's rigorously classical insistence on the ordering power of imagination and convention. What Sartre envisages [...] is a novel that would resemble the stone in its pure contingency, a novel so unselfconscious, so freed from artifice and convention, as to give us an unmediated image of the raw chaos of things, the world in its pure, meaningless 'being-there'.[7]

We, on the other hand, should argue that Roquentin's act of picking up the pebble is, in fact, a direct appeal to the reader to 'look where [his/her] hands are now'. This is just one example of a carefully worked stream of self-referentiality. In the overall scenario of textual seduction, this represents an ensnaring of the reader, an act of foreplay. The caress here appears to be primarily visual, forcing the pebble to yield. And yet the act of holding it by the edges reflects the reader's holding of the book. The act of looking does, as Serge Doubrovsky's work on the homotext suggests, stand for 'being looked at' but it may be hypothesized that it is in fact the book looking back at the reader, not simply the boys on the beach looking at Roquentin.[8] The book is paralleled by the shiny side of the pebble; it is one more mirror in which Roquentin is seen. The book, however, provides a

---

[7] C. Prendergast, 'Of Stones and Stories: Sartre's *La Nausée*', in *Teaching the Text*, ed. by S. Kappeler and N. Bryson (London: Routledge & Kegan Paul, 1983), pp. 56-72 (p. 61).
[8] For a synopsis, see S. Doubrovsky, 'L'Homotexte' in *'La Nausée' de Jean-Paul Sartre*, ed. by J. Deguy (Paris: Gallimard, 1993) pp. 216-19.

mirror in which he is seen as the reader interprets him, not as he sees himself. Roquentin adds ironically: "But I'm not going to amuse myself by putting that down on paper" (10). This quip, taken together with the masturbatory edge to the scene (the fondling of the stone, which both masks and discreetly points to Roquentin's desire), indicates the importance of refusing catharsis, of continuously seducing the reader (and maintaining the reader in a continuous state of seduction) without ever reaching climax.

The passivity of 'being looked at' is then shifted onto the gesture of picking up objects. Later in the novel, Roquentin will struggle to pick up pieces of text from the ground. Things progressively happen to him as he cedes power of interpretation to the reader: "There is something new, for example, about my hands, a certain way of picking up my pipe or my fork. Or else it is the fork which now has a certain way of *getting itself picked up*" (13 — author's emphasis).

Such instances of self-referentiality, which act as a desire to seduce the writerly reader, are veiled in the text. Sartre/Roquentin masks them by juxtaposing cruder examples of 'being read'. On the following page, for example, the Autodidact offers the hand of the reader to Roquentin. This hand will often be made object over the course of the novel, just as will be the case for Roquentin's own hand. These are two hands of the same persona: the hand of the reader meets the hand of the writer in their caress. When Roquentin immediately drops the Autodidact's hand, this ostensible fear of homosexuality doubles as a fear of being read. In the eyes of the reader, the refusal of this other reader's advances can be interpreted as the removal of a rival for Roquentin's attentions. Roquentin cannot be read by the Autodidact for the precise reason that the latter, with his unreflecting reading practice and inability to conceive of an unauthorized interpretation of the text, is not free enough to fulfil that role. The lover wishes to become the whole world for the beloved. Roquentin needs to be read freely:

> He wishes that the Other's freedom should no longer be free. He wishes that the Other's freedom should determine itself to become love [...] and at the same time he wants this freedom to be captured *by itself*, to turn back upon itself, as in madness, as in a dream, so as to will its own facticity. [...] In love it is not a determinism of the passions which we desire in the Other nor a freedom beyond reach; it is a freedom *which plays the role of* a determinism of the passions and which is caught in its own role. (*BN*, p. 367)

Translated onto *Nausea*, this desire becomes Roquentin's wish for the reader, by careful interpretation, to exist him as being-in-the-text, whilst being aware that s/he is trapped in his/her role as reader. The reader must read the text and believe in Roquentin at the same time as being aware of the text as text. This plea for a post-modern approach explains not only the text's self-referentiality but also the allusions to slaying the father (the end of the Rollebon project, for example) and the replacement of an easily identifiable image in Roquentin's mirror by a metaphorical subject that must be written in by the reader rather than seen. As previously mentioned, our reading here, which is an attempt to steer the text away from the *a priori* judgements made on it as philosophical treatise and towards a reading of *Nausea* as literature, is itself entwined in the philosophy of *Being and Nothingness*, the very retrospective philosophical guide from whose hegemony we are seeking to liberate the novel.

The core of a sensual reading of *Nausea* cannot lie in any one page for the simple reason that the entire text presents itself as erotic body (i.e. the text presents itself at every moment as text). We shall, however, limit our reading to an analysis of some of the key scenes involving hands.

Hands are a mid point; they not only function as an interface between the being for-itself and the world (hands as tools of discovery); they also stand for the caress between reader and writer. We may read with our eyes, just as the writer thinks with his cogito; the two intentional consciousnesses meet at that place where the writer physically pens the text and the reader handles the pages. This is why *Nausea*, as a text vitally aware of its being for-the-reader, whatever else it vehiculates, is fundamentally concerned with translating the philosophy of relating to other people into writing praxis.

The significance of hands in *Nausea* is made clear by Karen Gusto who analyses Roquentin's descriptions of them from the perspective of disembodiment and alienation.[9] Despite the relevance of such a thesis in terms of 'the problem of naming things', which is of prime concern to Roquentin in his understanding of the Nausea, this analysis is non-committal to the point of disingenuousness. Hands are, for example, the means by which Roquentin conceptualizes freedom.

---

[9] K. Gusto, '"Making it Strange": The Image of Hands in *La Nausée*', *Tropos*, 21 (1995), 36-44.

After his failure to pick up the pieces of paper, he announces: "I straightened up, empty-handed. I am no longer free, I can no longer do what I want" (22). Here Roquentin's inability to seize hold of an object is taken to be a sign that he is not free; he will, of course, realise that he is inescapably free, whatever he does. 'Having one's hands full' will prove to be a sign, not of freedom, but of a falsely reassuring means of validating one's actions: hands may, then, be read as indicators of bad faith. As chief bastard, Impétraz stands for authorial power in the text: "He holds his hat in his left hand and rests his right hand on a pile of folio volumes" (45-46). Not only does he hold the emblems of power, as Justice her scales, he crushes books (knowledge, power) "under his heavy hand" (46).

Roquentin mediates between Impétraz (the giver of the word) and the Autodidact (the blind receiver of the word, who refuses any free interpretation of it); he is between reader and writer, and as such will vacillate between hands-full and empty-handed states. He rejects Impétraz's authority but refuses equally to be loved blindly as by the Autodidact. As has been seen, he wishes to become the world in which the reader freely loses him/herself. For this reason, the reader of *Nausea* should be wary of the games that Roquentin plays with the Autodidact, as these are games in which s/he too is implicated.

The apparent androgyny of the Autodidact reflects his status as Other: when Roquentin elects to defeat him by turning his back on him, he is portrayed as a plump little sycophant with a chicken neck; when, on the other hand, Roquentin seeks to capture his objective gaze through seduction, the Autodidact is suddenly adorned with "a woman's eyelashes" (49). The description of these seductive eyes is enough to force Roquentin to unhand him, leaving him "with arms dangling" (49). In terms of this analysis, such a rejection of the little man's advances is not an act of homophobia or a repression of homosexual desire; it is simply an existential defence mechanism.[10] In the novel Roquentin opts for a solitary existence, adopting the armour of Impétraz as a way of repelling the Other. In the following description his hands are full to the point of petrifaction: "I am holding my pipe in my right hand and my packet of tobacco in my

---

[10] This is clearly not to deny a homoerotic reading of the interaction between Roquentin and the Autodidact. Indeed, Lawrence Schehr's chapter in the present volume attests to the strength of the sexual tension between these two characters.

left."[11] And yet "[his] arms dangle" (49-50). Frozen out of reach of the Other, Roquentin cannot act. This 'ignorance-is-bliss' reaction is an unviable solution to the problem of the being for-others; but it is not Roquentin's only reaction since he is not denying the Other altogether. For at all times, there is another whose full hands are vying with Roquentin for existing space in the text. Roquentin's indifference to the Other-in-the-text can be read as an attempt to seduce the Other-holding-the-text, to reveal himself as available for seduction. His freed hands invite our touch.

In the same way, the absence of satisfactory sexual relations in the text suggests a space for negotiation: the erotic body of the text beckons the reader to reciprocate Roquentin's love. *Roquentin enjoys caressing bits of paper; he likes to put them into his mouth.* Studies such as those by Andrew Leak and Peter Poiana's chapter in this volume attest to the viability of a Freudian reading of Sartrean texts, and it is clear that Roquentin's fascination with soiled paper may be legitimately interpreted in psychological terms (as an example of oral pleasure and infantile sexuality).[12] It is difficult, however, within the compass of this reading, to distinguish between a genuine slip of the tongue on Roquentin's part (a Freudian parapraxis, and, thus, expression of the unconscious) and a deliberately worked act of seduction (whereby words are left hanging in the air as an invitation to the beloved reader to respond). One thing is certain: we readers should not allow our guard to drop; Sartre's way of highlighting the depth of his message through off-hand statements certainly conceals more than at first meets the eye: "There's nothing much to say: I couldn't manage to pick up the piece of paper, that's all" (21). Roquentin wants to put words into his mouth. He cannot read himself objectively, only subjectively. He needs to empower the Other to read his pages, to put them into his/her own mouth and to make him exist as protagonist. As in so much of the text, meaning exists in reversal: if he could pick up the text and eat the words, he would have something to say. This is a

---

[11] Roquentin here fills his hands in the same way as Impétraz; a cardboard cut-out chef has his hands equally full later in the novel, at a point where a young couple engage in a joint act of seduction and reading over a menu: "Outside, a young couple has stopped in front of the menu which a cardboard chef is holding out to them in his left hand (in his right he has a frying pan)" (154).

[12] See A. Leak, 'Nausea and Desire in Sartre's *La Nausée*', *French Studies*, 43: 1 (1989), 61-72 and *The Perverted Consciousness: Sexuality and Sartre* (New York: St. Martin's Press, 1989).

desire to be read. *Quod erat demonstrandum.* He then muddies his hands, and in a primitive form of language, leaves his mark: "then I wipe the muddy palms of my hands on a wall or a tree trunk" (21). This gesture has all the sexuality of the Surrealists, for whom the expression of the unconscious was to be voiced directly, untrammelled by the formality of logical communication. In *Nausea*, Sartre will let his hands do the talking.

Whereas Karen Gusto dwells on the use of hand imagery in the novel as an indicator of strangeness, Georgiana Colvile goes beyond the divorce that hands and writing make apparent between things and their names, offering the writing act as a means of salvaging something from this loss of sense:

> At this point, only monsters remain, including the indolent hand of the writer. Without words Roquentin's thoughts are swallowed up [...] Language and writing are a lifejacket allowing a return to dry land.[13]

We should note the ostensible difference between the value of the Other for the Existentialist and the Surrealist: for the former the relationship with other people is logically a battle of 'overcome or be overcome'; for the latter, other people are, as Marie-Claire Bancquart notes throughout her work *Paris des Surréalistes*, a means to an end, consciousnesses by means of whose collective energy one can seek to achieve the ultimate synthesis of all binary oppositions.[14] *Nausea* has its hands in both camps.

Colvile notes the fetishistic fragmentation of the body that marks Sartre's description in the novel:

> The breaking down of the body into separate parts or the metamorphosis of the monster evokes Bellmer's mannequin, which he used to mutilate and reinvent as his fantasy took him. (Colvile, p. 25)

Amongst the 161 references to the word *main* that she records in the text, Karen Gusto draws particular attention to those usages of the disembodied hand that can be interpreted synecdochically. In reference to the scene in which the Autodidact strokes the boy's hand in the library, Gusto suggests that the passage "constitutes an extreme

---

[13] G. Colvile, 'Éléments surréalistes dans *La Nausée*: Une Hypothèse de l'écriture', *L'Esprit Créateur*, 17 (1977), 19-28 (p. 26-7) (author's translation).
[14] M.-C. Bancquart, *Paris des Surréalistes* (Paris: Seghers, 1972).

personification of the finger and also of other people's hands, as the sexual act is reduced to an action that takes place between two hands" (Gusto, p. 41). This symbolic use of the fetish attests to the novelistic properties of *Nausea*, the philosophical intent of the existentialist text being to reduce the body, in parts or *in toto*, to the rank of unrecognisable and unnameable existent.

Noting the predilection of the Surrealists for images of the hand, Colvile mentions the famous street scene of Buñuel's *Un Chien andalou*:

> The Surrealists were fetishists and erotomaniacs with a predilection for the symbol of the hand. An obvious example is the hand in Buñuel and Dali's *Un chien andalou* (1928), which an androgyne pushes with the end of a stick, and which captivates the crowd with a blend of horror and eroticism. Roquentin's nausea often resides in his hand. (Colvile, p. 25)

Colvile is right to point to *Un chien andalou*; in addition to a reference to a "dead donkey" (180), the sex scene that pits Roquentin against the *patronne* reveals a strong intertextual link between *Nausea* and this famous film: over the *patronne*'s genitals, which suddenly turn into a garden, "ants were running about everywhere" (89). If there is a marked absence of passionate relations between the *patronne* and Roquentin, there is intense intercourse between these two texts.[15] The *patronne*'s irrelevance and the supreme status of the text within the novel are intimately linked. From the point of view of concrete relations with the Other, sex scenes showcase not desire of this woman but desire itself. As formulated in *Being and Nothingness*, the caress is a way of enticing the Other to become body whilst keeping one's distance:

> Not as much to push or to touch in the active sense but to place against. It seems that I lift my own arm as an inanimate object and that I *place* it against the flank of the desired woman, that my fingers which I run over her arm are inert at the end of my hand. [...] I make her enjoy my flesh through her flesh in order to compel her to feel herself flesh. (*BN*, p. 390-91)

---

[15] The schoolboy's androgynous act of thrusting out his tongue in the library, as discussed here by Lawrence Schehr, can also be read intertextually: in *Un chien andalou* the lead female thrusts her tongue-made-phallus out in order to taunt and (further) emasculate the male protagonist, whose own androgyny is marked in various ways throughout the film.

Roquentin thinks of other things, losing sensation in his hand as he masturbates the *patronne*.[16] This suppression of feeling is interesting in terms of Gusto's synecdochic interpretation: the hand does not merely stand in for Roquentin metonymically; rather its loss points to a central absence. This is a fetishization of the text, in which words simultaneously veil and symbolise that which is absent. In this case, it is sex itself that is effectively removed from the picture. Even the patronne's defence mechanism involves a fetishisation of her own body: "If you don't mind, I'll keep my stockings on" (17). Whilst revealing herself as object of desire, she also fragments Roquentin's field of vision, forcing his view of her genitals to pass to a metaphorical level (the intertextual garden) and become suppressed as screen memory. In *Being and Nothingness*, Sartre himself points to the synecdochic value of body parts, which *Nausea* is generally considered to deny:

> But what is the object of desire? Shall we say that desire is the desire of a *body*? In one sense this can not be denied [...] To be sure it is the body which disturbs us: an arm or a half-exposed breast or perhaps a leg. But we must realize at the start that we desire the arm or the uncovered breast only on the ground of the presence of the whole body as an organic totality. (*BN*, p. 385)

Were the novel to present its reader with a catharsis, a pleasurable release of desire, through a graphic representation of sexual relations, there would be an outcome (the *patronne* would certainly play the card of the *vagina dentata*). As it is, however, both players maintain their distance, with the result that desire remains integral, unblemished by climax:

> Every subjectivist and immanentist theory will fail to explain how we desire a particular woman and not simply our sexual satisfaction. [...] Nevertheless it would be wholly inaccurate to say that desire is a desire for 'physical possession' of the desired object - if by 'possess' we mean here 'make love to'. Of course the sexual act for a moment frees us from desire, and in certain cases it can be posited explicitly as the hoped-for issue of the desire - when desire, for example, is painful and fatiguing. (*BN*, p. 384-85)

---

[16] As was alluded to earlier, the seduction of the reader functions similarly to the erotics of writing as expounded by Barthes, and has little to do with stark representations of sex in the narrative. In fact, sex itself is significantly made absent in the text.

The post-coital departure of the *patronne* also displays a clever use of metaphor on Sartre's part. As Linda Williams points out in *Figures of Desire*, the departure of a train is common cinematic parlance for the sex act;[17] in *Nausea* an opposite image is used, with the *patronne* announcing the end of the encounter as a result of the *arrival* of the train from Paris. This is an *anti*climax, a metaphor for the maintenance of desire and a deepening of the erotic encounter between Sartre/Roquentin and the only Other to be present throughout the intercourse: the reader.

The use of manifest fetishism (leg fetishism in this instance) at once to point to and to veil a fetishistic writing strategy is repeated throughout the text. A woman wearing a black hat in the Café Mably, whose "hands were moving all the time", orders her partner to tie her shoe; he agrees and "lightly touched her foot under the table" (106). She seems to avoid his caress by disembodying and fetishizing herself. Later a hand moves down to scratch mud from the hem of her skirt, and it is not clear to whom the hand belongs. The couple, it is revealed, are actors; the gaps in the text are the precise focus through which Roquentin forces the reader's gaze, and through which s/he reads the absent image. Whilst we should agree with Nicholas Hewitt and Sylvie Vanbaelen that Anny's value in the text is as missing love object,[18] she, too, is an actress in the text, the interpretation of whose role hinges on the active engagement of the key absent that is the reader. Indeed, Anny's explanation of perfect moments reminds the reader of the elaborate, and allegorical, courtship ceremony that is *la carte du Tendre*.[19] Hands are to the fore throughout the discussion in which Anny and Roquentin appear to have abandoned all attempts to gain the upper hand; Anny clasps her knee in her hand and then unclasps it before fading to grey:

---

[17] L. Williams, *Figures of Desire: A Theory and Analysis of Surrealist Film* (Urbana: University of Illinois Press, 1981).

[18] N. Hewitt, '"Looking for Annie": Sartre's *La Nausée* and the Inter-War Years', *The Journal of European Studies*, 12 (1982), 96-112; S. Vanbaelen, 'Anny, Syrinx de Roquentin : Musique et érotique dans *La Nausée* de Jean-Paul Sartre', *Romanic Review*, 90: 3 (1999), 397-408.

[19] It is interesting to note that Madeleine de Scudéry, who drew up *la carte du Tendre* in the seventeenth century, held court in her literary salon in Paris (where Roquentin meets Anny) but was born in Le Havre (usually considered to be the inspiration for Bouville).

We remain silent for a moment. Dusk is falling; I can scarcely make out the pale patch of her face. Her black dress merges into the shadows which have invaded the room. I automatically pick up my cup, which still has a little tea in it, and I raise it to my lips. The tea is cold. I should like to smoke but I don't dare. (217-18)

This urge to smoke could be read variously as a desire for a post-coital signpost, a means of picking up Roquentin's earlier display of infantile sexuality with the pieces of paper or, quite simply, as a way of occupying his hands.[20] Later Roquentin will hand the whip hand to Anny's companion, who has his post-coital cigarette in a blatantly imagined scene: "She is sleeping in a cabin, and on the deck the handsome sun-tanned fellow is smoking cigarettes" (222). It is no mere coincidence if there is a pointed lack of narrative distance between this wilfully oneiric scene and Roquentin's own meeting with Anny (i.e. both scenes have an equally imaginary status). Anny may well be more than an absent lover; she can be seen as being entirely absent, a construct written to seduce the Other who is present outside the text. Perfect moments are, after all, a defence of authorial power: Anny sets out rules for correct interpretation of the text whilst not revealing them to her actor/reader. Roquentin's attempts to play his role, to read his text, had relied on creativity, and it is this that necessarily comes to the forefront with the disappearance of Anny (and, following the removal of Rollebon – himself a self-referential literary device in the text - another death of the author).

Roquentin's attempts to draw the reader in with fetishistic images are repeated in the scene with the flasher. This functions as a *mise en abyme*, in which the gaze of the reader is forced to interpret a scene that is moved into position by Roquentin, and from which he removes his hand; the scene is a caress, disembodied through metonymy. The flasher is introduced by a synecdochic reference to "the cape" that here signifies to the reader "the man in the cape". The reader interprets Roquentin's gaze as he witnesses the flasher and the young girl contemplate each other. In an allegory of the author-reader relationship, the flasher exposes himself, waiting for her to interpret

---

[20] Drinking tea and smoking also parallel the likely environment in which Sartre would have written his novel, cafés being synonymous with the existentialist writing experience of that period. Any means of recalling Roquentin's similarity to Sartre the author stands to reinforce Anny's status as self-consciously literary character in the text.

him; his is an attempt to capture her objective view of his reality, to see himself as he really is.

The power of the caress is also turned against Roquentin himself. In an attack of Nausea that is particularly focussed on his hand, the latter becomes so disembodied that it lays itself onto his thigh: "I withdraw my hand, I put it into my pocket. But straight away through the material, I feel the warmth of my thigh" (144). Immediately after this caress, he stabs his hand with a penknife. The blood spills onto the page, obscuring the lines he had written and "stop[s] being [him]" (146). His thoughts then tumble into freefall, prompting the reader to question whether Roquentin is confessing to the murder of little Lucienne. As a diary addressing its reader, the text offers a fairly standard transfer of responsibility but, in the light of this analysis of seduction, the lines read more as a liberation of the reader; Roquentin has finally extended the death of the author theme to his own hand, seducing the writerly reader with the white expanses of the page. The confession begins as follows:

> I have the right to exist, therefore I have the right not to think: the finger is raised. Am I going to… caress in the splendour of white sheets the splendid white flesh… (147-48)

Struck down with Stockholm Syndrome, the reader wonders what crimes Roquentin may have committed; s/he responds to the caress, opening up all sorts of literary possibilities and making Roquentin exist.

At the end of the novel, *Nausea* has come full circle. The question of whether or not it is *the* novel that Roquentin was planning seems misplaced; it hinges on the fine distinction between Sartre-author and Roquentin-author. *Nausea*'s last line is famous for its literary turn of phrase (it talks about the weather, offering everything that Sartre openly despised in the work of François Mauriac et al.) and its suggestion of future time, of a reading to come: "The yard of the New Station smells strongly of wood: tomorrow it will rain over Bouville" (253). Whether or not the reader does reopen the book at page one, the fact that s/he has got to this line assures Roquentin of his place in history: he has become the world for the reader. The 'leaving Bouville phase' self-consciously vacates the central reading space of the text, the library, closing the door on reading itself, whilst counting down the amount of time remaining until the train leaves and the book is shut.

When Roquentin first becomes aware of the difficulties posed by leaving the library and shutting the book, the reader watches (reads) on from an external perspective. Roquentin's gaze stands between the reader and the scene, offering a mirror in which the reading act is reflected:

> 'Gentlemen,' said the Corsican, 'it will be closing time soon.'
> The young man gave a start and darted a swift glance at me. The young woman had turned towards the Corsican, then she picked up her book again and seemed to bury herself in it.
> 'Closing time,' said the Corsican five minutes later.
> The old man shook his head with an uncertain air. The young woman pushed her book away, but without getting up.
> The Corsican was at a loss what to do. […]
> 'Do we have to leave?' the old man asked quietly.
> (118)

At first this scene calls to mind the rather more famous example in *L'Étranger* where Albert Camus inserts himself into Meursault's trial as a young journalist in the gallery. Instead of the author, here it is the reader that appears in the story. And the overtones are more ominous: what would happen if the reader were to emulate his/her literary reflections?[21] Just as the sustenance of Alice's dreams appears to depend on key dreamers placed into the stories (the Dormouse, Kitty or the Red King), all of a sudden it appears crucial that the reading go on in the library in order for Roquentin to continue to be existed in *Nausea* by the Other-holding-the-text. And ultimately it is in the library that the reader is finally seduced into writing the ending of the novel.

As has been mentioned, the reading room of the library empties to the rhythm of the empting of the text; with a mere twenty pages to go before the famous last line, "the reading room was almost empty." Not only is this space the locus of reading and writing in the novel, it is at the epicentre of Nausea, safe in the eye of the storm: "it seemed to me that it scarcely existed and that the Nausea had spared it" (229). The scene that follows offers a pertinent *mise en abyme* for the dance of

---

[21] By including an old man and a young woman, Sartre has covered a wide demographic, multiplying the potential readers who will be able to recognise themselves in this scene.

seduction that, were it not for Roquentin's retreat into the future (reread), would end in a pleasurable climax for reader and author alike.

Inasmuch as he has devoured a large portion of the library's text(s), the Autodidact represents the library, and the novel *Nausea*, itself. He has read blindly, making himself a living vessel for the consciousnesses of all the authors whose word he has never challenged. Before the two schoolboys, however, his reading becomes a pretext, his hand coming off his book and straying, disingenuously dehumanised, into a place where a caress will occur. The targeted boy is drawn in, seduced. The caress is a textbook example of the lover becoming the world for the beloved: the boy, his own pretext for being there notwithstanding, is in a library, and the Autodidact contains that world: "The boy seemed to be drinking in his words" (233). And as the boy drinks in the Autodidact's words, so we the reader drink in the text. Roquentin, who is also there under a pretext (he is feigning to read the local paper), contemplates intervening in the scene; he is in a dilemma, there is an ineluctable sequence in train, which is beginning to look as though it may have the potential to make the scene "hard as steel". If Roquentin can keep up the pretence then he will, indeed, make the moment an adventure. His success hinges on his own ability to seduce, through the caress of the pages, the one witness who is not there on a pretext: the reader, to whom all responsibility for the ending has been transferred.

> Discouraged, I quickly turned my eyes away and returned to my paper to keep myself in countenance. Meanwhile the fat lady had pushed her book away and raised her head. She seemed fascinated. I could distinctly feel that the drama was going to begin; they all *wanted* it to begin. What could I do? I glanced at the Corsican: he wasn't looking out of the window any more, he had half-turned towards us. (234)

Does Roquentin want to prevent the scene, or does he, too, want to witness the drama unfold? This question is rhetorical as Roquentin's position is clearly perverse: he is (self-consciously) producing the text, and it is only through his mediation that the scene can occur. Whether the Corsican stands for master of reading ceremonies, Sartre the author or Napoleon himself, he is only playing a role; the fat lady is poised to sing but the act of pushing away her book cannot alter the situation. Only the reader of *Nausea* can close the library by closing the book and pushing it away. The whole scene is a set-up, a seductive trap set for us alone. Sartre's extravagant use of simile makes it clear that this is an example of how to seduce; like the waiter in *Being and Nothingness*, the characters are *too* self-conscious, *too* caricatured: the boy's hand "had the indolent nudity of a woman sunning herself on the beach" whilst that of the Autodidact "had all the grossness of a male organ" (234).

To capture his being for-others, to see himself as he really is, Roquentin must be loved freely. He must know that the reader wants the Autodidact to be caught. And if the reader has not yet realised that s/he is in control, is reading freely (writing *Nausea*), this final reminder leaves no doubt possible: Roquentin states that the Autodidact, the disenfranchised reader, has one last chance, i.e. "[to] put both his hands on the table, on either side of his book" (234). But, just as the boy gives himself freely to the Autodidact, Roquentin knows that the reader has become both seducer and seduced. In *Jazz* it is the narrator who has been "waiting for this all [her] life"; in *Nausea* it is the reader who finally realises that "being chosen [by him or her] to wait is the reason [Roquentin] can". S/he has been free to read/write *Nausea* and has chosen to follow the narrative to its end. Assured of the outcome, and knowing that it is one that has been accorded freely by the reader, Roquentin allows himself to remind the reader that s/he is about to make the finale ineluctable: "But I knew that he was going to miss his chance" (235).

As readers we have chosen the hegemony of authorial power because it is a power that, perversely, we alone can grant to the author by virtue of our reading of the text. Once the library scene is over and Roquentin has refused to punch the Corsican, thereby pulling the reader back from the brink of literary climax (one more example of *coitus interruptus*), Roquentin walks; he tidies up the remaining themes: Anny is removed from the text, being given the orgasm that we shall never have: "She is having her orgasm and I am no more to her than if I had never met her; she has suddenly emptied herself of me and all the other consciousnesses in the world are also empty of me" (240). Indeed, all Others in the text have abandoned the battlefield. All except one. For Roquentin has managed to become novel, founding his own existence via the writerly interpretation of his reader. He has disembodied his entire self, laid himself in reach, and we have understood, reached out and stroked. It is we, as readers holding *Nausea*, who have stroked meaning into the pages of the novel. In an act of erotic reading, we have stroked the protagonist who has prostrated himself before us, and he, in turn, has relished the seduction: "I can no longer manage to feel myself. […] I give a long, voluptuous yawn" (241).

Notes on Contributors

AMANDA CRAWLEY-JACKSON lectures in French at the University of Sheffield. She has published in the fields of contemporary French prison writing, Existentialist fiction and philosophy and the visual arts in France.

CHRIS FALZON is a lecturer in philosophy at the University of Newcastle, Australia. He is the author of *Philosophy Goes to the Movies* and *Foucault and Social Dialogue: Beyond Fragmentation*.

DEBRA HELY is a former science teacher. She has recently completed her B.A. (Hons) and plans to pursue her MCA in creative writing. She has recently focused on poetry but isn't afraid to flirt with other genres.

TOM MARTIN teaches philosophy at Rhodes University, South Africa. His research interests include existential phenomenology, self-deception, race and gender. He is the author of *Oppression and the Human Condition: An Introduction to Sartrean Existentialism*.

PETER POIANA is Lecturer in French Studies at the University of Adelaide. He has published in the areas of Twentieth-Century French Literature and Comparative Literature.

ELIZABETH RECHNIEWSKI is Senior Lecturer at the University of Sydney where she teaches in the French, European Studies and Comparative Literature programmes. She has published widely on Bourdieu, the cultural field and intellectuals in France, including *Suarès, Malraux et Sartre : antécédents littéraires de l'existentialisme*.

ALISTAIR ROLLS is a lecturer at The University of Newcastle, Australia; he teaches in the disciplines of French and English within the School of Language and Media. He researches primarily in the areas of Twentieth-Century French literature, including Boris Vian, Sartre and the Roman Noir. He is the author of *The Flight of the Angels: Intertextuality in Four Novels by Boris Vian*.

LAWRENCE R. SCHEHR is professor of French, comparative literature, and gender and women's studies at the University of Illinois. He has published widely on French realism, French modernism, queer studies, and various areas of nineteenth-, twentieth- and twenty-first-century French cultural studies.

KERYN STEWART first became interested in theories of intertextuality while completing an Honours Degree in English at the University of Newcastle. Her research interests include the negotiation of disclosure in contemporary Australian literature and the politics of true crime narratives.

GEORGINA WOODS is currently completing her doctoral thesis at The University of Newcastle, Australia. Whilst her area of study is early modernist poetry in English, George is also an environmental activist.

Bibliography

The following bibliography provides a selection of the critical texts cited by the contributors to this volume. Also included are some of the important fictional works drawn on in these essays.

Arisaka, Yoko, 'Spatiality, Temporality, and the Problem of Foundation in Being and Time', *Philosophy Today*, 40:1 (1996), 36-46.

Bancquart, Marie-Claire, *Paris des Surréalistes* (Paris: Seghers, 1972).

Barnes, Hazel, *Sartre* (London: Quartet Books, 1974).

Barthes, Roland, *S/Z* (Paris, Seuil: 1970).

_____ *The Pleasure of the Text*, trans. by R. Miller (New York: Hill and Wang, 1975).

_____ 'The Death of the Author' in *Image, Music, Text*, trans. by Stephen Heath (New York: Hill & Wang, 1977), pp. 142-48.

Beauvoir, Simone de, *Mémoires d'une jeune fille rangée* (Paris: Gallimard, 1958).

_____ *La Force de l'âge* (Paris: Gallimard, 1960).

_____ *Adieux: A Farewell to Sartre*, trans. by P. O'Brien (Harmondsworth: Penguin, 1984).

Benjamin, Walter, *The Arcades Project*, trans. by H. Eiland and K. McLaughlin (London: The Belknap Press of Harvard University Press, 2003).

Borch-Jakobsen, Mikkel, *Lacan: The Absolute Master* (Stanford (CA): Stafford University Press, 1991).

Boschetti, Anna, *Sartre et Les Temps Modernes* (Paris: Editions de Minuit, 1985).

Bourdieu, Pierre, 'Le Marché des biens symboliques', *L'Année sociologique*, 22 (1971), 49-126.

Buck-Morss, Susan, *The Origin of Negative Dialectics* (Sussex: Harvester, 1977).

Butler, Judith, *Bodies that Matter: On the discursive limits of sex* (London: Routledge, 1993).

Catalano, Joseph, *A Commentary on Jean-Paul Sartre's 'Being and Nothingness'* (Chicago: Chicago University Press, 1974).

Chapman, Rosemary, 'Autodidacticism and the Desire for Culture', *Nottingham French Studies* 31:2 (1992), 84-101.

Choay, François (ed.), *L'Urbanisme: utopies et réalités, une anthologie* (Paris: Seuil, 1965).

Cohen-Solal, Annie, *Sartre : 1905-1980* (Paris: Gallimard, 1999) [Translated as *Sartre: A Life* (London: Heinemann, 1988)].

Colvile, Georgiana, 'Éléments surréalistes dans *La Nausée*: Une Hypothèse de l'écriture', *L'Esprit Créateur*, 17 (1977), 19-28.

Contat, Michel, 'Sartre et la gloire', in *La Naissance du phénomène Sartre, raisons d'un succès 1938-45*, ed. by I. Galster (Paris: Seuil, 2001), pp. 29-41.

Contat, Michel and Rybalka, Michel, '*La Nausée* : Notice', in Sartre, Jean-Paul, *Œuvres romanesques* (Paris: Gallimard, 1981), pp. 1657-78.

Curtis, William J.R., *Modern Architecture Since 1900* (London: Phaidon, 1996).

Danto, Arthur, *Sartre* (Glasgow: Fontana/Collins, 1975).

Deguy, Jacques, *'La Nausée' de Jean-Paul Sartre* (Paris: Gallimard, 1993).

Descombes, Vincent, *Le Même et l'autre* (Paris: Minuit, 1979).

Doubrovsky, Serge, 'Phallotexte et gynotexte dans *La Nausée* : "Feuillet sans date"', in *Sartre et la mise en signe*, ed. by M. Issacharoff and J.-C. Vilquin (Paris: Klincksieck and Lexington, KY: French Forum, 1982), pp. 30-55.

Evans, Deborah, '"Some of These Days": Roquentin's American Adventure', *Sartre Studies International*, 8 (2002), 58-74.

Falzon, Chris, 'Sartre: Freedom as Imprisonment', *Philosophy Today*, 47:2 (2003), 126-37.

Favre, Yves-Alain, *La Recherche de la grandeur dans l'œuvre d'André Suarès* (Paris: Klincksieck, 1978).

Fox, Nik Farrel, *The New Sartre: Explorations in Postmodernism* (New York; London: Continuum, 2003).

Freud, Sigmund, *Introductory Lectures on Psycho-analysis*, trans. by J. Riviere (London: George Allen & Unwin Ltd, 1922).

_____ *Inhibitions, Symptoms and Anxiety*, trans. by A. Strachey (London: Hogarth Press, 1936).

_____ *The Standard Edition of the Complete Psychological Works of Sigmund Freud. Vol. 19. The Ego and The Id and Other Works,* trans. by J. Strachey (London: The Hogarth Press, 1961).

_____ *Art and Literature*, trans. by J. Strachey (Harmondsworth (U.K.): Penguin Books Ltd, 1987).

_____ *Dora: An Analysis of a Case of Hysteria*, trans. by A. and J. Strachey (New York: Touchstone, 1997).

Galster, Ingrid (ed.), *La Naissance du phénomène Sartre : Raisons d'un succès 1938-45* (Paris: Seuil, 2001).

Goldmann, Lauren, *Sciences humaines et philosophie* (Paris: Editions Gonthier, 1966).

Gore, Keith, 'Lucienne, Sex, and Nausea', *Forum for Modern Language Studies*, 26:1 (1990), 37-48.

Gusto, Karen, '"Making it Strange": The Image of Hands in *La Nausée*', *Tropos*, 21 (1995), 36-44.

Harvey, Robert, *Search for a Father* (Ann Arbor: University of Michigan Press, 1991).

Heidegger, Martin, *Being and Time*, trans. by J. Macquarrie and E. Robinson (Oxford and Cambridge, MA: Blackwell, 1995).

Hewitt, Nicholas, '"Looking for Annie": Sartre's *La Nausée* and the Inter-War Years', *The Journal of European Studies*, 12 (1982), 96-112.

Hollier, Denis, '*La Nausée*, en attendant', in *La Naissance du phénomène Sartre, raisons d'un succès 1938-45*, ed. by I. Galster (Paris: Seuil, 2001), pp. 86-100.

Holtsmark, Erling B., 'The *Katabasis* Theme in Modern Cinema', in *Classical Myth and Culture in the Cinema*, ed. by M. M. Winkler (Oxford: Oxford University Press, 2001).

Howells, Christina, *Sartre: The Necessity of Freedom* (Cambridge: Cambridge University Press, 1988).

Kabbani, Rana, *Europe's Myths of Orient* (Bloomington: Indiana University Press, 1986).

Keefe, Terry, 'The Ending of Sartre's *La Nausée*', *Forum for Modern Language Studies*, 12 (1976), 217-35.

Kershaw, Angela, 'Autodidacticism and Criminality in Jean-Paul Sartre's *La Nausée* and Edith Thomas' *L'Homme criminel*', *Modern Language Review*, 96:3 (2001), 679-92.

Kolakowski, Leszek, *Main Currents of Marxism volume 1: The Founders*, trans. by P. Fella (Oxford: Oxford University Press, 1978).

Kritzman, Lawrence, 'To Be or Not to Be: Sexual Ambivalence in Sartre's *La Nausée*', *L'Esprit Créateur*, 43:3 (2003), 79-86.

Lacan, Jacques, *Ecrits: A Selection*, trans. by A. Sheridan (London: Tavistock Publications Ltd, 1977).

_____ *The Four Fundamental Concepts of Psychoanalysis*, trans. by A. Sheridan (Harmondsworth (U.K.): Penguin, 1979).

Lacouture, Jean, *Malraux, une vie dans le siècle* (Paris: Seuil, 1973).

Leak, Andrew, 'Nausea and Desire in Sartre's *La Nausée*', *French Studies*, 43:1 (1989), 61-72.

_____ *The Perverted Consciousness: Sexuality and Sartre* (New York: St. Martin's Press, 1989).

Le Corbusier, *The City of Tomorrow and its Planning* (London: Rodker, 1929).

Lefebvre, Henri, *La Révolution urbaine* (Paris: Gallimard, coll. Idées, 1970).

Lévy, Bernard-Henry, *Le Siècle de Sartre : Enquête philosophique* (Paris: Grasset, 2000).

Lévi-Strauss, Claude, *Tristes Tropiques*, trans. by J. and D. Weightman (London: Jonathan Cape, 1973).

Levy, Neil, *Sartre* (Oxford: Oneworld Publications, 2002).

Macquarrie, John, *Existentialism* (Harmondsworth: Penguin, 1972).

Magny, Claude-Edmonde, 'The Duplicity of Being', in *Sartre: A Collection of Critical Essays*, ed. by Edith Kern (Englewood Cliffs, NJ: Prentice Hall, 1962), pp. 21-30.

Manser, Anthony, *Sartre: A Philosophic Study* (London: Athlone, 1966).

Martin, Tom, *Oppression and the Human Condition: An Introduction to Sartrean Existentialism* (Lanham, Md.: Rowman and Littlefield, 2002).

Merleau-Ponty, Maurice, *Phenomenology of Perception*, trans. by C. Smith (London: Routledge, 1962).

Michaels, Anne, *Fugitive Pieces* (London: Bloomsbury, 1998).

Nagel, Thomas, *Mortal Questions* (Cambridge: Cambridge University Press, 1979).

Prendergast, Christopher, 'Of Stones and Stories: Sartre's La Nausée', in *Teaching the Text* ed. by S. Kappeler and N. Bryson (London: Routledge & Kegan Paul, 1983), pp. 56-72.

Pivcevic, Edo, *Husserl and Phenomenology* (London: Hutchinson, 1970).

Prince, Gerald, *Métaphysique et technique dans l'oeuvre romanesque de Sartre* (Geneva: Droz, 1968).

Porter, Dennis, 'Orientalism and its Problem', in *Colonial Discourse/ Post-Colonial Theory : A Reader*, ed. by P. Williams and L. Chrisman (London: Harvester Wheatsheaf, 1993), pp. 150-61.

Rechniewski, Elizabeth, *Antécédents littéraires de l'existentialisme, Suarès, Malraux et Sartre* (Paris: Minard, 1992).

Riffaterre, Michael, 'Compulsory Reader Response: The Intertextual Drive,' in *Intertextuality: Theories and Practices*, ed. by M. Worton and J. Still (Manchester: Manchester University Press, 1990), pp. 56-78.

Rifkin, Adrian, *Street Noises: Parisian Pleasure, 1900-1940* (Manchester: Manchester University Press, 1993).

Rolls, Alistair, *The Flight of the Angels: Intertextuality in Four Novels by Boris Vian* (Amsterdam; Atlanta: Rodopi, 1999).

_____ '"This Lovely, Sweet Refrain": Reading the Fiction back into *Nausea*', *Literature and Aesthetics - The Journal of the Sydney Society of Literature and Aesthetics*, 13:2 (2003), 57-72.

Russo, Vito, The Celluloid Closet: homosexuality in the movies (New York: Harper & Row, 1981).

Sartre, Jean-Paul, *Situations III* (Paris: Gallimard, 1949).

_____ *Being and Nothingness*, trans. by H. Barnes (London: Routledge, 1958).

_____ *Words*, trans. by I. Clephane (London: Harmondsworth Press, 1967).

_____ *The Psychology of Imagination* (London: Methuen, 1972).

_____ 'Existentialism is a Humanism', in *Existentialism from Dostoevsky to Sartre*, ed. by W. Kaufmann (New York: New American Library, 1975).

_____ *Œuvres romanesques* (Paris: Gallimard, 1981).

_____ *Lettres au Castor, 1926-1939* (Paris: Gallimard, 1983).

_____ *Les Carnets de la drôle de guerre, novembre 1939-mars 1940* (Paris: Gallimard, 1983).

_____ *Mallarmé: La Lucidité et sa face d'ombre* (Paris: Gallimard, 1986).

_____ *Les Ecrits de jeunesse* (Paris: Gallimard, 1990).

_____ *La Reine Albemarle ou le dernier touriste* (Paris: Gallimard, 1991).

_____ *Nausea*, trans. by Robert Baldick, with an introduction by James Wood (London: Penguin, 2000).

Sayre, Robert and Löwy, Michel, 'Figures du romantisme anti-capitaliste', *L'Homme et la société*, 69-70 (1983), 99-121.

Schehr, Laurence, *Alcibiades at the Door: Gay Discourses in French Literature* (Stanford: Stanford University Press, 1995).

Scipion, Robert, *Prête-moi ta plume* (Paris: Gallimard, 1946).

Simenon, Georges, *Maigret et la vieille dame* (Paris: Presses de la Cité, 1951).

Soler, Colette, "Literature as Symptom" in *Lacan and the Subject of Language*, ed. by E. Ragland-Sullivan & M. Bracher (New York & London: Routledge, 1991), pp. 213-219.

Spargo, Tamsin, *Foucault and Queer Theory* (Cambridge: Icon Books, 1999).

Suarès, André, 'Pour Gabriel d'Annunzio' *Écrits nouveaux, t. VII*, 1921, pp. 3-7.

_____ *Sur la vie, I* (Paris: Emile-Paul, 1925).

_____ *Sur la vie, III* (Paris: Emile-Paul, 1928).

_____ *Voici l'homme* (Paris: Albin Michel, 1948).

_____ *Cette âme ardente: choix de lettres d'André Suarès à Romain Rolland, 1887-1891* (Paris: Albin Michel, 1954).

_____ *Bouclier du zodiaque* (Paris: le cherche midi, 1993).

_____ *Le Condottière et le magicien, correspondance choisie, établie et préfacée par François Chapon* (Paris: Julliard, 1994).

Taylor, Charles, 'What is Human Agency', in *The Self*, ed. by T. Mischel (Oxford: Blackwell, 1977), pp. 103-35.

_____ 'Embodied Agency', in *Merleau-Ponty: Critical Essays*, ed. by H. Pietersma (Lanham, Md.: University Press of America, 1990).

Thody, Philip, *Introducing Sartre* (Cambridge: Icon, 1999).

Vanbaelen, Sylvie, 'Anny, Syrinx de Roquentin : Musique et érotique dans *La Nausée* de Jean-Paul Sartre.' *Romanic Review*, 90:3 (1999), 397-408.

Wetzel, Michel, *Sartre : La mauvaise foi (L'Être et le néant)* (Paris: Hatier, 1985).

Wilson, David, *Love and Nausea* (London: Abacus, 1995).

Zizek, Slavoj, *The Plague of Fantasies* (London: Verso, 1997).

Zeki, Semir, 'Art and the Brain', *Daedalus: Proceedings of the American Academy of Arts and Sciences*, 127:2 (1998), 71-104.